CLIMATE TECH BRANDING

HOW TO BUILD A SUSTAINABLE TECHNOLOGY BRAND.

Strategic Brand Building For Climate Innovators in the New Era of Sustainable Technology

Joseph D. Simpson

To request permissions, contact the author at:
joseph@climatetechbranding.com

Joseph D. Simpson
Amsterdam, The Netherlands.
Cliamte Tech Branding

For Abel, Jake, Rupert, Ollie & all the others yet to come...

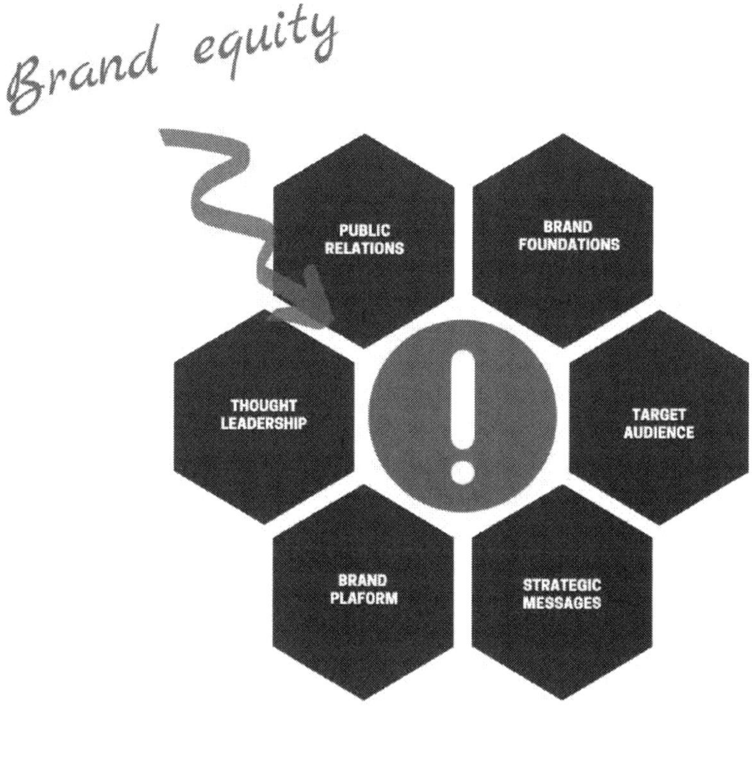
Brand equity
PUBLIC RELATIONS
BRAND FOUNDATIONS
THOUGHT LEADERSHIP
TARGET AUDIENCE
BRAND PLAFORM
STRATEGIC MESSAGES

TABLE OF CONTENTS

FORWARD

If you are reading this then there is a good chance you have dedicated your life to addressing some of our planet's most significant challenges.

First of all, I just want to take a moment to acknowledge how big that is. It takes a special breed of person to do that. So, on behalf of myself, my family and the rest of us, thank you.

We need more inspirational people like you in this crazy period of history.

Because the world is going through a shifting paradigm now, we need as many people as possible to help us through the storm.

A technological revolution is afoot. A global pandemic has torn entire economies into shreds, and there's an even greater disaster looming. We are pushing ourselves to the edge of the petri dish.

What the Corona Virus crisis has shown us, is that we are incapable of dealing with disasters of a global magnitude in future tense. Whether it's a biodiversity collapse, climate change, or global migration, today's problems will be exacerbated by an unpredictable and volatile future.

I believe, however, that today, not only can we rebuild our economies in a post-Corona world, but we can actively build a future worth getting excited about.

As climate tech entrepreneurs and sustainability professionals, we are going to be front and center in this new reality. We are going to build tomorrow's sustainable economy.

I'm proud that we are embarking on this journey together.

Sincerely,

Joseph D. Simpson

1.

AN INTRODUCTION

Sustainability over the last few decades has been defined by three distinct eras. Each the dominant way of creating positive environmental impact in their own period. Each a product *of* their own time.

ERA:	GREEN	SOCIAL	CLIMATE TECH
DEFINING BUSINESS MODELS:	NGO CHARITY PHILANTHROPY	CSR, ECO-FRIENDLY, SOCIAL IMPACT	ENTREPRENEUR TECHNOLOGY BUSINESS
PERIOD:	UP TO 2000	2000-2021	2021

We began with the Green Era, defined by NGOs, charities, and philanthropy. This era saw the rise of great organizations like Greenpeace and WWF. As a society, we decided that this was the best way to create impact at scale. However, as the years moved on, and environmental challenges mounted, we were forced to reconsider. Perhaps the private sector also needed to be involved in this effort — and not just by donating to a philanthropic cause after all their profits were divvied out. The Green Era ran all the way until about 2000.

Then came the Social Era. Businesses started to contribute to creating a positive impact through being "socially responsible" — all whilst continuing to conduct their business as-usual. Others began creating new products in an attempt to be "eco-friendly". However, after two decades of this social narrative dominating sustainability, we failed to move the needle and the climate crisis became ever more pressing.

Today, we have just entered a new era of sustainability: The Cliamte Tech Era — where business is the key component. Driven by the massive flow of investment in sustainable technology, the Climate Tech Era is using innovation and entrepreneurship to solve our most pressing environmental challenges. To thrive in this new era, Climate Tech founders need to shed their product-driven mindsets, become true entrepreneurs, and embrace the commercial side of their business.

However, the problem is, many Climate Tech brands still communicate from the Social or the Green Era. These narratives struggle to convince today's investors, talent, customers, and business partners to join their journey and don't demonstrate a growth mindset. Today, many Climate Tech brands still use the playbook from both these eras, rather than playing the growth focused game needed to scale innovative tech startups. And this has created four key problems for entrepreneurs in the Climate Tech Era:

- First, sustainability is no longer a market differentiator that founders think it is. Many sustainable brands lead with a variation of "to accelerate the transition towards a sustainable future" and expect that it sets them apart. But the competition is growing rapidly in the Climate Tech space and sustainability is no longer the market differentiator it once was.

- Second, potential investors and customers don't necessarily understand sustainability or its complexity. They certainly don't understand when you preach to the choir with industry-specific jargon like, "we're an circular and systemic ecosystem with an innovative technology to accelerate the current state of sustainability in the world" and then ask them to give you money, time or both.
- Thirdly, investors aren't interested in founders who fall back on their social roots and put impact ahead of growth. Using a narrative that falls back on social roots — "save the whales, buy our product" — demonstrates a lack of a "growth mindset"; a big red flag especially when you're spending someone elses money.
- And this leads to problem number four: Climate Tech founders give far more priority to their innovation than in their growth. Or perhaps I should say, Climate Tech founders pay far more attention to their product, than their brand. This is a huge problem because investors aren't interested in founders who put their product or innovation ahead of their business's development.

That's why we need to ditch the outdated green/social narrative and embrace the commercial side of their business. Because groundbreaking technology is only going to be impactful if businesses know how to bring them to market and scale them. Because growth and impact are no longer two separate concepts. And, because to accelerate the transition towards a sustainable future, we first have to bridge the gap between sustainability and entrepreneurship. And that starts with building a brand, not a product.

It doesn't matter how groundbreaking your idea is... The only way to create a sustained positive impact is by convincing the right people to help you build it. When you're building a sustainable technology company, you need access to capital, an ecosystem of partners that believe in your solution, top talent, and customers who want to "accelerate the transition towards" whatever world your building. But if no one understands what you do, how you do it, or why — except for that your climate tech brand is "sustainable" — it's going to hold back your potential impact.

A brand showcases a business's potential to create value and significant positive impact at the same time. A strong brand highlights a thriving business and a strong business-minded leader. A brand will also help you weather an unpredictable future, which as the Corona Crisis has demonstrated, is going to be stranger than you could have ever imagined. The perception of your brand also determines the behaviour of potential partners and investors. For instance, founders who are considered thought leaders attract more media coverage, can build stronger relationships with organizations, and they're more likely to be a trusted recipient of investment. And if you've made a solution to a global problem, you're going to need access to capital.

If you want to build a company that can go on and play a role building the sustainable economy of tomorrow, then we have to move away from our roots and create a strong brand. To do that, we have to start with the way we present ourselves, the story we tell, and the way that we communicate.

BRAND EQUITY

Warren Buffett's investment strategy is so simple: Invest in businesses having a wide and long-lasting moat around them. What Buffett's describing is a proverbial deep, wide ditch to defend your company. In this metaphor, your moat is a brand, so just like with a medieval castle, your brand protects and enriches those inside the fortress from outside attackers. The reason your climate tech business will succeed is because you have built a brand, not a product or solution. As a climate tech brand, you have a competitive advantage because sustainability is a core element of your business. Yet, competitive advantages invariably erode, so it's your brand that will help convince investors, partners, clients and talent to join your businesses journey.

The reason your business will succeed is because you have built a brand, not a product. As an Climate Tech brand, you have a competitive advantage because sustainability is a core element of your business. But competitive advantages always erode. It's a fact of modern economics. And with boom in Climate Tech investment, the space is becoming more competitive than ever. As your competitive advantage erodes, it's your brand is what will keep your business thriving. A brand can help you protect your long-term market share and wade off attacks from competitors. What's more, investment in it now indicates you'll take this matter seriously in the future — a key point for investors and venture capitalists. And a strong brand can help weather an unpredictable future, which as the Corona Crisis has demonstrated, is going to be stranger than anyone could have ever imagined.

The thing is, investors don't invest in a product, they invest in a brand's current — and future — equity. Brand equity is a term which describes a brand's value, which is in turn measured by perception of and experiences with, that brand. For companies with higher brand equity, it's easier to charge premium prices, increase market value and boost funding opportunities. For individuals, if you're considered a visible expert or thought leader in your field, you can earn more and significantly improve your career opportunities.

Now I know what you are thinking: I am reading this because I want to build a product or service that is going to have a significant impact on the state of sustainability in our society. If that is the case and you've chosen to do it through entrepreneurship, then you are in the right place. Hear me out: If people think highly of your brand, it will have a positive brand equity. When climate tech brand have a higher brand equity, people will trust what you say, and will pay more for your services. If your primary business function is creating a positive environmental impact, your impact can be scaled. The perception of your brand also influences the behaviour of potential partners or investors. Thought leaders attract more media coverage. They can build stronger relationships with organizations and they are more likely to be a trusted investee. If you have created a solution to a global problem, you will need access to capital.

The basic premise of this book is to help you build a brand and not a product. Why? So you can convince a) potential clients that you deserve their attention, b) and potential investors to part with their hard-earned dollars; and c) for potential partners to join you in your journey. Your company will thus be instrumental in scaling its impact to saving our planet from the looming climate catastrophe.

The reason 'why' I have written this book is far more elementary:

Sometimes the smartest person in the room is the worst at presenting ideas. We have a small window to make a significant change in the world and change must come — at least in part — through entrepreneurialism. You, as a Climate Tech entrepreneur have the duty to scale your business, disrupt the market, and challenge the status quo. But if you do not better your fundamentals of branding, there is a chance you will never get the resources you need to scale your impact, which is plainly, unacceptable. This book will aim to help you leverage the intersection of branding, communications, sales and marketing and teach you to kickstart your entrepreneurial journey towards climate impact. I'm going to teach you to build a moat.

SUSTAINABILITY IS THE NEW DIGITAL

Over the past few decades, every business in the world has embarked on the beginnings of what would be their digital transformation. Out went the old whirling desktops and fax machines and in came "the internet". In just a few short years since, the internet has morphed, bringing huge social changes and with it, new ways of doing business. Total digital businesses. The sharing economy, Software-as-a-Service and everything in between. At the turn of the dot-com crash, the internet was growing at a rate of roughly 2,300% per year, according to Jeff Bezos.[1] Whilst many at the time of the Dot-com crash and even well into 2008, believed that digital business was a fad, likely to pass, what's happened in the decade or two since has been the most rapid transformation of business the world

1 Jeff Bezos quote, CNBC.

has ever seen, akin to only the discovery of the Americas or the Industrial Revolution.

The periods between these transformations — where the world economy adapts to radical advances in technologies — are becoming shorter and shorter. Whereas before, you may have to wait several lifetimes for the global economy to transform, the shift from the birth of the internet to the Industry 4.0 revolution has only been 40 years. Less if you take into account the widespread practical application of digital business in the private sector. As these periods grow shorter, we even begin to feel multiple transitions in parallel. The next transition is likely to happen before the last one has even finished. The transformation of our economy towards a sustainable state. Innovation and impact are colliding.

As the economy grows and becomes more intertwined, it becomes less sustainable because more planes, more coal, more food, means less water, less space, and fewer resources. The transition to a sustainable economy is thus, inevitable. That which is not renewable is finite. Anything surrounding this concept is noise and ideology. This transition begs the question, when, how fast and who wins?

This is taken straight from Elon Musk's playbook which frames Tesla's ascent in the dormant auto industry. Or Patagonia's eco-activist domination of the outdoor industry. Ben & Jerry's, Unilever, Impossible Foods' founders, as well as activists like Greta Thunburg and David Attenborough, all have digested this mindset and their actions have set the stage for action.

But perhaps Blackrock's announcement in late 2019 is the greatest sign of the times changing. The world's largest asset manager and investment fund, made sustainable investing a defining priority in its investment strategy, spurred on by the awakening of millions of citizens across the globe in the 2019's September climate strikes. In an open letter, Chairman and CEO Larry Fink put it bluntly, "The evidence on climate risk is compelling investors to reassess core assumptions about modern finance. Research from a wide range of organizations — including the UN's Intergovernmental Panel on Climate Change, the BlackRock Investment Institute and many others, including new studies from McKinsey on the socioeconomic implications of physical climate risk — is deepening our understanding of how climate risk will impact both our physical world and the global system that finances economic growth."[2] Shortly after the announcement, the fund achieved a record $1 billion first close for its Third-Vintage Global Renewables Fund. Whilst public and private investor pressure undoubtedly played a role in their announcement, the firm acted of their own accord. No government pushed them into it — heck in Trump's America, the US government was probably livered by the announcement — they simply decided because it's good business.

This transition will be the defining factor of the next decade. The 20s are going to be the decade that the transition towards a sustainable economy receives access to the capital it needs to become a reality. On a fundamental level, the sustainability revolution is going to cause mass disrutption to business-as-usual. The advent of this new economy is accelerating at a pace which very few would have predicted only a few years ago. As Bain & Capital puts, "The sustainability revolution is unstoppable."[3] And just like with the revolutions which came before it, the movers and shakers of today will be those that end up as leaders in

2 Larry Fink, 2019.

3 Bain & Capital, 2020.

tomorrow's impact economy.

A growing number of investors are incorporating impact metrics into their values. Whilst governments around the Anglo-world continue to argue about the existence of climate change, it's become obvious that the private sector is no longer taking the risk of inaction. It's a simple financial metric. Now I'm not going to pretend to be an economist — maths has never been my forte — but what I can say with an unwavering degree of certainty is this: As with any transition in the economy, there will be winners and losers.

The winners are the ones who invest early, getting ahead of the pack and when society catches up, they will be able to profit from their position. The losers, on the other hand, are likely to be wary of change, have a wait-and-see approach and to continue along the path of business-as-usual.

It's possible to find examples throughout history of this transition. For instance, bicycle manufacturers at the advent of the automobile. But for argument's sake, let us focus on recent history

We all know the story of the big come up of Netflix. Out of nowhere, it seemed that the streaming company grew to dominate the global digital TV industry overnight. What most don't know however is that before "Netflix and chill" became a mantra for a lazy night in with a significant other, Blockbuster had a chance to purchase Netflix for a lousy $50 million in 2000.

In a book released in 2019 titled That Will Never Work, Netflix's co-founder Marc Randolph outlines what happened in the meeting that must make literally everybody who was involved cringe: "The dot-com hysteria is completely overblown," said Blockbuster's general counsel

Ed Stead, who believed Netflix was a joke.[4] Randolph recounted of the meeting later, "It was tiny, involuntary and vanished almost immediately. But as soon as I saw it, I knew what was happening: John Antioco [ex-Blockbuster CEO] was struggling not to laugh." The meeting soon went downhill after his comment and the Netflix team walked away with nothing. Ten years later, Blockbuster went bust, laying off 25,000 employees. Today Netflix is worth upwards of $200 billion.

History has demonstrated the profound effects of transformation in the global economy, whether it is caused by new technology or shifts in the social fabric of our society. The rush is on for those who want to be the new Netflixes in 2030, not the Blockbusters. The stakes are just as high and compelling.

The companies which fail to embrace sustainability are going to find it difficult to compete. Thus, the growth of sustainable technology, combined with environmentally-conscious consumers, can be compared with the technology entrepreneurs of the digital technology revolution.

At the turn of the millennium, digital natives were barely entering their teens. Technology was only harnessed by the early adopters and innovators.[5] Both the early and late majority were still playing the wait-and-see game. That all changed roughly the same time when you got a desktop as a kid (unless your parents were part of those primary movers). Technology grew from a privileged few to a necessity of the many. Then the digital natives began to enter the workplace and the market. The earlier generation was told they could be whatever they wanted, yet silenced by the realities of the previous generation. Our natives began to

4 Marc Randolph, 2019.

5 Joe Bohlen, George Beal and Everett Rogers, 1957.

tear down these institutions with a wave of new tech startups.

The same thing applies today with sustainability. The early adopters and innovators are now becoming conscious about what they buy, where it comes from and what effect it has on the earth and the people who inhabit it: Fairchain, vegan, eco-friendly, carbon neutral, planet positive, organic, B Corp certified, GE-Free, the list is endless. What was once touted by hardline hippies and eco-warriors, has become a driving force in the way we choose products. Employees are also looking for impact-driven workplaces to fulfil a depth of meaning in their workplaces. For-profit sustainable workplaces have the pick of talent without the price tag. These are the foundations of a booming sector. What was a niche is becoming mainstream; the beginning of a tipping point. Driven by the visible effects of climate change and a new, energized and driven generation, climate impact, sustainability and purpose are becoming common boardroom terms. As a society, we are crossing the chasm.

Economically, the warning signs are evident. Forget even for a moment the grave warnings from the IPCC, the UN and climate scientists all around the world. Let us begin instead to look at financial institutions, insurers and investment funds. According to a report by global consultancy Oliver Wyman released in February 2020, the world's financial firms risk $1 trillion in losses if they are slow to act on climate change. "Our analysis shows that there are strong commercial reasons to act — the financial risks are material and need to be incorporated into decision-making," James Davis, a partner at Oliver Wyman said. "This is an opportunity for the industry to lead."[6]

Another example lies in the Black Summer, the name Australians

6 Oliver Wyman Report cited by Reuters, 2020.

have given the bushfire season spanning 2019-2020. Ecologically, the Black Summer was a disaster. Economically, it ravaged the country. Not only was it unprecedented in size, but it was also unprecedented in time. Around the same time, the country was inundated by floods from torrential rain. To make matters worse, the usual help Australia received from Californian firefighters was delayed due to an elongated American wildfire season. The scale and intensity of extreme weather events like fires, droughts, floods and cyclones across the Australian island have been predicted by scientists for many years. Whilst these matters are ecologically catastrophic, they also place humans in grave danger. As a result, properties across the country will increasingly be prone to destruction. Directly affected by climate change, one in 10 Australian properties may become uninsurable by the end of this century. According to a leading climate risk analyst Karl Mallon, "If we see emissions continuing in the current direction, the level of warming continuing in the same direction and if we continue to see a sort of blind attitude to what's happening, then our risk will rise to about one in 10 properties."[7]

Whilst this may only be a small part of the picture, it tells a greater story. There is a real and present danger through inaction, caused by the fragility of our choices. With the majority of governments squabbling or stalling on climate action and the non-profit sector unable to make much headway, real action can only be achieved by business.

These words should resonate to anyone reading this, particularly for those who have started a new business aware of the importance of incorporating an equal balance of impact and capital in mind. I imagine that you are likely to be someone who truly believes in their solution. Yes,

7 ABC News Australia, 2020.

you want to take your product to the world but you want to make an impact, and your solution is truly going to make a difference.

The problem, however is that you are not alone in discovering this trend. Many are riding the bandwagon of impact because it's smart business, and whilst you may think that your solution is unique, the fact remains, your competition is growing by the minute. I to look at this in two ways: whilst there is no doubt people are acting to curb the effects of climate change; build more resilient societies which includes a diverse sustainable economy, there is — not unlike that of our natural resources — only a finite amount of opportunity to scale. Unfortunately, most businesses still fail, whether they are impact-driven or not. It is simple math.

A lot of entrepreneurs and especially Climate Tech entrepreneurs, believe that they and they alone can change the world. That the world truly needs their solution and without it, there are going to be significant challenges in the future. Otherwise, why would they go to all the trouble to invent it, build it and take it to market? Eventually, they shoot themselves in the foot, by underestimating what it takes to commercialize a technology. As the saying goes: "Build it and they will come." Unfortunately, that's not quite the case in today's day and age. Whilst we have unparalleled access to capital as entrepreneurs, there has never been so much competition. And investors are looking for entrepreneurs that demonstrate the ability to go the distance. This means that you must invest not only in your solution but also in your brand.

Now I can hear you saying what you are saying from behind my keyboard, and I get you. As a Climate Tech entrepreneur, you're more likely to be a scientist, an industrial ecologist or an academic rather than a marketing guru. I've worked with clients that completely brushed off the whole concept of branding as money-wasting-magic. Marketers were people who come in and feed off the hard work of the educated to make a quick buck and then disappear. Sure, it's true in some cases, however, it is usually the same people expressing this who are least likely to understand that business development and sales are inextricably linked to brand. This is how so many climate tech brands fail. They fail to take into account the importance of concepts like branding, thought leadership, public relations, digital content marketing, social media and strategic messaging. This is exactly what I am covering in this book; specifically adapting to the plight of the Climate Tech entrepreneur.

Living and working in Amsterdam — one of the world's fastest-growing Climate Tech hubs — as a brand strategist and copywriter, I've been privileged to work with some of the most innovative and pioneering companies this country has to offer. What I've found throughout this experience is that the founders who take branding seriousy are the ones who successfully build their client base, attract investment and scale their business. I want to make sure that you're not on the other side of the table, five years down the track, saying "I now understand the value of communications, but I wish I had put it to work in my brand." It is my mission to help you, the founder of a Climate Tech brand, bridge the gap between sustainability and entrepreneurship. Climate Tech Branding will help you come to terms with the basics of brand building in the twenties. The majority of the time when Climate Tech brands communicate they do one of two things; they tout their own horn or they shoot from the hip. This book will take you through the six pillars of branding for positive impact and in turn, will help you to avoid the most common mistakes that your peers will continue to make.

Whilst my background as a branding specialist will give you the ability to dive in the deep end, I'm not going to pretend that I am by any means an expert on all the subjects I cover in this book. It is for this reason that I've reached out to several peers to comment and share their experience from a top-down perspective. I will avail you the best possible information when you are seeking to build a scalable Climate Tech brand. Although this book is relevant to a global audience, it is impossible to explore the depth of the global impact investing scene. Rather, I will cover the options from a European perspective where the majority of movement is focussed. Falling in line with the EU's Green New Deal, with Amsterdam, Berlin and Vienna taking their share of the innovation pie, I will ensure all the information is at your fingertips, to increase your brand's equity, and make it investment-ready.

DON'T LET A CRISIS GO TO WASTE

We are ready for a new wave of sustainable innovation set in motion by the turning tides of the coronavirus. Crises come and go. In my lifetime, I've experienced three economic downturns. The dot-com crash, the GCC and now the Corona Crisis. Out of the ashes of the first two, we saw a new era of companies bent on building the future. Today, it will be no different. The companies who rise like phoenixes from an economic downturn are more often than not, the ones to integrate pressing societal challenges into their core existence. Microsoft, General Electric and IBM are all examples of companies that were either born in or consolidated during a recession. Just like in 2000 and 2008, today we're going through a defined shift in our economy.

Twenty years ago, we witnessed a global crisis of confidence. Whilst it may not compare with the Corona Crisis,with so much pain and miserywe can draw some similarities. During the five years leading up to its peak, many internet companies as they were called then, were borne to gain market share through brand building and networking. The focus was solely to capitalise on an insane bull market. Rather than identifying and solving real challenges extant in society, they launch their product through an IPO, without having profitability in sight.

The Dot-com bubble burst at some point in March 2000 while a plethora of overvalued, underperforming brands went bust. By April, the Nasdaq had lost 34.2% of its value. Those who survived, did so because they innovated their way out of the crisis; and because they had an inherent reason to exist in the first place.

Those who survived possessed a "change the world" mentality. Amazon, eBay, Adobe and others who traversed 2000 can testify to this fact. Sure, Amazon and eBay are not what you would call the most sustainable companies in the world, but back then, changing the world wasn't viewed in the same way either. To change the world through business was to solve unwieldy inefficiencies, like cueing for a taxi or booking overly expensive hotels; Some streamlined or sidestepped ingrained cultural tendencies, like charging late fees at the video shop. The hard yards were left to NGOs and governments.

Come 2008, another crisis comes and goes. The bursting bubble of the American housing market sends shockwaves throughout the world. Some go bust. Others prevail. A new world is born. This time, the focus is on the sharing economy, fast-casual restaurants and, of course, the rise of the smartphone. Imagine talking to your grandfather when he was

20 and saying these words. "In 50 years, we're going to have a device in our hands that you can literally ask any question and you'll get a correct response." He wouldn't have believed it for the world. The introduction of the smartphone created a new era of tech brands, the most successful of which were resilient, innovative and purpose-driven.

Today's most pressing social issues undoubtedly lie at the intersection of environmental sustainability and economic growth. Could this latest crisis kick off a new wave of consciousness?

The link between financial decline and a spike in innovation is well known to economists. Periods of turbulence bring about the end of eras and the start of new ones. Whether it's the Dot-com bust (which CleanTech enthusiasts will remember with a bitter taste in their mouth), the global financial crisis or the end of Tulip Mania in 17th century Holland. Some of the strongest companies grow in the periods following a crisis.

Today is the day when tomorrow's giants are going to be borne and tested. If Covid can do anything positive for the world, it will end today's divisiveness to environmental issues and enliven a race towards a new global economy, where sustainability becomes the new digital and where Climate Tech companies are pusued by Silicon Valley investors, as tech startups were over the past two decades. Why? Because we are beginning to see a convergence between capital and impact. As a result, the brands born today, which have climate at their core, are more likely to receive further support funding and grow into the Google and Facebook of tomorrow. Or as Blackrock CEO Larry Fink says, the next 1,000 billion-dollar brands will be in Climate Tech.

What Does This Mean For Sustainability?

Crises are essentially a filtering mechanism. They test founders and give societies a chance to see how valuable we find ideas, businesses and movements. Severe economic upheavals caused by a crisis allow brands to flex their muscles. They ask entrepreneurs to be entrepreneurial. The weak are cast aside. Only the strong survive. The coronavirus has changed the world in ways that we could not have believed possible only a few months ago. Some companies will survive. Others won't. This time, "changing the world" or "fixing social inadequacies" will not cut the muster.

Today, we are ready for a new wave of sustainable innovation, set in motion by the economic damage left by Covid. It is a wakeup call caused by a virus that is atypically not human.

This is important because human beings are not programmed to respond to threats from a non-human origin. It's just not in our nature to fear what doesn't hate or grieve or laugh or cry. As Daniel Gilbert, an author and Harvard Professor of Psychology puts it, "global warming lacks a moustache." As humans, we are concerned about human responses acts over natural events. "That's why we worry more about anthrax than influenza", he says. "Influenza is a natural accident, anthrax is an intentional action and the smallest action captures our attention in a way that the largest accident doesn't."[8]

But Corona may be changing all of this. We are opening up to the effects of a common non-human enemy on our planet. It will threaten the very economies on which we depend for our survival,

---

8 Daniel Gilbert, 2006, in his amazingly titled LA Times article, "If only gay sex caused global warming".

and provoke action before rather than later.

For Climate Tech entrepreneurs and sustainability innovators, this is a shift in mentality which will drive us into the future. Climate impact used to be an afterthought. Now it's front and center. And now is the time to double down on future-building. We are at a crossroad and our societies are awakening to the changes needed right now.

CLIMATE TECH IN A SHIFTING GLOBAL LANDSCAPE

Investors are more interested in sustainable businesses than ever before. They consider brands that solve some of the world's greatest challenges — climate change, deforestation, rapid urbanization, etc. — as the foundations of a new economy. A sustainable economy, in combination with public-private partnerships, are attracting funds in unprecedented numbers. BlackRock's recent pivot creates an insight to this economic transformation. "Sustainable investing was once viewed as a trade-off between value and "values." Today it is not.

"More granular data, more sophisticated analysis and shifting societal understanding of sustainability as well as growing awareness that certain factors — often characterized as environmental, social and governance or ESG — can be tied to a company's long-term growth potential." Any good bet comes with a heavy dose of long-term strategic planning. A sustainable economy is not being borne out of wishful thinking, but out of necessity. Companies which fit into today's economic model may still thrive in 20 years, moreover, the companies who build tomorrow's model, certainly will.

But as the global landscape changes and investors' priorities move with them, attitudes towards brands have not. The focus is still on making money. To attract and hold their attention, it is important that your brand presents itself as a company that can do just that. Climate tech brands, no matter what their focus, are being built all over the world by passionate entrepreneurs with a greater purpose at heart. But they are still in the business of being in business. There are certain rules they must follow, to give investors the impression that they are serious.

As an impact entrepreneur, you are more likely to be a scientist, an academic or a Delft University genius than a marketeer. But communications and branding are far too important to ignore, especially if your solution is worth this much effort. Investors — whether they are from a private equity firm, venture capital or a public-private partnership — want to see a certain level of dedication to these topics, before they are going to invest. It shows that you've got a growth mindset. That you are prepared as an entrepreneur and a leader to put yourself out there. And that you are serious about scaling your business as well as your impact.

THE DELFT EFFECT

In recent years, I've worked with a dozens of entrepreneurs who are building a sustainable companies and looking for funding. I've seen the passion these founders put into their projects and I've seen the mistakes they have made over and over again, when it comes to communicating what they do. My greatest experience which has influenced my outlook was my time working with a sustainability consulting firm based in the Netherlands as its communications manager. It was a big step into the world of the sustainable economy, venture building and impact entrepreneurship.

I had worked with the team's director to transform the company's brand, and digital assets, into a modern version of themselves. The director has a brilliant and inspiring mind, a force in the sustainable development world. Yet, he struggled from an affliction which I call The Delft Effect. The term derives from students who have been educated at Delft University of Technology or TU Delft; an advanced level scientific university in the south of The Netherlands. TU Delft is the oldest and largest Dutch technical university, ranking as the best university in the country. It's safe to say those educated at Delft are some of the sharpest tools in the shed. Notable alumni include many Nobel Prize winners as well as CEOs of both Shell and Philips. Whilst the Netherlands is a leader in sustainable innovation, Delft is one of the world's most important breeding grounds for these permutations. Delft university attracts a certain type who can thrive in this atmosphere.. They operate on a level that would befuddle the average person in the street. On a visit to TU Delft, I went inside a nuclear reactor where PhD students had set up fishing rods next to the blue light. They had been testing the reaction that certain materials would give when placed next to radiation, testing their hypothesis towards creating new sources of energy and energy storage. They are sufficiently trusted to be seated next to a nuclear reactor, with a fishing rod of experimental onjects placed next to uranium. Gifted as they may be, these types often suffer from what is called, The Delft Effect. It is where they begin to believe that everybody in the world is on their level and should understand their every argument and theory. These are the same people who continue to make sustainability or impact-driven businesses, are often prone to using high-level reasoning in their communications and marketing. In the real world, however, when you are bombard by scientific jargon and a salesman tries to sell you something, you are more likely to walk away thinking, "who's the madman" rather than, "yeah, I gotta get me some of that".

My old boss suffered from The Delft Effect, believing he needed only to express himself and the company in the loftiest academic language, verging on the poetic, to capture the attention of his clients who were on his level. But communicating from a business perspective, you have to appeal not to yourself, but to your customers. The firm struggled with this, as did I as its communications manager.

I may be accredited with university education but I'm certainly no Delftman. I've studied hard at sustainable development and international law and post-conflict studies. I'm a communicator, that's what I am good at. When I write copy for a press release, a script for a short film or a blog post — I found many a brick wall. Every time I submitted something for quality control, it came back with a few edits, having to start again. I once wrote a press release over twenty times, and when it finally ready for release, the newsworthy event was long gone, simply a waste of time. In the end, when we parted ways. I felt I had achieved far less than desired, because instead of moving forwards, we were unable to converse on a lower level or arrive at a common point.

Their website was outdated and a blog was barely updated every couple of months. We had an email list of a couple of thousand people which had been dormant for nearly a year by the time I had arrived. The company needed to make big changes in the way it communicated but instead of being progressive, it dwelt on small details, neglecting to fix the big issues. To this day, a year on, the company's website, remains dormant.

The reason why I am telling you this story is because it is an extreme case study. It is the platform from which I began to develop my branding philosophy which I use in my work ever since. It is a common character trait of Climate Tech entrepreneurs to suffer from The Delft Effect; it is natural for a person from a scientific or an academic background, but to build a brand for investors, but it is imperative we learn to see these symptoms for what they are and work towards overcoming them. An inability to do so will inhibit your brand from scaling. Witnessing this shortfall up close and personal, helped me develop the concept of The Delft Effect, and eventually, the writing of this book.

BUT I DON'T SUFFER FROM THE DELFT EFFECT?

Recently I was working with a particular climate tech startup. The founder and I have a great rapport and when I told her about this theory, she admitted to me that she saw some of these characteristics in her behaviour as well. She became aware because she noticed her team told the story of the company, they all told a different story. They were well versed to the solution they were bringing to the market, but when it came to their mission, vision and purpose, they were unaligned. This anomaly was reflected on their website and social media. It is a small issue that can have monumental consequences.

Many people think that branding is all about logos and colors. When you've got both in order, then you can move onto more important parts of building your product or service. Your website, social feeds and your staff are your brand. When they tell a different story, it is no wonder your message becomes diluted. In the Western world, digital marketing experts estimate, that we are all exposed to up to 10,000 pieces of advertising per day. All little stories trying to vie for your attention. If the messaging is off, it is only natural, our attention span will be minimized.

If you are an investor and you see a company failing to align its messaging, it says to them that there's a startup not taking their brand seriously. As branding is inextricably linked to sales and business development, they are probably not going to trust your company with their capital.

The value of having your messaging aligned throughout your communications can, however, bring you the reputation of being an expert in your field, a front-runner in your market, able to charge a premium on your product. It's the difference between a name that puts a solution on the table and a name that asks the question, "what do those guys do again?" Although your brand has nothing to do with how solid your solution is, it says much about how you, as an entrepreneur, conduct your business.

According to an experienced entrepreneur and angel investor Scott Goodson, founder of New York-based advertising agency StrawberryFrog, "people don't have relationships with products, they are loyal to brands… brands can rally people for or against something. Products are one dimensional in a social media enabled world, brands are Russian dolls, with many layers, tenets and beliefs that can create great followings of people who find them relevant. Brands can activate a passionate group of people to do something like changing the world. Products can't really do that."[9] This is the basis of brand building: no matter how much a game-changer it is, your product, without a brand behind it will only be worth the weight of its raw materials. This may sound like a strong and potentially contentious comment. This may sound like a strong comment, but branding is just as important as the problem which your solution solves. Following one, without paying attention to the other, means your business is unlikely to scale.

Another common misconception about branding is that people only start to pay attention to it after you invest effort in it. It's a good feeling when someone compliments you on a blog post or your new website, but whether you put effort into it or not, your branding will always be in the background. As Jeff Bezos says "branding is what people say about you when you are not in the room". Following along these lines, your brand's equity is thus the combination of your reputation and your story. Your reputation is what people hear from others about you, and your message is what you mediate to the world. To build your brand's equity, it's important that you take the reins of both; because if you don't both your message and your reputation will rely on outside forces. Plus, with the growing influence of social media, paid media and the decline of the traditional method of advertising, investing in your brand, overcoming the Delft Effect and communicating from the Climate Tech era can have a huge effect on your success as a business.

So, where Should I Begin?

In this book, I will explore what a strong Climate Tech brand consists of; and the theories which will build your brand's equity. Firstly, we will

9 Scott Goodson, 2012.

look at the old way of creating a positive impact in the world, concomitant with the shift already happening in the global economy, towards impact — and what this means for Climate Tech entrepreneurs.

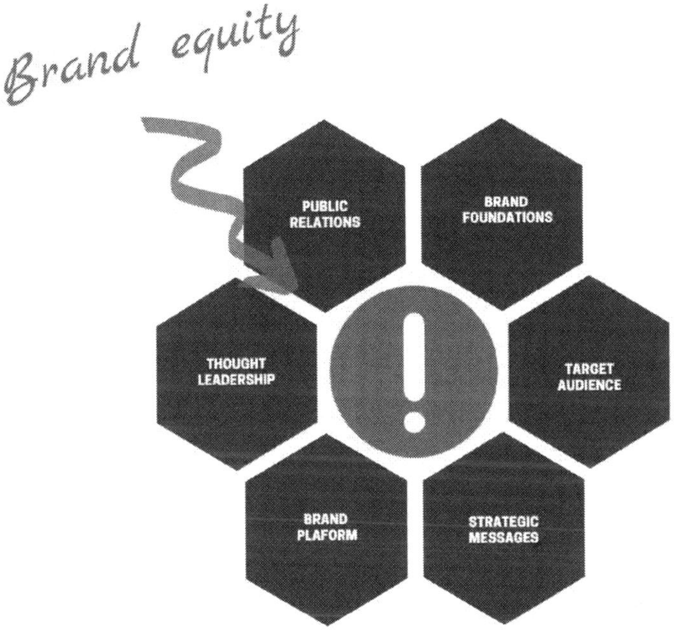

We will then look at how we can leverage biology, psychology and communications' theory to create the narratives underpinning our branding efforts. After theory, we will cover the six pillars of building brand equity in the Climate Tech ecosystem:

1. **Brand Foundations.** The foundations of your brand is integral to all of your future branding efforts. It's easy to skip this part — because you already know what you do, right? — and move on to the more exciting stuff like web design, social pages etc, but in reality, without a clear understanding of how to explain what you do, what you stand for, your perspective on the future and your brand's story — beyond environmental sustainability — you're holding yourself back in the long run. In this chapter, *Brand Foundations*, you will learn how to define your brand's mission, vision, values, translating them into a brand manifesto and identity.
2. **Target Audience.** Crafting your niche is one of the things that we have traditionally struggled with in the impact ecosystem. As Climate Tech entrepreneurs, it's easy to think that everyone will want what we're building because it will make the world a better place. In reality, it's simply not the case. So how do you make your idea cut through the noise? How do you differentiate yourself from your competition? By targeting the right audience. Market segmentation is the process of dividing all of your potential customers into smaller groups, based on certain characteristics. I.e., industry, company size, annual revenue or challenge. This is undeniably important when it comes to communicating your position in the market and your value proposition. If you don't have a clear target audience in mind when you begin to communicate, your value is going to be spread too thin. By segmenting our market, we can identify a profitable market for early traction, tailor our message to that specific audience, position our solution for success in that market and create value for those potential customers within our content.

3. **Strategic Messaging.** Whenever you communicate as a brand or an individual, how you frame your message will determine whether it will be successful. When a message is framed well, it leaves a lasting kernel in your target audience's mind. If you've just started your business, then you'll essentially be targeting a problem which your ideal market segment and target market holds. You want to become known as an expert in the eyes of your market. That's your first aim. Once you have a foothold in their mind, you want to give them strategic messages which will empower them to achieve their goals.
4. **Brand Platform.** Your brand is much more than your logo, but your visual identity will be remembered as a brand. And like everything that we will cover in branding, consistency is key. In this chapter, we will cover the basics of brand identity and your brand's personality as well as your digital footprint; your website, your online customer funnel and the content which enables it and your social channels. Having each of these assets in place and in a form that represents your potential is essential to show potential investors and future partners that you're in this for the long haul.
5. **Thought Leadership.** Building your personal brand is key to giving your sustainable innovation the best possible chance at scaling your impact. I know, you're much more likely to be a computer scientist, an academic or an engineer than a marketing guru, but the fact is that half of your brand's reputation rests on the shoulders of its founder or founders. And most of your personal brand is online: visable on LinkedIn, your blog, your Twitter or

Instagram. Your social channels are the first place an investor will look when deciding whether to invest in your company or not...and you get to choose what they find. What you post, what you write and care about, and your insights as a leader will all be on display, and you know they will be looking. So you'd better make it sure as hell that it says something positive. This chapter will take you through the essentials of personal branding, why LinkedIn is your digital resume for investors and how to leverage social media for your personal branding efforts.

6. **Public Relations.** An investor will look into your personal channels, and at your public record. What have you written and if it has been published? What has been written about you as an indicator of your leadership. For instance, are you a thought leader in your industry? Have you been featured in Forbes, Fast Company or Inc? What about in smaller blogs or industry publications? Or do you not value these types of pursuits? Leveraging public relations can be a great way to attract new partners and investors. Bill Gates started his journey focusing on sanitation in the developing world after reading one news article. Similarly, the partners you are looking for, are out there, but whether you leverage this mighty medium to reach them says a lot about how you are going to act as a leader. This section will take you through why you should get featured in the press, the different types of PR content, and how to pitch to journalists.

I don't expect you to follow each and every step in detail, but I hope that with this book, you will appreciate the importance of branding, and choose those core elements which will boost your brand's equity. Give yourself time to work on these concepts and consolidate each before moving on to the next. It took me over a year to fully comprehend the concept of a niche audience, so believe me, I get that it is foreign. You will continually refine, but remember what LinedIn's founder Reid Hoffman, stated, "If you are not embarrassed by the first version of your product, you've launched too late." The same is true of your brand. Someday you will come back to it and say, "what the hell was I thinking." Throw out the piece of paper and start again. Print it out and stick it on the wall. Ask yourself, "does this really represent me?" Over time you will adapt it and that's okay. Nothing is set in concrete.

Spread out your time, you are a busy entrepreneur. Make sure you dedicate time each week, fortnight or month. Perhaps it's only half an hour a week or one morning a month. It is consistency that will lead to success with branding. When you begin to look at scaling, if your brand is not solid, if your communication strategy is shoddy or your footprint as a founder is off, then it's going to hold you back. Investors and partners choose to work with you based on how professional you appear; how invested you are in your own company; and how much effort you have put into building business's equity. If your brand doesn't represent you or your product, it shows that you are more interested in your product than your company, and interest in joining your journey will wane quickly.

Time and time again, I see people in the Climate Tech industry communicating from the Social or Green Era. Essentially, everything in this book is an attempt to remedy this. This book intends to give you the tools to build your business's brand and communications effectively, so that you will be able to scale your impact through branding and storytelling.

We will be drawing on some of the most well known marketing and communications theories including Simon Sinek, Seth Godin and Everett Rogers. The theories you will be exposed to in this book will represent a good chunk of my own theory. It is necessary to build on top of solid concepts proffered by these writers. As climate tech leaders, you are not inherently different from other founders and much of what works for them, applies to you too.

Essentially, I am going to help you translate your technical impact jargon into a language that we understand, and put it in front of the right people using tried and tested branding strategies.

AN INTRODUCTION

2.

FROM CHALLENGE TO OPPORTUNITY

Climate Tech businesses struggle to communicate their value with the wider world. I've seen it time and time again in my work. Because of the fine line between impact and profit, at times we fall back on our social tendencies or technical jargon. It's understandable: Climate Tech entrepreneurship is a new genre. As we are experiencing a transition from social enterprise to for-profit impact enterprises, we are likely to hold on to our past. A past when impact was delivered by charities and NGOs. We also hold onto multiple biases which we have inherited from this era. These biases will hold us back in our pursuit of impact and profit. For example, the belief that impact-driven organizations don't deserve to be paid as much as regular enterprises. Or the bias that for-profit organizations are only interested in increasing their return on investment, and for them, climate impact is an afterthought.

We have grown up with these line-in-the-sand distinctions between charities and for-profit enterprises, and if you have come from a social background, you might have been wary of capitalism. It is understanable in your private life, but bear in mind, in the past decade a transformation has taken place. Before, impact was relegated to nonprofits and governments whilst capital generation was left to the private sector. Today, we've seen a complete 360 degrees, with entrepreneurs taking their solutions and scaling them on the open market, delivering positive social, environmental or cultural impacts alongside profit.

In this section, we will look at the social and cultural changes which brought us to this point as well as the biases that we need to shake in order to move forward. We will examine the shift from nonprofit to impact-driven organizations, how organizations who deliver impact at scale — think about global NGOs — they struggle to incorporate innovation into their operations and why that translates to bad practice for the modern Climate Tech entrepreneur. We will then translate these challenges into a theory I like to call *The Sustainability Lecture* and dive into why communicating in this way is both ineffective and detrimental to our overall cause. Lastly, we will bring all these concepts together in order to determine the best path forward: Shifting the perspective of sustainability from challenge to opportunity.

...AND NONPROFIT TO CLIMATE TECH ENTREPRENEURSHIP

We used to rely on charities and nonprofits to create environmental, social or cultural impact. In for-profit businesses, impact was mostly relegated to an afterthought. Yet relying entirely on these mechanisms alone to deliver positive impact hasn't been as effective as we would have liked. Before I go on, I want to express that I do not take issue with NGOs. Greenpeace and MSF have their place in the world as do local charities that tend to the needs of those that society has overlooked. They are a fundamental and essential service and the world needs them. However, I do, however, believe that they are incapable of addressing some of the most pressing global issues today. They are flawed because of their reliance on aid and charity, their lack of ability to innovate and their scarcity mindset.

These flaws might be acceptable in isolation, but to adopt or replicate them in entrepreneurship, can hold back your growth. If you operate like a nonprofit, you effectively inhibit your own growth. This is an issue for many Climate Tech entrepreneurs. Inherently, as Climate Tech entrepreneurs, we are also social beings. Without speculating on which side of politics you find yourself on, I am more likely to be to the left-of-centre than the far-right. Creating an impact business is a social undertaking in itself. It is no coincidence the conservative side of politics has taken an anti-climate change stance. Thus, many Climate Tech entrepreneurs believe in creating companies which toe the line of not-for-profit.

By adopting this approach, we struggle to convince investors, to articulate our place in society and we struggle to scale. By standing still, our solution (and the impact we've dedicated so much energy into creating) doesn't reach those who need it most.

To tackle global problems, we need scalable solutions. Yet nonprofits struggle to grow in both reach and impact due to one simple factor: They struggle to reinvest in themselves. Dan Pallotta, the American entrepreneur, author and humanitarian activist, best known for his involvement in multi-day charitable events with the long-distance Breast Cancer 3-Day walks, AIDS Rides bicycle journeys and Out of the Darkness suicide prevention night walks, believes this is because society stunts the growth of charities. In his Ted Talk on the subject titled *The Way We Think About Charity is Dead Wrong* underlines the reason behind this. "This ideology gets policed by one very dangerous question which is: 'what percentage of my donation will go to the cause versus the charity's overhead?'"[1] Pallotta goes on to explain that there are two problems with this question. First, he says, that it makes us think that overheads are negative. That it is somehow not a part of the cause which, in turn, creates a second and much larger problem. "It forces organizations to go without the overhead things that they really need to grow in the interest to keep their overhead low." However, when considering creating the biggest impact possible, growth is a necessity.

With an inability to invest in overheads like marketing, top tier employees or risky projects, charities can stunt their own growth. They are at times put on a pedestal for failure, yet they don't have the ability to make great investments in themselves. Often, they can't afford to hire the best candidates and if they did, the choice would be scrutinized by donors. "Couldn't this job be done by someone cheaper?" With all these limitations, charities struggle to make the impact which can usher in a new, sustainable economic reality. Pallotta frames this concept by asking a few further questions: Why have our breast cancer charities not

1 Dan Pallotta, 2013.

come close to finding a cure for breast cancer? Why have our homeless charities not come close to reducing homelessness in any major city in the US? Why has poverty been stuck at 12% of the US population for the past 40 years? "The answer is that these social problems are massive in scale and our organizations are tiny up against them and we have a belief system that keeps them tiny." This belief system has created a separate rule book for charities and NGOs as opposed to the rest of the economy. According to him, it's an apartheid, in the for profit sector, the more value you produce, the more money you make. However, society doesn't like non-profits to use money as an incentive for people to produce more in social impact. We have a visceral reaction to the idea that anyone would make a lot of money helping other people. On the other hand, it's interesting that society doesn't have the same reaction to the notion that people would make a lot of money not helping other people. "If you want to make $50 million selling violent video games to kids, go for it. We'll put you on the cover of Wired Magazine. But if you want to make half a million dollars trying to rid kids of malaria, you're considered a parasite," Pallotta said.

This came to light recently in my birth country of Australia. After the burning bushfires over the November-February 2020 period, the Australian Red Cross received over AUD $115 million in donations in order to aid those worst affected. The charity however said it would distribute less than a third of the money raised and it could take up to three years before some bushfire affected victims receive anything at all.[2] Such overheads were seen by Australian residents as unacceptable inefficiencies and a later announcement that a further AUD $11 million

2 7 News Australia, 2020.

of that relief funds will go towards admin only poured salt in the country's wounds.[3] Overheads were seen by Australian residents as an unacceptable inefficiency. A later announcement of a further AUD$11m of relief funds will go towards administration, only pouring salt in the nation's wounds. Australians were keen to have their money go directly to helping bushfire victims, not to the people who would distribute the funds.

Our global society is facing one of humanity's greatest challenges, and no longer are charities seen as a solution. Unable to innovate and evolve, their mere existence has created a reliance on them. Charities and NGOs lag behind in keeping up technological developments. This may be due to overhead restrictions but it does render them less efficient, in comparison to their for-profit peers.

We live in an age of constant disruption, new and better ways of doing things, but when you play by the charity rulebook that Pallotta describes, you limit your organisation with a scarcity mindset.

BIASES FROM THE SOCIAL AND GREEN ERA

As Climate Tech entrepreneurs, we find a strong bond with the idea of creating good in the world, yet these social tendencies could also hold us back. It is common among us to hold onto old classic charity character traits. It is a belief we are not able to make profit for ourselves because it would mean taking money away from our cause. Investing in our own

3 Daily Mail UK, 2020.

growth would take time and effort away from where it is needed most. The notion that advertising is a waste of revenue when it could be spent on business lines which directly create change: product development or implementation. Some fear that taking risks is going to be criticised by the community, or is a waste of valuable resources. This can thwart growth because people are reluctant to take those risks. To fail and to feel like business lines contributing to growth are a waste of resources; creating a doubt in our mind which holds us back. In the capitalist play book, and in the venture capital world of tech startups closeted in San Francisco, this is called a scarcity mindset.

In sales and marketing, scarcity is often used to manipulate people into buying. You would have seen those late night ads with people selling something "for a bargain to the first 100 callers". Or the internet ads on a website you have never been to previously, where you click onto a page, a clock begins counting down until the time to purchase is up. They are employing scarcity tactics, or leading you to believe the product or deal will disappear later. The scary thing is it actually works. I have been on these websites many times and thought, "who buys this rubbish?" but lo-and-behold, they work, because they convert your thinking.

Scarcity when entrenched in your mentality can hold you back. In life, just like in business, the belief that there's a limited amount of funds or partners out there, leads to missed opportunities and experiences. When it comes to creating impact, we become caught up with these narrowed beliefs. It is necessary to remember that a scarcity mindset is just that; a mindset. It is possible to change our way of thinking, open up a world of opportunity to grow and scale our impact. To do so, it is important to recognise the pitfalls in the first place.

Here is a incomprehensive list I have observed in my work:

1. **Thinking small.** It's quite common to see an impact organization that doesn't want to grow above a certain number of people. Even though we have big dreams for the world, it's easy to get stuck thinking local. This can be caused by a number of different beliefs, like an aversion to the corporate world or the belief that working with existing companies will damage our reputation. When we adopt a mindset that we don't want to grow our startup, we take away opportunities to scale that impact to those who need it most.
2. **Scared of the spotlight.** Coming from a social background, many Climate Tech entrepreneurs find it difficult to embrace taking a stand in the public domain. Rather, we prefer to operate in an echo-chamber of our own making. Telling people who are already on board with our opinions rather than taking the leap into the public sphere.
3. **Believing that money stinks.** It's natural for Climate Tech entrepreneurs to want to build a foundation on the side of their main business. This shows that they're really dedicated to their cause. That they're not in it just for the money and that what they really want is to make an impact. Whilst there's nothing inherently wrong with this, using your business to fund charity evokes the sentiment that you're not in this for growth. In the world that we live in, money accompanies success and the only way to successfully scale your impact is to become financially sustainable as well.
4. **Acting like a charity.** Another common pitfall that I've seen affect Climate Tech entrepreneurs is believing that, because they are not just in it for themselves, others should receive less for working with

you. On a number of occasions, I have worked on projects where work is outsourced to friends or peers with no financial expectations in return. And when outsourcing work, it's not uncommon for social startups to pay less than their commercial peers. Saying "I don't have enough money" and "we'll have to go without" instead of "let's invest in ourselves, we can always get more money", creates scarcity when it's not necessary. This type of scarcity mentality does not attract the top talent or high-quality work that will see your company grow.

5. **Relying on impact instead of ROI.** Another mistake is believing that impact is enough to sell your product or service. Impact without a return on investment is unlikely to attract investors or customers. The impact you are making must tangibly correlate to a specific return on investment for your customer or target audience. Without it, you're only selling an idea of a better world for people to donate to. This is not a long term or sustainable business model.

A scarcity mindset goes back to our primal instincts. Down to fight or flight. It's the difference between a cup half empty and a cup half full. A victim of the world, business and our previous generations rather than a visionary. When you get trapped in a scarcity mindset, it slows your growth as a leader, as well as the growth of your company because it's one -dimensional. You can't focus on what's happening outside because you teach yourself to believe that you're lacking in your business. By failing to see the big picture, Climate Tech entrepreneurs often struggle to access the resources and external network available to make their impact global.

When Climate Tech entrepreneurs adopt an abundance mindset, they see these challenges for what they are: opportunities. Problems waiting to be solved. To overcome the scarcity mindset, it's important to develop a mindset of abundance. However, for sustainability experts, this can be a difficult exercise. "Abundance? That's the type of thinking that got us into this mess!" I can hear the outrage coming from you as I type the words. The idea that there is plenty in the world has pushed us far beyond our planetary boundaries and contributed to our failure to make significant steps towards reversing climate change. I agree that when a capitalist wields an abundance mindset, it can be devastating for our planet. But when an entrepreneur who believes in the triple bottom line — people, planet, profit — an abundance mindset can be a force for good.

THE PSYCHOLOGY OF CLIMATE COMMUNICATIONS

This chapter has attempted to give context to the large global transformation which is underway: The explosive growth of the global impact economy, impact vs. philanthropy, the burdens charities face in the modern age and growth vs. scarcity mindset. I wanted to cover all of these subjects here before we move on to communications and branding. It is my belief that to build a sustainable economy, **we have to create positive impact and not reduce negative impact.** If you're still reading, I'll assume that you believe that too. Because we both share this mentality, we are put in a unique situation. At the forefront of a growing section of a new economy. Which means that we have to realize — and move on from — some of the old ways of doing things. Specifically the way we communicate about sustainability using negative messages like "just stop flying already" or "stop eating meat... the planet will thank you" — what I call the sustainability lecture.

Over the 20th Century, we became increasingly aware of the large environmental challenges that our planet faced and in the period since we've found many ways to address them. Yet there has always been a distinct challenge for those selling the solutions to the public. Conveying both localities (distance), proximity (in time) and direct effect (on our lives) from the climate crisis at hand has been complex, to say the least. To maximize the effectiveness of our campaigns and communicate about our impact, it's important to understand what messages resonate beyond the "impact bubble" and how the general public responds to certain messages.

The imagery used to convey climate change provides a unique example of this challenge. Imagery has always been able to distil abstract concepts and events for those at a distance. Consider the Tiananmen Square Massacre or the Vietnam war. What comes to mind? An image of a man standing in front of a tank and the image of a 7-year-old South Vietnamese girl running from a cloud of napalm smoke. Now think about environmental challenges. Imagine concepts such as deforestation, rising sea levels and climate change. What do you see?

Let's take a look at this concept through a historical lens. At first, we were shown direct action. Images of men and women tying themselves to trees in the US and UK dominated the public discourse. Empowered by the injustices of the Vietnam war and a radically transformed society, people began to fight back against "the man". Corporates and politicians called them hippies, sympathisers called them activists and they managed to change the world. But as the world became more global, we realized that we couldn't focus on saving trees as a solution. The problem became more global and so did our necessity to cooperate internationally. As a result, the imagery which represented environmental challenges adapted by becoming global in nature.

Direct action was replaced with images of polar bears in the Arctic. The theories went something along these lines: Hippies are despised by the corporate world, but they (corporates) can't hate animals and children in the same political way. This era was defined by great global movements such as the Live Aid concert to raise funds for the famine in Ethiopia, the Reduce Reuse Recycle campaign and WWF's campaign against deforestation in Indonesia and Brazil. The imagery that was used changed from black and white to colour. It became more vivid. It became starving East African children, beaches filled with plastic pollution and orangutans or pandas trying to survive in the vestiges of decimated rainforest. The imagery evolved to face the challenges of the day. However, research suggests that charities or cause appeals which use particularly emotive images (such as explicit images of suffering children) may not be as effective as less heavy-handed ones.[4]

Climate Visuals, an organization which draws on psychology to change the imagery we use in climate change communications, argues that the decision to begin associating climate change with an iconic animal like the polar bear has provided a simple visual shorthand for the issue. However, it has also reinforced the impression that climate change is a distant problem and arguably "closed down" the climate discourse around a concept that is remote from people's day-to-day lives.[5] The

4 Katherine White , David J. Hardisty, & Rishad Habib in the Harvard Business Review

5 Climate Visuals, 2015.

organization's director Adam Corner believes that because the images don't contain people in them, they're unable to tell a human story.[6] Images telling stories about climate change are now all about hitting home.

The Sustainability Lecture

Localization and humanization are key to crafting climate narratives which change minds rather than switch them off. The polar bear, just like the starving child and the activist had their place in their own individual contexts, but today they've become obsolete. After receiving this advice from Climate Visuals, The Guardian announced in late 2019 that they would change the way they used visuals to cover climate stories and consider showing the direct impact of environmental issues on people's daily lives as well as trying to indicate the scale of the impact.[7] Just as the imagery has to change to fit the day, so too must the way that we communicate about sustainability in the evolving impact economy.

When you lecture people about whats and the hows without giving them context, people begin to switch off. Lecturing can be defined as to talking seriously or angrily to someone in order to criticize their behaviour and bring about change. Whilst it sounds obvious that this doesn't change behavior, this is the basis for the majority of climate communications. For example, it's not uncommon to hear brands talking about the pressing challenges — i.e., climate change, plastic pollution or deforestation — and why they require change and then saying "buy our product". The sustainability lecture usually hinges on three distinct

6 Diego Arguedas Ortiz, BBC, 2018.

7 Fiona Shields, The Guardian, 2019.

emotions: Fear, being trapped and guilt.

- **Fear.** Marketers typically avoid fear in their advertising, because consumers tends to associate that negative feeling with the brand itself. However, when communicating sustainability, the most common tactic is to employ fear to spread our message. Opting for fear-based messages can turn consumers off to your message before they even know about your product or service.
- **Being Trapped.** Telling the masses what to do makes them actively fight back against it. Research shows that when someone is told that they can't do something, it makes them want to do it even more. It's obvious in children's behavior but you can also recognise it when adults are exposed to climate change messaging. Reactance Theory states that people are convinced they possess certain freedoms to engage in so-called free behaviours and when a loss of those freedoms is imposed on them, it motivates them to restore it.[8] In layman's terms, it causes a knee jerk reaction to resist.
- **Guilt.** Whilst research also suggests that guilt can be an effective motivator, when it's too forceful, it turns people off to the message entirely.[9] This was demonstrated in a controlled public experiment where two focus groups who were shown the same fairtrade tea options with two different messages. A subtle option and a forceful option, both conveying the emotion of guilt. In the subtle scenario, consumers reported anticipating future guilt if they failed to shop for green products and chose fair trade options 84% of the time. In the second scenario, customers became angry, upset or irritable and

8 Christina Steindl et al., 2015.

9 John Peloza, Katherine White, & Jingzhi Shang, 2013.

only 40% chose the fair trade option.

The Psychology of Inaction

"We ourselves are the process of evolution, just like any other animal." says Kate Jeffery, a neuroscientist at UCL. I reached out to Kate to get a better understanding of why humans are so slow to react to an existential threat like climate change. "We are creatures that have been designed by natural selection to exist in the conditions that we've experienced...those conditions that shaped us, shape the way we think and act." Scientists have been warning us about climate change for years. The science itself over the past half-century has only become more conclusive and more striking. It points to more and more dire scenarios for rich and poor alike, yet we've not made the dramatic changes necessary to avert a climate disaster. What is stopping us then? "Ultimately, human behaviour is hard-wired with all its quirks and faults," Kate says. "We are unfortunately prone to these viral processes which affect our operations. For example; authoritarianism or vaccine denialism or climate change denialism. And the internet's fast speed of information transformation has made us act much more quickly than we used to." But before we look at deep-seated climate denialism, let's take a look at the three broad categories of psychology. "There are multiple mentalities and identity issues that feed both climate action and climate inaction. They all begin with the three broad categories of psychology; perception, cognition and action. These are not discrete categories, but they feedback into each other." Together they paint a picture of the why behind climate inaction in our society.

- **Perception.** How we make sense of all the things coming in through our senses. The term has been used to describe a range of psychological phenomenons including beliefs, attitudes, concerns and perceived risks.[10] We're not very good at perceiving slow things overtime or things at scale. According to Jeffrey, this is due to our perception's inability to report truthfully on reality; something that's often referred to as *The Parable of the Boiling Frog*. If you put a frog in hot water, it'll jump out, but if you put a frog in cold water and slowly warm it up, it will adapt to the changing environment until it's too late and the frog boils alive. Human beings act in a very similar way. "For one thing, we don't actually perceive the entire visual world in front of us. That's an illusion in our brains. At any one moment, you're only looking at a tiny spot which moves all over the place. Your brain stitches together and makes you think you're looking at a film screen." Perception is the first step towards action. However, this divergence between what we perceive and what is actually happening on the ground can lead us to misinformation affecting the decision-making process.

- **Cognition.** How we organize that information to formulate internal representations of the world that will allow us to adapt to that environment. People don't react to risk rationally, but rather what we've found in psychology is that they're applying a whole bunch of heuristic and cognitive biases. "You can think of those as shortcuts, quick ways of thinking about things that don't require any calculations". These biases include loss aversion, that society as a whole is very reluctant to forego immediate gains for the benefit of longer-term gains, temporal distancing, how much time (e.g.,

10 Psychology and Climate Change: Human Perceptions, Impacts and Responses edited by Susan Clayton & Christie Manning, 2018.

past or future) separates between the perceiver's present time and the target event and confirmation bias — when you already believe something — you interpret all evidence on the subject with your position already determined. "So if we're not getting our beliefs on logic, what are we basing them on?" According to Kate, a very strong determinant of our beliefs are the beliefs of people in our trusted circle. "We tend to form groups of people we feel bonded to. During evolutionary history this would have been our tribe, our neighbours and our immediate family." The parallels with the climate change argument are obvious and striking. Over the past 20 years, in the United States, climate change has become increasingly political. In 2001, roughly 50% of Republicans and 60% of Democrats believed in Climate Change. Today it's roughly only 30% of Republicans vs 70% of Democrats. "This makes us understand that when people aren't acting on climate change, it's not because they don't have the facts. So it's not a matter of pouring enough facts into somebody and then they'll stop denying climate change and start acting."

- **Action.** Just like beliefs, actions — i.e., how we convert that information into behaviour — are not always rational. There's a very famous example called *The Tragedy of the Commons* which exemplifies a big part of our inability to act on climate change. The Commons is a piece of land where three farmers have their livestock. As each farmer increases the number of their cattle on the land, the land starts degrading. Eventually, it won't have any grass at all and all the animals will die. The rational argument for each farmer is to add another animal because it will add a big personal benefit but a shared cost. The tragedy is that because everyone is focused on their own return on investment, everybody loses out in the long run. This is one way to explain the inaction between countries on climate change. The "why should we change our behaviour when China or India aren't going to change theirs," argument. Another irrational factor which influences our actions is that we often go beyond personal cost-benefit and focus on looking at the people around us. "What tends to happen with climate is that everyone's looking around and living life as normal. It doesn't seem to be much of a problem. But if you're sitting in a cinema theatre by yourself and you smell smoke, you'll probably leap to your feet, but if you're sitting there and you're surrounded by people and no one does anything, you're less likely to do anything either."

The denial of personal impact by the majority of the developed world is underscored by some uniquely biological character traits. Just like humans process information through perception, cognition and action, we are also programmed to respond to an imminent threat in one of three ways. When we feel fear, we freeze, fight or fly. With a slow-moving, conceptual challenge like the climate crisis, the threat mechanism isn't likely to be triggered. That is, we're not highly likely to respond in the face of an abstract problem. According to Daniel Gilbert, a Professor of Psychology at Harvard University, the human brain evolved to respond to threats that have four distinct features. "Features that terrorism has and that global warming lacks." [11]

- **Climate change lacks a moustache.** Gilbert states that humans are congenitally prone to fear human actions. "Global warming lacks a moustache. No, really. We are social mammals whose brains are

11 Daniel Gilbert, Los Angeles Times, 2006.

highly specialized for thinking about others. Understanding what others are up to — what they know and want, what they are doing and planning — has been so crucial to the survival of our species that our brains have developed an obsession with all things human. We think about people and their intentions; talk about them; look for and remember them." Climate change is not something that has been set upon us by a person, intent on destroying our way of life. Because climate change lacks a human persona, it's difficult to characterise its motives.

- **Climate change doesn't violate our moral compass.** Acts or events that challenge our moral sensibilities are the ones that drive us to act. When the President of your country stands up and makes a fool of himself, it violates your sense of national pride, driving you to vote in the hope that you bring about change. Climate change doesn't desecrate any moral code, nor does it profane over religious rules about sex, gender bias or food. Unfortunately, no human societies — regardless of creed or colour — have moral rules about atmospheric chemistry. "Moral emotions are the brain's call to action," Gilbert explains. "The fact is that if climate change were caused by gay sex or by the practice of eating kittens, millions of protesters would be massing in the streets."
- **Distant in the future.** The third reason why global warming doesn't trigger our concern is that global warming is seen as a far away occurrence. We are programmed, like all animals, to respond to clear and present danger. Our brain has been engineered to react to the world around us and predicts danger before it occurs. "Our ability to duck that which is not yet coming is one of the

brain's most stunning innovations...But this innovation is in the early stages of development." Without the feeling of an imminent threat to individuals, a future unseen is too far away to respond to. "Unfortunately, we see climate change as a threat to our futures — not our afternoons."

- **Climate change doesn't strike in real-time...until it does.** Lastly and perhaps most importantly, our brain can detect changes to our environment in real time when they happen. Changes in light, sound temperature, size and weight, if they happen fast enough. However, if a change happens slowly, say for instance like a river losing a meter of width every couple years, the changes can go undetected. We are highly adaptable beings and whilst we like to reminisce about the "good ol' days", we tend to accept the present and adapt to it. Gilbert gives an example of traffic in Los Angeles. "The density of LA traffic has increased dramatically in the last few decades and citizens have tolerated it with only the obligatory grumbling. Had that change happened on a single day last summer, Angelenos would have shut down the city, called in the National Guard and lynched every politician they could get their hands on." Unfortunately, whilst we in the impact bubble may be alarmed by the rate of change, many aren't confronted by any of these changes when they happen and as a result, they go by undetected.

These factors combined are demonstrated when we take into account two catastrophic events in our recent history — the Twin Towers attack where 3,000 people died and the 2003 heatwave in Europe where between 30,000-70,000 people died. Although the heatwave was at least ten times worse than 9/11 in terms of fatalities, Jefferies says that most people wouldn't even remember the event. "The difference is that one of them was a predatory attack while the other was a slow and insidious event. We reacted to one, we didn't react to the other."

When I asked Kate how we can move forward, if our human condition is obstructing our starting point, she said "Things are starting to change. It's getting harder to maintain a strong sense of climate change denial. Even Trump has reluctantly muttered that the climate may be changing." But still, with the issue being inherently political and thus one of identity, she was of the view, "You can't turn people's attitudes around overnight. And you certainly can't push on people and expect them to change their attitudes."

So then, considering the current climate, I asked, what should we rely on to build a sustainable economy? Money is a good starting point, she says. "Money is the one thing that every individual understands. It's the universal language and I think that might be the starting point because I don't think there's anything else that can work. XR was very anti-capitalist, but ultimately, we are in a capitalist system and it's the only tool that we have that's universally understood. Appealing to people's better natures on their own is not enough. The bottom line comes down to self-interest."

To translate that into the context of the identity divide — between those who advocate for climate action and those who don't — if you want to appeal to people who are inherently averse to climate action, you should appeal to their sense of economic utility maximization (opportunity). "It's best to focus on the economic costs of climate inaction, the loss of revenue and the harm that non-sustainable decisions can make for businesses in general," she says. "For example, to invest in solar power, not because it's going to "save the planet" but because it's more economical in the long run. People will buy if it makes their expenses cheaper or solves their problem better than other options on the market even if the added environmental benefits are not the main motivations."

By phrasing climate change and sustainability as opportunities to get ahead in the new economy and telling success stories as opposed to stories which evoke feelings of being trapped, fear and guilt you're essentially flipping the challenge on its head.

THE CLIMATE TECH ERA MUST BE FRAMED AS AN OPPORTUNITY

When I grew up, I was always told that if we just turned the lights off, if I just showered for a couple less minutes and if we recycled then we could solve our biggest problems. But has climate change slowed down? Has plastic waste in the ocean reduced? No. It's accelerated. This framing of climate change and sustainability as a challenge hasn't worked over the past 30 years. So why would work today? When we pedal the same negative narratives — that reducing consumption rather than consuming better brings about the change we need to see in the world — we aren't solving anything. Rather, we're adding to the problem.

Now I'm not saying that as individuals we can't make a difference. But I am saying that we cannot rely on pressuring individual to take action to bring about systems change. Beyond eating less meat, flying less and investing in sustainable alternatives, there is very little that we as individuals can do to change the sustainability of our society as a whole. That's why we need entrepreneurship to disrupt business-as-usual and build us alternative options (think hyperloop or plant-based protein or carbon-neutral jet fuel).

Spurred on by The Paris Agreement, this rapid race to create a sustainable, low-carbon economy has pave the way for a new global race for innovation. Since the signing of United Nations Framework Convention on Climate Change's Paris Agreement in 2015, the costs associated with decarbonisation have reduced so rapidly, they're creating a new wave of prosperity for businesses, investors and countries who choose to chase them. "This is a story of opportunity. It's a story of growth," says Sir Nicholas Stern, Professor of Economics and Government & Chair of the Grantham Research Institute on Climate Change and the Environment at the London School of Economics.

"We know that inadequate action translates into massive and costly climate risk. The Paris Effect makes it clear that it also puts economies at risk of falling behind the next wave of the creation of prosperity. That wave is already gathering pace and will become a dominant force in growth and transformation over this decade. Wise policy makers and investors will aim for the opportunities, jobs and resilience that can be delivered only through a net-zero economy." [12] According to *The Paris Effect: How the climate agreement is reshaping the global economy,* whilst in 2015 low-carbon technologies and solutions were considered uncompetitive, today they're at cost parity in a quarter of the economy and by 2030, low-carbon solutions could displace carbon intensive technologies across nearly three

12 Nicholas Stern in The Paris Effect: How the climate agreement is reshaping the global economy, Sistemiq, 2020.

quarters of the economy. The scale of the opportunity in itself is simply mind-boggling. And people are starting to catch on.

Once seen as mutually exclusive, creating positive impact and maximising profits have become aligned. Whilst investors were initially wary of having financial trade-offs for sustainable investing, the overwhelming majority of investors today, believe companies that engage in leading ESG practices have the potential to be more profitable than their purely for-profit peers. They are also considered to be better long-term investments.[13] What's more, 8 out of 10 investors are interested in investing sustainably. And this grows to above 90% when considering millennial investors. Given the pressures arising from a changing climate and other environmental factors, together with millennials overtaking Baby Boomers as the dominant generation, it isn't unthinkable that this growth will be exponential. However, underscoring the high returns is something that runs much deeper into the veins of society: The shift of the perception of sustainability from a challenge to an opportunity.

This huge growth in the impact ecosystem has created new opportunities for investors and entrepreneurs alike. For investors, a whole new sector, once relegated to philanthropy, foreign aid or nonprofits, not only became profitable but began to overtake other asset classes. For Climate Tech entrepreneurs, the additional attention soon translated into projects developing into scaling for-profit companies. "There is also now empirical practical evidence built over the last 10 years that shows impact investment funds returning double digits and above comparable portfolios," states impact investor and thought leader JP Dallmann.[14] Yet

13 Sustainable Signals survey by Morgan Stanley Institute for Sustainable, 2019.

14 JP Dallmann, 2018.

the ecosystem is only in its infancy and still defined as an emerging asset class.

The end destination is what McKinsey & Company call an impact economy. "An impact economy is a very different kind of system from a traditional capitalist economy that prioritises only financial returns. In an impact economy, consumers and shareholders will challenge entrepreneurs and executives to show that they generate their profits in a manner that contributes to the public good." [15] The consultancy implies, within the public good, are looming social and environmental challenges like climate change, overpopulation, food security and finite resources. Given the global scale of these challenges and the difficulties governments have in addressing them, society is turning to the private sector and especially Climate Tech entrepreneurs to take their solutions to the world. And as these challenges increasingly become underlying factors of everyday life, investors, governments, cities and organizations are being galvanised into action.

Innovative and impact-driven companies such as Tesla, Beyond Meat and Northvolt are living proof of the potential of the impact economy. And this trend is likely to continue. The energy transition, electric vehicles and sustainable agriculture are all some of the fastest-growing industries on the planet — and direct solutions to global challenges. But to accelerate these solutions, we cannot continue to drive change with the negative narrative which worked in the golden era of NGOs and charaties. We need to highligh this opportunity. We need to show success. And we need to explicitly define that there will be winners and losers. The winners are those who will build tomorrow. The losers are

---

15 McKinsey & Company, 2018.

those who continue to drag their feet.

If you're an entrepreneur and you have an early-stage startup, this growth in the impact ecosystem will inevitably change the way that you operate. It too, must change the way you think: From challenge to opportunity.

3.

BUILD A BRAND, NOT A PRODUCT

When Warren Buffet decides to invest in a company, he looks for a business that has a wide moat around it. A defence system. Just like when a castle comes under attack, a company in jeopardy needs something that keeps the attackers at bay. In the olden days, they used to attack with iron and steel. Now they replicate your product or idea and take it to market under their own name. "The key to investing is not assessing how much an industry is going to affect society or how much it will grow, but rather determining the competitive advantage of any given company and, above all, the durability of that advantage. The products or services that have wide, sustainable moats around them are the ones that deliver rewards to investors," Buffet says. He described the moat strategy in an article with Fortune magazine in 1999, back when the share price of Berkshire Hathaway was only — eh only — $58,000. Today it's around $300,000 for just one share. I'm not going to go over why it's important we listen to Buffet. However, I think it's sufficient to simply say that his advice has some merit.

The moat which Buffet is referring to is a company's brand. These days, it's very easy to copy a product and a service. You may believe that your innovation is unique or your solution is one of a kind, but chances are, there is someone, somewhere, doing something similar. It's your brand that, when things get hairy, is going to keep you floating above the water. Your brand attracts business partners and top talent. It's your brand that attracts investors to join your journey. And it's your brand that turns your customers into your fans. Now at this point, it should be obvious that I'm not talking about your logo or your name. While these things may be distinctly you, what I'm talking about is how people perceive you; how you perceive the future and your ability to build a community.

Before investing, what Buffet tries to figure out is: "Why is that castle still standing? And what's going to keep it standing or cause it not to be standing five, 10, 20 years from now. What are the key factors? And how permanent are they? How much do they depend on the genius of the lord in the castle?"[1] The narrative around the moat has taken a prominent position in the investing community today. Essentially, this insight into one of the leading minds in investing shows that the robustness of a product or service is only part of the equation. This is especially true, since you may not have a viable product from the get-go. But investors invest in a vision, potential to grow and the ability to protect what's within the castle walls. A particular solution — as brilliant as you think it maybe — is only another brick in that wall. Simply a means to an end.

---

1 Yahoo Finance, 2020.

Before we go into how to build a moat around your business and create a brand which investors will love, let's look at some of the fundamentals of *what* and *why*? The most difficult part about building a brand is in recognising that you have to do so in the first place. This chapter aims to give you knowledge about the importance of branding, as well as some of the historical and cultural changes that will underscore success in the Climate Tec Era. These include the development of the impact ecosystem, the diffusions of innovations theory and the difference between the primal brain and the rational brain. Whilst these concepts may not directly impact your endeavours, the points taken from biology and psychology are interesting concepts that are adaptable to the way that we communicate as impact-driven pioneers. Next, we will touch on theories which seek to explain the uptake of new ideas and innovations in societies and about the way that great leaders communicate.

WHY A BRAND?

A brand is worth many times the value of the company itself. It is "the capitalized value of the trust between the company and the consumer," James E. Burke, CEO of Johnson & Johnson.[2] A company can itself be measured by the building they own, the technology stack they use, the people they employ, their equipment and their intellectual property. Whilst it is difficult to measure a brand's true value, it's not uncommon to hear that it can be valued anywhere between 2x and 100x the value of the company itself. Take for instance Uber, Tesla or Amazon. Each

2 James Burke quoted in John Quelch and David Harding's 1996 Harvard Business Review article.

is wildly valuable, yet their values far exceed their sales. That's because their current valuations are not just based on current sales. Rather, their worth is based on their potential — or their future sales. In our case, their potential is also based on their future impact, which is why measuring your project impact is becoming so important. When combined, they present your brand's equity.

Brand equity is more of an art than a science to measure. It's for this exact reason that many impact entrepreneurs find it difficult to commit resources to. In tangible terms, a brand is simply visual. A logo, a colour palette or a design that people associate with a company. However, a successful brand is much more than that. It's the potential to grow exponentially. **Your potential is your brand**. It is the promise which you make your customer, your potential to grow and your ability to deliver on both. To get a rough idea, we must start with a brand's value and work backwards. And brand value, on the other hand, is easy to measure: How much is another company willing to pay for your company? Your brand's equity is the value of your brand, minus all of the hardware and IP. What's left is your potential. Your potential to enact your vision of the future. Your potential to change the world. Your potential to make a significant profit. Your potential to disrupt the status quo. Your potentail to fundamentally change the future of your industry. These all have value, even if it can't be seen explicitly. A successful brand brings them to life.

Brand equity is a term often used to describe the interaction between a consumer and a B2C company. Whilst I am using it in a different context — the context of your brand's potential to create impact through it's primary, for-profit business activities — the fundamental principles are the same. Marketing communication agency Young & Rubicam (Y&R)

has developed a brand diagnostic tool called the BrandAsset Valuator (BAV) to measure and track brand equity which has four principles:

- **Differentiation.** The defining aspect of a brand and what distinguishes it from all others.
- **Relevance.** The personal appropriateness of the brand to consumers (usually correlated with market share).
- **Esteem.** The extent to which consumers like a brand and hold it in high regard.
- **Knowledge.** The extent to which consumers are aware of the brand and understand what it is for.

According to their methodology, the degree to which a brand is both differentiated and yet relevant to consumers drives the brand's strength in the marketplace. In terms of a startup, branding can be more than just interactions with customers. Your initial traction will be a culmination of your interactions between customers, partners and potential investors. Success for startups is not only found on the marketplace, but rather in their connections and networks. Building your brand's equity will not only help increase knowledge of what you're doing but also of your vision and your customer promise.

Before we go on, let's look at a few of the most common pitfalls in climate tech branding today. Whilst every climate tech brand is different, they've all got a lot in common. They're trying to break into the mainstream because they believe the world would be better if they did. They all want to challenge the way things are currently done and put forward a new solution to an existing problem. And they all struggle with time and money. Branding is, for many, the last thing on their mind. They're busy looking for proof of concept, product-market fit or for early adopters of their new solution. They're busy hustling to keep the doors open rather than bother with the interior design. This leads to three main challenges which all climate tech brands struggle with in terms of branding and they are all a result of being either lazy with, or dismissive of, communications: Inauthenticity, over-complexity or being non-confrontational.

1. **Inauthentic.** Inaction is the antonym of authenticity. Some climate tech brands will say whatever it takes to get clients. They rely on cheap manipulations rather than a long-term strategy. This is a major pitfall of a climate tech brand not investing in their own brand. If you don't know what your values are and what you stand for early on, you're going to be shooting from the hip. This uncertainty doesn't create great morale for team members and it won't help to breed a desirable working culture. Or even worse, founders align themselves with a cause and then don't follow through with action. Half-arsed or absent action is rarely a replacement for words. Silence speaks volumes. But when you do say something, make sure you back it up with action.

2. **Over-complex.** Just because what you do is complex, doesn't mean that's the way you need to explain it. It's not just you though, if that gives you any solace. A large chunk of entrepreneurs — regardless of field — struggle to communicate what they do in a succinct manner. They focus either on industry-specific jargon or business jargon words like "innovative" or "solution" which in essence don't add much meaning to your pitch. Your audience wants to comprehend exactly what your unique selling point (USP) is and what they can expect when dealing with you. They shouldn't walk

away confused or puzzled from the interaction.

3. **Non-confrontational.** Climate tech brands sometimes become uncomfortable with challenging social expectations. Even though they're out there challenging what society is doing and putting a new solution into the world, they're afraid to go outside the realm of what we understand is "normal" behaviour. At times they're too afraid to take a stand over topics they care about for the fear that it will create a negative impression with their peers. We live in a world where we're completely overrun by numerous options in almost every industry imaginable. The only way to stand out is to pick a set of rules, norms or conventions and break them.

To overcome these challenges and build an authentic brand that impact investors will love, you have to ensure that your approach is authentic, relevant and different from your peers. To do so, you have six mechanisms at your disposal to build a moat around your impact-driven business. Each is a process rather than a lever, but when utilized correctly, together they can be extremely powerful and valuable. In my experience, every climate tech brand is at a different stage with each of these concepts, so what I recommend doing is an organizational sweep to determine your position before moving forward. They are the basis of the Climate Tech Branding Methodology:

- **Brand Foundations.** Solid foundations mean a solid house. A brand's foundations are its stories, its vision of the future, and its purpose to exist, split into internal and external. The internal aspect is your brand's manifesto. The external aspect is your brand's strategic narrative. In my experience, a manifesto is a fantastic way to exemplify all of these concepts together in a story: It's the why, the how and the what all in one piece of copy, told with passion. By connecting your own experiences as a founder with the things that drove you to start your business, you can create a solid base from which to scale. The second part is your brand's strategic narrative — the story that you will tell externally. A strategic narrative wraps the facts you want to get across (your product's features and impact metrics) within a story (of your view of the future). These two will in turn be the basis for many of the other branding endeavours like creating a brand position or determining your visual identity.

- **Target Audience.** Defining your target audience is an essential mechinism in business development, yet one which many climate tech brands downright fail to do. The process itself, market segmentation, can be defined as the aggregation of prospective buyers into groups or segments with common needs and who respond similarly to a marketing action.[3] Often, impact entrepreneurs struggle to define our target audience due to an unwillingness to narrow their scope of impact. We want to help everyone. But if everyone is your ideal customer, how do you tailor your message appropriately? Segmenting your audience and pinpointing exactly who you're going to target lends clarity to the rest of the branding process.
- **Strategic Messaging.** Strategic messaging is the process of crafting a message or a story for a specific decision-maker in your target market. Once you have a clear idea of exactly who your target market is, it's time to find out what problems they have and how you can craft stories using your product as a solution. By tackling the major

3 Investopedia, 2020.

pitfalls of impact communicating with strategic messaging, this step shows how you can add value with your communications and position yourself in your target audience's mind as a viable solution when it comes time to buy.

- **Brand Platform.** A brand's platform is where all this information comes to life. All the work you've put in building your foundatons, defining your target audience and birthing your strategic message. And will be the middle ground between marketing and sales. It's the combination of your visual identity, your digital assets and your social presence. Whilst I've said many times that a brand may be much more than its logo, its colours, your look and feel are a key component of differentiating your brand. But it goes deeper than that, just like a person's identity isn't only visual. Your brand identity includes your personality (e.g. is your brand optimistic, genuine?) as well as its tone of voice. All of these concepts feed into your website's design, your written content, your customer funnel — i.e. your customer's journey from completely unaware to customer — and which social platforms you choose to own.
- **Thought Leadership.** A major part of building a brand is having a founder who inspires, builds a network and exudes confidence. Personal branding is 50% of the work. A strong brand starts with a compelling brand vision — the way a brand wants to present itself — and a founder that embodies that vision is a valuable asset. Speaking opportunities, publishing articles and engaging in meaningful debate around your niche are all ways in which you can tell your brand's story and boost your reputation as a thought leader. It's the way you can position yourself, rather than let those outside

do it for you.

- **Public Relations.** As public relations lies outside your direct sphere of influence, it's the most difficult aspect of brand building to tame.Getting press coverage is difficult when no one cares about your product or solution. It's downright frustrating when you send out 100 emails and you get no responses. But by leveraging your personal brand and using it as a stepping stone, you can begin your PR journey with the best foot forward. By harnessing this strategic branding medium, you can actively get third-party verified information in front of your potential partners, investors and clients. Furthermore, press coverage can be extremely valuable when the right story is presented to the right person. For instance, Bill Gates began his journey in water & sanitation after reading a new article. When employed correctly, this medium can fuel explosive interest in your topic of interest and can assert your position as a viable option to confront the challenge.

It doesn't matter if you think that you've got the most forward-thinking and innovative X that's out there... if two other companies are offering similar services, how does the purchaser choose? The reason your climate tech brand will succeed is simple: Your vision of the future is better than your incumbent market leaders and you've told the right stories to the right people. It's not, however, because you've got the most sustainable X on the market. That competitive advantage will always erode, it's a fact of modern economics. Yet impact entrepreneurs are prone to believe their methodology or their solution can compete because it's "more sustainable" or "more innovative" than anything else out there. We believe that we stand out from the crowd. And maybe it's true...for a while. But it doesn't last forever. Every solution can be replicated. Every innovative business model can be copied. You might have the solution to solve a specific problem now, but what happens when someone solves it for cheaper? Or is backed by a bigger company? In the current climate, sustainability won't be your competitive advantage for long.

Why? Because **sustainability is a business value** and **not a market differentiator.** Every day, new climate tech brands are being built. Imagine you're in the market for a non-plastic straw. Ten years ago, this market was a niche. You could have called yourself Eco Straw and had a green logo. Today, there are so many Instagram accounts selling sustainable straws, you couldn't count them on the feet of a millipede. So what differentiates one from another? They all sell long, round bits of metal, bamboo or recycled plastic that you can drink through "guilt-free". They're all claiming to be sustainable. They all solve the consumer's problem: Not wanting to use single-use plastic. The sustainability of their product isn't their defining feature anymore. So how can they compete for market share?

Now I know that there are some people out there thinking: "They shouldn't have to compete...there should be enough people out there that don't want to use plastic straws and they all should survive." This is a thought process that derives from our social days. We so often think that our solution shouldn't have to compete because it stands alone; the only sustainable option on the market. As such, it's survival is guaranteed by humanity's humanity. In reality, however, the truth is much less secure.

People buy solutions. Sustainability isn't quantifiable for most consumers; it simply is or it isn't. They're not looking for the most sustainable thing on the market and they don't have time to check the specifics of a product against your competitors. They have a problem and they value sustainability. If you're in the market of solving a sustainability pain point, all your competitors will be too. As that problem becomes more mainstream, more people will see value in solving it.

Just like plastic straws, reusable water bottles and packaging-free soaps were niches a decade ago, there are hundreds of unique solutions today that will grow into profitable markets. You might think you own the problem you're solving. But if you succeed in making a profitable business from solving it, it's only a matter of time until you have company.

WHY INVEST YOUR TIME IN BRANDING EARLY ON?

Whilst every climate tech brand is different, they've all got a lot in common. They're trying to break into the mainstream because they believe the world would be better if they did. They all want to challenge the way things are currently done and put forward a new solution to an existing problem. And they all struggle with time and money. Investing in branding early on can save you both in the long run, by helping you:

- **To differentiate your company from the competition.** When it comes down to it, your customers or clients are human beings. When they're not shopping for your product or service, they're busy picking their kids up from daycare or polishing off that annual report. They don't have the mental capacity to judge and measure exactly how impactful or sustainable your solution is compared to the competition. When all product features align, how you present yourself can be a decisive way to set yourself apart from the competition.

- **To demonstrate leadership.** Potential partners and clients are looking for leaders to express long-term vision for the industry, not just in their cause. Because sustainability is a business value, not a market differentiator, they need to see more than just a sustainable solution. Especially in our fast-paced, internet-driven community, your climate tech brand has to show your adaptability to concepts outside of your specialty. A strong brand helps you protect your long-term market share and investment in it now indicates that you'll take this matter seriously in the future.
- **To attract the right investors.** One of the most important things for investors is to invest in businesses with a wide and long-lasting moat (brand) to protect them. In the first few years of existance, the majority businesses fail. One of the main reasons is that they struggle to get access to the capital they need to stay in business. By investing in your brand early on, you will find it easier to attract the right type of investors and showcase your potential. Failure to do so may prevent you from getting your concept of the ground at all.
- **To leave a good impression.** Every time anyone has an interaction with your company, it leaves an impression. The only thing in your hands is whether you take ownership of this or leave it up to chance. If you're looking to grow, a bad impression can be a make-or-break moment. A good impression however can result in a check with lots of zeros on the end. Branding is when you decide to take control of the interactions which your company

has with the public. It can be the difference between whether that impression is "they seem like they're in control of their future" or "they're inconsistent and they'll never get anywhere".

BUT I'VE ALREADY GOT A LOGO?

If you're building a company that's going to take a bite out of some of the biggest challenges of our time, then chances are you're not going to be able to do it alone. Whether that's by partnering with governments, private investors, crowdfunding or venture capital is up to you. But with the current state of affairs, we need to scale our impact as quickly as possible... and unfortunately, those of us who weren't a founding partner at Paypal have to compete on a level playing field. At the same time, branding is, for many, the last thing on their mind. Between product launches and MVPs, it's all about the quality of the solution: Right? However, consider this. Founders spend roughly half their time raising capital. If a founder works for 10 hours a day, that's 25 hours a week. If you managed to cut that number down to 30% — becuase your business already speaks the same language, generates outside interest, shows a certain level of professionality and is consistent in its message — isn't that a win? By focusing on your developing your brand as your product develops, you can actively save time and effort in future tense.

I'll say it again: Branding is much more than your logo, the colours you use or the font on your business card. Branding is about the stories that you put into the world. And your stories are your strategy. It's what people say about you and your business when you're not there to defend yourself.

The visual assets are simply shorthand for these stories. A brand's stories are it's most valuable assets. Stories that are easily digested and shared. If you're a B2C company, it's the stories that your customers can tell their friends about your product. If you're a B2B company, it's the stories which your potential customer will use to help them sell the investment to their boss.

For instance, think about Patagonia. They have a logo and colours. But when you see them what do you imagine? I think about their Black Friday Sale where 100% of their global retail and online sales went directly to grassroots environmental nonprofits. When I think about Netflix, I think about the time when their founders pitched to Blockbuster only to be laughed out of the room. When I think about BrewDog, I think about the time they stuffed 11 bottles of beer inside a deceased wild animal and sold them for hundreds of pounds.

Now not everyone agrees with these stories. Followers of liberal economics would be repelled by Paragonia's actions. Netflix's story appeals to the entrepreneur in us. And BrewDog...well, it's divisive, to say the least. You either find your own values in them or you don't: Stuffing beer in dead squirrels probably isn't your cup of tea, but you'd be damn stupid to believe that those bottles didn't sell out in minutes. There's one thing that binds them all together; they're memorable because they don't explain a problem or a product.

Telling stories is a key concept in branding. **No one cares about your product or solution.** People invest in solving their problems and want to tell a story when it's done. The story that you tell shouldn't be aimed at everyone (this is the segmentation mentioned earlier). If you have to water down your message so that it appeals to everyone, you've already failed. But that doesn't mean that you should confuse your audience with industry-specific jargon either. A great story is easy to remember and recite. A great story can be the difference between a startup that receives investment and a startup that doesn't. And a great story can be the difference between a lineup of alternative straws. But it's not about the sustainability of your service or product, because in time, that will fade and you'll blend into a bland background of others who forgot to tell a great story.

For example, if you type in "ecofriendly" on Instagram you will find a whole range of brands are peddling the same concepts; soaps, metal straws and faux-leather goods. The vast majority use the same green branding and images of the ocean. They're all essentially the same brand. So how can you grow exponentially if you don't differentiate yourself? If sustainability and impact are becoming mainstream, then we must evolve with this development.

THE INNOVATORS BELL CURVE

Just like we have to watch the words that we use in the story we tell, we have to ensure that we're telling the right story to the right people. Ideas, when they're told to the right people, spread. When an idea is told to the wrong person, it doesn't. The difference between an idea that spreads and an idea that doesn't is the person which it's told to. If your story doesn't resonate with them, if they don't feel involved in it and don't subsequently pass it on, your story won't spread. You may imagine that as a brand, you'll say or do something and it will reach an audience. Like an antenna distributing one signal to 100 people. Sender, receiver-style. However, in reality, it's more likely to work like this. You have an idea and you tell one person. That person loves your idea so much, they tell a further two people. Those two people are so enthusiastic about your idea that they tell two more. Sooner or later, you have an audience of 100 people, but it all starts with telling the right story to the right person first. That's because people spread ideas. And because people believe people they know or are connected to in some meaningful way. They don't believe strangers selling stuff. Identifying who the right people are and creating a story not only for their consumption, but which they will be happy to spread is key in ensuring that your idea spreads.

Just like a story spreads, so too does new technology. The adoption of new information leads to innovations which challenge our existing world view. Challenge a world view, you challenge the world order. And this is by no means a new phenomenon. Going back in history, we can find many concepts which challenged the dominant ideology of the day. The idea that the world was round was floated for the first time in the 5th century BC by Greek philosophers. The paradigm was gradually adopted throughout the Old World during the Middle Ages and by the time it was widely accepted, technology had evolved significantly. The adoption process of this concept paved the way for the first voyages across the Atlantic ocean. Christopher Columbus's determination to find a direct water route west from Europe to Asia was underlined by this thought process. However, the existing world order is, almost always, resistant to change. Only a few years after Columbus made his voyage, Italian diplomat and political theorist Niccolò Machiavelli said the following words: "There is nothing more difficult to plan, more doubtful of success, nor more dangerous to manage than the creation of a new order of things…Whenever his enemies have occasion to attack the innovator they do so with the passion of partisans, while the others defend him sluggishly, so that the innovator and his party alike are vulnerable".[4]

Today's resistance to addressing climate change can in many ways be compared to the historic resistance to new ways of thinking.[5] One way that we can learn from the comparisons that they draw is through the lens of acceptance, a concept that American sociologist and communication theorist Everett Rogers brought to light in the mid 20th Century. Considered a founder of modern communications theory, Roger's Diffusion of Innovation, examines how ideas spread through society. An innovation, for Rogers, is an idea, practice or project that is perceived as new by an individual or other unit of adoption. Diffusion analyses the conditions that increase or decrease the likelihood that an innovation — a new idea, product or practice — will be adopted by a group. Because new ideas are not adopted by all individuals in a social system at one time, Roger's combined these two concepts into a sequence of adoption. "One reason why there is so much interest in the diffusion of innovations is because getting a new idea adopted, even when it has obvious advantages, is often very difficult," says Rogers.

Adoption of technology or change to the status quo by an individual takes five steps. It begins with awareness and knowledge; the acknowledgement of the presence or existence of the new innovation or technology, as well as a general understanding of what it might entail. Next come persuasion and interest; the act of processing information associated with the

---

4 Niccolo Machiavelli, 1532.

5 Lynn White Jr, 1967.

innovation, inspiring the individual to find out more about the product or services. The third is decision and assessment; Having considered the persuasion factors, the individual will at this point make a decision — by gathering evidence, data or opinions — about whether to adopt or reject the innovation. Fourth comes the implementation and exploration phase; The series of activities wherein the innovation is put to use for the first time. The success of this stage solidifies the adoption of innovation in the individual's mind. Lastly comes the confirmation and adoption stage; this is where behaviour is reinforced by the innovation's actual delivery against the claims of relative advantage.

As a Climate Tech professional, you're undoubtedly trying to solve a global issue in a new or novel way. This newness is inherently uncertain in its applicability. And just like there was resistance to the science of climate change, the spherical earth theory or the theory of evolution, there will undoubtedly be resistance to your solution. To make sense of this process of acceptance, Roger's theory splits society into five distinct segments. They include innovators, early adopters, the early majority, the late majority and laggards.[6]

- **Innovators (2.5%).** Innovators are the first individuals to adopt an innovation. Innovators are willing to take risks, are the youngest, have the highest social class, have great financial lucidity, are very social and have the closest contact with scientific sources and interaction with other innovators. Risk tolerance has them adopting technologies which may ultimately fail. Financial resources help absorb these failures.
- **Early Adopters (13.5%).** This is the second-fastest category of

6 Evertt Rogers, 1957.

individuals who adopt an innovation. These individuals have the highest degree of opinion leadership among the other adopter categories. Early adopters are typically younger in age, have a higher social status, have more financial lucidity, advanced education and are more socially forward than late adopters. More discrete in adoption choices than innovators. Realizing judicious choice of adoption will help them maintain a central communication position.

- **Early Majority (34%).** Individuals in this category adopt an innovation after a varying degree of time. This time of adoption is significantly longer than the innovators and early adopters. Early Majority tend to be slower in the adoption process, have above average social status, contact with early adopters and seldom hold positions of opinion leadership in a system.
- **Late Majority (34%).** Individuals in this category will adopt an innovation after the average member of society. These individuals approach an innovation with a high degree of scepticism and after the majority of society has adopted the innovation. Late Majority are typically sceptical about an innovation, have below-average social status, very little financial lucidity, in contact with others in late majority and early majority, very little opinion leadership.
- **Laggards (16%).** Individuals in this category are the last to adopt an innovation. Unlike some of the previous categories, individuals in this category show little to no opinion leadership. These individuals typically have an aversion to change-agents and tend to be advanced in age. Laggards typically tend to be focused on "traditions", likely to have lowest social status, lowest financial fluidity, be oldest of all other adopters, in contact with only family and close friends, very

little to no opinion leadership.

Understanding how society adopts new technology and accepts new ideas is crucial to creating a communications strategy for a brand in the climate technology space. Because as impact entrepreneurs, we're social beings, we inherently tend to focus on the largest social group possible. The whole. However, according to Roger's bell curve, we should be focusing our efforts on communicating with those most open to change. Our businesses are built on better ways to do things. Because these news ideas challenge the existing status quo, the greatest chance we have to have them grow our innovations into socially accepted alternatives lies with convincing the innovators and early adopters first.

They're the ones who are likely to be most open to your solution. To be willing to give you the benefit of the doubt and help you leverage their network for the sake of bringing your solution into the world. In other words, they're imperative to your success as an impact entrepreneur. But where do you find them? Innovators and early adopters of new innovations:

- Are actively seeking a competitive edge.
- Have the ability to find new uses for an innovation.
- Seek out and sign up for early trials and beta tests.
- Like to be unique and share new products because it makes them feel good.
- Are technological leaders in their organizations.
- Are willing to use a product that isn't complete.

Innovators don't have the solutions but they have the problem that you're in business to solve. These problems aren't global — like climate change or plastic pollution — they are business issues like "my investors want me to measure my impact but I don't have the capabilities" or "how do we communicate about sustainability without sounding like we're greenwashing". Identifying the problem is key to positioning your product or service as a solution. As we have seen, the first step of adoption is awareness and knowledge. To bring awareness to your solution, it's imperative to have a solid pulse on the issue, who suffers from it and how it affects their lives. As your startup introduces a new product to the market, find the place where your target audience is talking about the problems that your product addresses. Whether it's in traditional media, online forums, blogs, social media, etc, find them and contribute to the conversation. And when you find them, showcase your passion for solving their problem rather than your product.

If innovators are those who create new ideas or tools that are more efficient than their predecessors, then the early adopters are their first users of the cutting edge technology of the day. Both are catalysts for new ideas. Innovators are likely to, if they complete all five stages of adoption, pass on their experience to the early adopters. The early adopters are the influencers of the early majority and so on.

TARGETING THE INNOVATORS & EARLY ADOPTERS

How do we frame our solutions to such problems like climate change and food insecurity in a way that will trigger a call to action? As an climate tech brand, it's normal to believe that your business is united with the cause that you're dedicating so much time and energy to solve.

Consider that Diffusions of Innovations graph represents 100% of the industry you're trying to serve. Those in at the beginning (the innovators and early adoptors) are at the forefront of change, those at the backside are those lagging behind. Every industry, every population segment has these categories: Of those who are open to change and those who aren't. Sustainability is a big transformation and just like any other big change, there will be those who want to embrace it and those who will oppose it — be it on political, ideological, or religious grounds. It's not your job as a Cliamte Tech brand (yet) to convince the masses to adopt your product.

We spend far too much time on is convincing the yellow and red section of the industry the benefits of "going green". In other words, we lecture to a general audience. We waste our breath lecturing the early majority to try and turn them into innovators. And it's far less efficient than helping the section in green. Your ideal target audience already wants impact — they just don't know HOW to achieve it. When you communicate, don't try and convince them to act, show them how.

But when you harp on about a global problem, as we've talked about earlier, people tend to switch off. If your goal as a business is to change the views of the general population in regards to sustainability (or any other cause you hold dear) and have them change their ways, you're not in business, you're trying to build a social movement. Social movements communicate with a sole goal in mind: Change the way society acts in relation to a cause. They target large audiences with similar messages in the hope that they inspire enough people to reach a tipping point for change. Examples of social movements are the Civil Rights Movement, the Me Too Movement and Extinction Rebellion. But if you've decided to create a product that you need to sell to grow your impact, then you have to communicate like a business. Why? Because the biggest section of the pie, the majority, are good at ignoring what you have to say. They're simply not interested in joining your movement if they've never heard of it before, just like if they have no need for your product.

Seth Godin, American author and one of the forefathers of modern marketing theory, states that there are two major reasons why you shouldn't target the majority:[7]

1. **They don't want to hear what you're saying.** "They have problems that they find far more significant than the ones your product solves and they're just not willing to invest the time to listen to you".
2. **They don't always listen to the innovators on the left of the curve.** The majority "want protocols and systems and safety that new products rarely offer." Because of this, many new businesses never get the chance to target the majority at all.

If you're a small business, targeting the majority with your messages about the dangers of sustainability and climate change is a waste of breath. You're unlikely to change any minds and if you do, they're unlikely to be in the market for your product due to other constricting factors. As Godin puts it, "If they're not going to listen to their friends, why should they listen to you?" Informing the innovators with a message about the dangers of climate change is just as futile. Innovators already know about the significant challenges which we face. If they don't, they can't possibly be innovators.

---

7 Seth Godin, 2002.

Our goal with communications as sustainable businesses should be to define the struggles that these innovators are experiencing and work hard to solve them, not try to bring about a social tipping point by educating and informing the masses. We should be outlining the problems our company solves, our solutions and why the company has chosen to take up this battle. In short, it should be to help our company grow. However, I quite often work with climate tech brands who are committed to spreading their knowledge or disseminating information with their communication campaigns. Instead of growing their company, they want to "inform the public" on the perils of climate change or the necessity to transition towards a sustainable society.

These general messages can span anything from going vegan to getting solar panels at home or driving an electric vehicle and they're, generally, ineffective. Informing the public about stuff you care about is the equivalent of standing on top of a cliff with a megaphone. If your goal is to scale your impact, then the more people you bring along on your journey, the better. But you have to start one by one and let those people help you build.

Communication goals for climate tech startups should look something like this:

1. Underscore the challenge that you're facing and why your company has chosen to focus on solving this challenge
2. Increase brand awareness of your company for potential customers or partners by identifying the problem that you're solving
3. Demonstrating that you are an authority in your niche and that you're the one who's best positioned to confront the challenge

4. Create demand for your products and drive it into your sales funnel
5. Create awareness for fundraising (VC, angel investors or corporate partners) and building brand's equity

Communications can help turn strangers into fans, introduce your brand to the market and help your future clients become aware that you exist. It's the top of your sales cycle and it's a key element that provides the fuel for growth. If your goal is to grow your business and take your solution to the world, it can be the way to let the world know you're coming. But if your goal isn't to be recognised on the market as a leader in your field, but rather to inform or challenge general public opinion, you've fundamentally misunderstood the task at hand for two reasons.

Firstly, to grow your user base and your network of potential partners and investors, it's important to target the people who will become your biggest fans. Focusing on changing the general public opinion about a topic so broad as deforestation won't lead to increased action on the topic, but rather it will just add to the white noise surrounding it. See, the thing is that you don't just walk up to the masses and give them something unique and obscure. You give it to the innovators — those lining up for days for a new iPhone or pair of Nike Airs — and let them tell the masses for you. Following the innovators' curve, if you've created a new and innovative solution you're in your first year or two of business, you should be directly communicating to the top 2.5% of innovators who might actually use your product. If you've already got a client base, then perhaps it's time to start looking to the top 15% of early movers and innovators. Your job marketing your startup is to wow this small demographic, excite them and then retain their attention.

This demographic may not need to be convinced that the problem exists. They already know climate change is an issue and they know the challenges we face in solving it. They're desperately looking to leverage their utility to find solutions. What they don't know exists is your solution. Getting your solutions into their hands will increase the likelihood that you can reach the critical mass of society. They're the Evangelists, the unabashed cheerleaders and salespeople for your product and, if you are creating a new market, for your company vision. If you talk down to or lecture evangelists, they're far less likely to advocate for your brand. This leads me to reason number two.

When you, as a marketeer, try to penetrate the masses with your messaging they're likely to turn off or view it as offensive or untrustworthy. Imagine you're walking down the street and somebody stops to tell you that you should change your superannuation to a fund that has divested from fossil fuels. Your reaction is likely to be one of disdain or annoyance. "Who do you think you are and why should I even care?" But now imagine that you have a good friend who tells you the same thing at a BBQ. Would you hear them out? Maybe hear more than just what you need to do? Maybe even the why? When a message is delivered by someone you know and trust, you're much more likely to be receptive rather than sceptical. These messengers are called evangelists and they're your brand's biggest fans. They're the ones who grow brands and they're the ones you should be targeting.

I'll give you a personal example. Since I moved to The Netherlands, I've had a massive problem with banking. I originally banked with Rabobank but after getting stuck in the Middle East without any money on three separate occasions, I knew I needed to change. The solution would have been to give me a Visa or a Mastercard, but because I was a foreign national, they refused. Next I went to ABN AMRO, after three trips to the bank where their system was down, they also refused to give me a bank account with a card that would work outside of Europe. Then I found BUNQ, a Dutch challenger bank. It was more expensive than the rest, but I had my account within an hour. I had my visa card within a day. Now I'm a BUNQ evangelist. Whenever I pull out my card and people ask me, I tell them with fury about my struggles and how BUNQ solved them. I've convinced multiple friends in similar scenarios to swap banks too or open business accounts with them. Heck, I even read a book on the company and I hate banking! Although I'm aligned with their mission, it was their ability to solve problems for me that turned me into an evangelist.

Your first job as a marketer is to turn innovators into evangelists. If you believe you have succeeded in this, then next your focus should be to give your evangelists the information that they need to spread your message for you. Innovators are usually extremely preoccupied by being the first to get their hands on something. They take pride in being the first to know that something exists, before everyone else...and they'll want to tell others.

Ultimately, if you tell someone what to do, they're likely to do the opposite. But if you give people an alternative, you can build the economy of the future. In this way, marketing goes beyond telling the customer about the problem but offering them a way that they can actually make changes. For many companies however, this is difficult because it forces them to reassess their brand promise[8] — what is the effect or result that

8 A brand promise is a statement made by an organization to its customers stating what customers can expect from their product and services. This is in terms of the benefits and experience — the tangible and

clients will have when they work with that company?

PRIMARY VS. RATIONAL BRAIN

Before we had images and recordings, we had stories. Stories relayed the truths of the past and they continue to define how we engaged with our environment and those within it. As humans, our brains are constructed in a way to help us digest and internalise stories. Our ability to do that far exceeds our ability to digest facts or figures. Why? Because stories create emotions.

See, our brain is split between our rational brain and our primal brain. Our primal brain — similar to that of other mammals — makes decisions based on instincts. It interprets the world around us and analyses whether something is a threat, whether something is tasty or whether it's attractive without us processing it. Rather, we feel it and react. For instance, if you saw a lion in the wild, before you realise you're scared the hairs on the back of your neck would already be standing up.

Our rational brain on the other hand was developed later in our evolution. It's what gives us the ability to make decisions based on rational facts. For instance: A monkey would never leave a banana uneaten just because you tell him that he can have unlimited bananas in monkey heaven. But with the developed rational brain, humans can listen to facts and figures, crunch the numbers and come to a conclusion that while you could eat the banana, it may be more rational to leave that banana there, if there is

---

the intangible, i.e., the value proposition.

a good chance that monkey heaven exists on the other side of the door.

The primary brain influences our instincts and is both impulsive and rash when it comes to decision-making. Whilst we may be highly informed about the options available to us and can consistently and uniquely rank all options according to our preferences, we can consistently justify choosing against the best option for something that aligned with our interior motives. And it's something that big brand names have been capitalising on for years. Why choose BMW over Mercedes?

Why choose iPhone over Samsung? The rational brain may lead you to believe that it's the functions of each product; i.e. the equation of performance and features divided by price. This is what marketers call Rational Choice Theory and it's something that only comes into effect when that overwhelming urge is missing. For instance, if you're an Apple diehard and you have to buy an Android, but you have no idea where to start and no affinity with any of the products. You'll quite rationally begin to look at the features of all of the options on the table. How much do they cost? What's the storage capacity, how big is the screen? I'm the same, I buy Apple because I truly identify as being an Apple man. I find the concept of buying an Android discomforting and for the brief period I used one when my iPhone broke, I hated it, even though it had a bigger screen than my iPhone and was faster. That's what a brand does. It sways your rational brain and allows you to make irrational choices because they feel right.

WHAT DOES THIS HAVE TO DO WITH

BRANDING?

So many startup founders and managers say words to the effect of: "We tried branding but it didn't pay off". Many of them have received expensive advice and unnecessary campaign suggestions from branding agencies (who would undoubtedly carry out the work). A few were tried and tested, but most branding exercises stayed on the shelf, accumulating dust. This aversion to branding is normal. It's impossible to judge by the same metrics by which you would judge an advertising campaign. Every $1 spent doesn't turn into $2. It just seems all too hard, doesn't it? I'll tell you a secret. It was never going to be easy, but when done right, branding can help guide an investor's hand towards their chequebook or an executive's towards a handshake. And you'll be happy to know, in most circumstances, right doesn't have to mean expensive.

For example, let's say that you're an investor looking at a range of startups to invest capital in. They have narrowed the option down to three companies who are all in the process of raising capital. All three have solid books. All three have potentially game-changing products. All three have a scalable business model. But like most things in life, all things are not made equal. And humans have an inherent desire to discriminate, judge and analyse, even if it's a process that happens in the subconscious.

We are instinctually programmed to make decisions in a matter of milliseconds regarding pretty much anything we come into contact with. Is it dangerous? Should I be wary? Can I relax? Such cognitive bias happens in a place in your head called the subconscious brain. Let's go back in time a moment and consider the difference between the evolved apes we are today and the primal apes we once were. What sets us apart is our ability to take in, digest and contemplate complex bits of information. Whilst we have evolved and have developed a consciousness, this primal instinct is still guiding us through everyday life. When targeted, it can override rational thought processes.

Going back to our example, the day comes when you will have an initial interview with all three candidates. One stands out in terms of their scalable business model and you're more interested in them than the other two. Let's call them Startup A, B and C. Imagine that Startup A's founder arrives for the interview and is all over the place. Their presentation doesn't work and their clothes look like they haven't been ironed properly. Rationally, they're the best option of the three on paper, emotionally however, your interaction with Startup A is subpar. It's the same reason we wear a suit to a job interview or put on lipstick when we go out for a date. Because we understand that on the other side of the table, someone will make a split-second decision on whether they trust us or like us or not. However, Startup B nails the social interaction. They ask questions. They tell stories. They seem engaged. They may not have the best product, yet. But there's just something about them; they've got an aura of success about them. Startup C just talks about their solution. Who do you think gets the second interview?

Unfortunately, today, it's not only the appearance of your founder that can sway the primal brain of investors. It's every interaction that that investor could have with the startup, be it a blog post, an article in the newspaper, your website, your business card and of course what that investor's peers say (or don't say) about your brand. Obviously, you can't control what people say about your brand or everything that they can find online, but you can and should be able to sway that table by crafting and pushing one continuous message and telling it to the right people.

This is especially necessary because generally, people tend to be less trustworthy of new entries in the market. Startups have to fight harder to prove themselves as a result. But when you create a strong brand, it shows your target audience — be it investors or customers — that you're going to be sticking around. That you mean business. To gain people's trust, your company must be authentic, credible and recognisable. By developing a strong brand from day one, your business can enter the ring with longstanding companies and begin to challenge, disrupt and compete. Failing to do so can mean that your potential customers/ partners don't identify with your startup or see your product as a solution to their problem. It can create a disconnect between your company and the ecosystem that will support it. At best, it will be a hindrance that you will have to fix at a later stage. At worst, a poor brand will slow you down and deter partnerships, talent and investors from taking interest in your company. In short, to give your startup the best chance of success, you must put effort into crafting a brand which represents your potential.

When it comes to presenting yourself to the world, winning customers and building a reputation, it's imperative that you start on the right foot. startup branding is going to be critical to your success. No matter how much your solution will help create a sustainable ecosystem or impact our planet's greatest challenges, at the end of the day your venture is one out of thousands who are fighting for growth and attention. Setting yourself apart from the pack is the only way to scale your impact. For every brand or entrepreneur, the path is different. But to move from MVP to investment-ready, certain things need to be in order. Maybe your product is still only a concept. Perhaps, you've not even launched yet. Whilst there is no one path, there are certain steps that need to be followed to build the foundations of your company's brand. They will help you in understanding how you should be communicating. They will help you build your strategy. And they will help you act in a manner which is perceived as authentic.

START WITH ~~WHY~~

How sustainable your products are, is a feature, not your differentiating factor. Your brand's differentiating factor is its purpose, its reason to exist: Your why. Why you exist in the first place. Understanding the difference between these two concepts is integral to creating a communications strategy that builds a brand rather than sells a product. Consider this quote by author, motivational speaker and instructor of strategic communications at Columbia University Simon Sinek: "People don't buy what you do; they buy why you do it". Sinek is the author of Start With Why, a best-selling book on how great leaders communicate.[9] He contends that great leaders in their respective fields, from Martin Luther King Jr. to Apple all communicate similarly. That they start with their why. Not their what or their how.

For instance, consider a new coffee company which claims that they have a sustainable supply chain. They are fair trade and they are carbon neutral. But like so many other brands, they communicate by saying: 'Hey, we're a sustainable coffee company, we're fair trade and we're carbon

9 Simon Sinek, 2009

neutral. Buy our coffee, it's great for the planet and it tastes great too'. It's a good sales pitch. It may even get clients, but when it comes to scaling, it's not going to be enough. They started with what and then supported it with their how. In the long run, there may be hundreds of new coffee companies that claim to have a sustainable supply chain and are carbon-neutral, they can all operate independently of each other and claim to have a similar impact, but something is missing. Their why.

"If you talk about what you believe, you will attract those who believe what you believe," says Sinek. Let's flip the coffee example on its head. Imagine a coffee company that says: 'Hey, we're a company that exists to stop deforestation in the Amazon and empower local Brazilian farmers. We're a sustainable coffee company. And we're fair trade as well as carbon neutral. Buy our coffee, it tastes great.' By flipping it on its head, you begin with something which connects to your customer's why immediately.

This all comes back to the primal brain. For instance, let's take the example from earlier about the BMW and the Mercedes and throw a Tesla into the mix. You, as a sustainable entrepreneur, believe that electric vehicles are the future of private transportation. That's a belief that you hold internally and no amount of advertising can make you change your mind on that. Now consider that BMW and Mercedes have just come out with electric vehicles. The specs are on par with Tesla's and they are all roughly around the same price mark. Both Mercedes and BMW are serious about sustainable transport but they were both late to join the party. Both are coming out with cars to rival that of Tesla. But the messaging around it? I just checked both their websites. Mercedes says: "The art of luxury, built on science". BMW talks about "pioneering the future of mobility" and then gives a list of benefits of going electric.

Tesla, in everything it says and does spread this message: "Our mission is to accelerate the world's transition to sustainable energy." This message connects to peoples why and it resonates somewhere within them. The result is that there is very little choice between the three brands and can act as an explanation for Tesla's massive growth over the past decade. I'll be touching on Tesla as a case study a lot in the rest of this book, so whether you love them or you hate them, it's important that you recognise their commitment to strategic communications.

Now, you're probably thinking, "I've heard of Simon Sinek and I know about the Goldern Circle." The reason I've introduced it here is because it's an important concept to know in the recent history of brand building. But I'd like to expand on this for a moment. Sinek hypothesized this concept in the days where impact was still delivered by NGOs and charities, and business was slow on the uptake of purpose. As the worlds of impact and profit have collided, this no longer stands true.

As impact entrepreneurs, we find a strong bond with the idea of creating good in the world. For everyone and not just ourselves. Yet these tendencies also hold us back. So many early-stage sustainable businesses communicate to convince the general public why we need to act on climate change. They only communicate their why! They tell stories of melting ice caps, and endless CO2 emissions, and plastic in our oceans. They tell us about the necessity to "act now". The problem with these messages lies in their misguided intention: To educate the general population. Every day, I hear someone tell a general audience that they have to minimize negative impact on the planet. Why does this matter? Negative impact actions = negative messages = inaction. Then when it comes time for an impact entrepreneur or climate tech startup to answer the question, "What do you do", we usually preach to the converted, by:

- Speaking in overly complex industry jargon. Many of those who dedicate their life to solving the greatest challenges of the day are undoubtedly some of the sharpest tools in the shed. You're more likely to be an academic or scientist and on the other, you're an inherently social human being. But it's likely that their target audience lives outside our impact-bubble and have little to no idea what you're talking about when you say stuff like "We are an AI-driven multidisciplinary innovation ecosystem leading the systemic transition to a planet-inclusive circular economy through Industry 4.0 technology". BUT WHAT DO YOU DO?? The scientific or academic route is a classic impact entrepreneur character trait: It's a complex subject and you want to show that you're qualified. However, this often drives us to speak to our peers, not our target audience. Essentially, it leaves us preaching to the choir. And when you speak in complex industry jargon to investors or partners, they simply turn off.
- Leading with negative social messaging instead of value. When you're a social-first communicator, you often forego speaking about what you can do for your clients and customers and focus solely on the problem at hand or the global-level actions/challenges we face. "Think of the polar bears," or "Plastic is bad for the planet," or "Stop eating meat". This is relatively pointless from a communications perspective because a) your ideal customers are already concerned with this subject so you don't need to convince them, and b) you're not adding anything valuable to the conversation. For this group, the main thing which hinders their communications is their goal.

> In both instances, it comes down to communications theory. It's easier to appeal to yourself than to others. But that's simply not how ideas spread. And if you have an idea — or an innovation — that's going to build the foundations of the impact economy, then you have to go beyond social issues and bring value to the table.

When we employ Sinek's Golden Circle but fail to consicely articulate what we do or how we do it, we create a gap between impact and capital: A major red flag for investors. I was recently on a call with a potential client who told me that this is one of their greatest challenges. In investor pitches, they know exactly how to explain "why" they do whey do, but eyes start glazing over when talking about the specifics of their technology. In our business, making the "what" and "how" tangible is just as important as leading with "why".

4.

BRAND FOUNDATIONS: MISSION, VISION & STORY

In my last full-time position, I had the responsibility of creating a new website and brand film for the company. It was a job that required a lot of content and I knew that before I got started, I needed more information. Why did we exist as a company? What did we want to showcase? What impact did we intend to have in the future? What was our north star? Before we got started with these projects, I began to press the director about these subjects. The company had a clear mission statement but it was vague: "To build the foundations of a sustainable society." We were a small company, how could I possibly showcase such a grand mission? And what did it mean for us anyway? When I began to work on these projects, it became obvious that there was a disconnect between what we did and what we wanted to be known for. For instance, you can build "the foundations" of a sustainable society with knowledge. But you can also build it with materials or energy. Which direction should I take? Before

I could continue with either project, I knew that we had to get more specific. We had to get to the core of our brand's story before we started building. This experience, I have come to learn, is a common one. We create a website before we know what to put on it. We write a blog post before we know who our audience is. We start communicating before we know what our goal is. It's the equivalent of building a house without laying the proper foundations.

So when it comes to building a brand, what should your goal be? To build authority, authenticity, and show leadership. Whether we're trying to leverage our position to create impact or make our voice heard, it's important to demonstrate clarity, decisiveness and passion. Leaders are clear and concise, their vision is unwavering and they know what needs to be accomplished to achieve a goal. This gives others the opportunity to internalize their ambitions and choose if they'll join the leader on their change journey. Whether they'll support their cause. However, few people generally know what they want, and much less how to get there. Instead, they will gravitate towards those who appear to have a clear picture in mind and a compelling end destination. Clarity leads to action and action leads to impact.

Your brand's foundations are essentially your purpose and your vision as well as your brand's story. Once defined, each has its place in both internal and external communications. This chapter, we will look at all three components seperately.

Firstly, we will start with your brand's mission and vision. Cliamte Tech entrepreneurs are prone to believe their methodology or their solution can compete because it's "more sustainable" or "more comprehensive" than anything on the market. We believe that we stand out from the crowd, perhaps because we're green. Maybe it's true, for a while. But if we can learn anything from modern economics, it's that competitive advantage doesn't last. Every solution can be replicated. Every innovative business model can be copied. You might have the solution to solve a specific problem now, but what happens when someone solves it for cheaper? And in the current climate, sustainability won't be your competitive advantage for long. That's why it's important to spend time and craft your purpose carefully. Construct a mission and a vision that's bigger than you and that will differentiate your business.

Secondly, a Climate Tech's brand story — or sustainability narrative as I like to call it — is essentially a way to relay your brand's place in the world so that people actually remember it. Far too often, do we as impact entrepreneurs start by telling people — from potential clients to investors — about how great our technology is. That it's going to change the world. But we don't wrap it in a story. As a result, when we pitch, eyes start glazing over. Biologically, human beings are 22x more likely to remember stories over facts.[1] This means that to avoid death-by-numbers and to help keep your audience engaged when you're talking about your startup, a strategic narrative is key.

Without taking the time to build solid brand foundations, all of your branding efforts won't be as effective as possible. For example, many brands struggle to differentiate themselves and when it comes to communicating, they fall back on industry jargon or explaining global issues because it's what they know. To prevent this, it's essential that

1 Kate Harrison in Forbes, 2015.

you identify and internalize your brand's foundations before you begin with your marketing endeavours. While much of your brand foundation may never be visible to the outside world, the stronger these foundations are, the more unique, the more your messages, identity and strategic communications will support your desired position in someone's mind. Essentially, by investing early-on in your brand, you'll be setting yourself up for long-term success.

Why? Because every time anyone has an interaction with your company, it leaves an impression. The only thing in your hands is whether you take ownership of that impression or leave it up to chance. Whether that impression says "they seem like they're in control of their future" or "they're inconsistent and they'll never get anywhere", is up to you. By taking ownership over the interactions which your brand has with people, you can communicate your worth — and potential impact — both consciously and subconsciously.

And it's essential that you take a proactive approach because ... Every. Moment. Counts. When you fumble about what you do, who you are or why you do it, that's a potential fan lost. Just like Simon Sinek says, most people can explain what they do. Some know how they do it. But few know why. We on the other hand know why we do what we do — climate change, plastic pollution, etc. — but we struggle to explain how our solution connects to these global challenge. Very few impact entrepreneurs manage to articulate all of these sentiments in their elevator pitch. Your brand's foundations (mission, vision and story) are going to be the building block from which you build your entire brand. A stable factor that will propel you into the future. Yet many businesses confuse their foundations with their technology or solution. This gets worse when a company is impact-driven. If your solution is the most forward-thinking and innovative X that there is, but if two other companies are offering similar services, how does the purchaser choose? How do investors know where to invest? Your story is your strategy.

THE ELEPHANT IN THE ROOM

What's the most common sentence in climate tech? "To accelerate the transition towards...". Now, don't get me wrong, that's Tesla's mission statement and Tesla is undoubtedly one of the great success stories in the Climate Tech world. But that doesn't mean that we should all base our purpose on theirs. Remember: you're building your brand to set your business apart from the competition. However, so many businesses in Climate Tech— large and small — do just the opposite. For example, here are a few brands that use the term "accelerate" in their mission statement:

- Tesla: To accelerate the advent of sustainable transport.
- ENGIE: To accelerate the transition towards a carbon-neutral economy.
- Fastned: To give freedom to electric drivers and accelerate the transition to sustainable mobility.
- Gispen: To accelerate the transition towards a circular economy.
- The Natural Step: To accelerate the transition to a sustainable society.
- Circle Economy: To accelerate the practical and scalable

implementation of the circular economy.

- Ellen MacArthur Foundation: To accelerate the transition to a circular economy.
- WBCSD: To accelerate the transition to a sustainable world.
- Circularise: To accelerate the transition to a circular economy.

Think about it. If someone's going to remember one thing about your brand, do you want that one thing to be the same as 100 other climate tech brands on the market... Probably not. Just because we're all working towards the same common goal doesn't mean you can't differentiate your own brand and what you stand for...beyond being "green" that is.

Let me put it another way: If Nike was a sustainable technology brand, what would their mission statement be? "Accelerating the creation of a world where more people play sport"; doesn't that sound rediculous? Or what about these others:

- Apple: Accelerating the adoption of computers with the best user experience.
- Starbucks: To accelerate the transition to a world where more people drink more coffee.
- Ted: To accelerate the transition to a world where ideas spread.
- Google: To accelerate the transition to an interconnected world.
- Uber: To accelerate the transition to seamless transport solutions.

Just because it works for Tesla, doesn't mean the phrase "to accelerate the transition towards" should be in your mission statement as well. So here's saying it: Don't be afraid to draw a line in the sand. Get creative. Be authentic. Make something new. After all, you're building a climate tech brand because you want to challenge the status quo, right?

So what's an example of a great purpose or mission statement? The best place to start is by looking to companies and brands you admire and reading their purpose/mission statements or their manifestos. I consider Patagonia's as one of the best from our generation. It's direct and it's provocative:

"We're in business to save our home planet."

It's big, it's bold and it's brave. It's a step beyond their previous mission statement: "Build the best product, cause no unnecessary harm, use business to inspire and implement solutions to the environmental crisis," don't you think? While both give you a sense of what the outdoor clothing brand represents whilst they're on their journey towards reaching their purpose, the former drives it home. Other notable examples which I like include:

- Vattenfall. Fossil-free within a generation.
- Tony Chocolonely. Making all chocolate 100% slave-free across the globe.
- Climeworks. To inspire one billion people to remove carbon dioxide from the air and fight climate change.
- Impossible Foods. To make the global food system truly sustainable by eliminating the need to make food from animals.
- Northvolt. To enable the future of energy.
- Lilium Aviation. Building radically better ways of moving.

MISSION STATEMENT

A mission is WHY your brand exists: The reason for being in business beyond "making a profit". Its purpose is to attract the right people to your organization's journey, repel the wrong people, and motivate your organization as a whole. As an climate tech brand, you probably already know why you exist: To save the planet from a catastrophic climate meltdown. But saying that your brand exists to "solve climate change" doesn't cut it. There are thousands of businesses—new and old, big and small—out there today who are dedicating their existence to "solving climate change". It's a free-for-all and if you want to stand out, it's nonsensical to use the same non-specific jargon as your competitors.

In this new era of sustainability, the Climate Tech era, a mission statement has to be specific. Authentically you. So ask yourself, "what exact challenges are we addressing?" and "why are we best suited to tackle this over the other challenges that our industry faces". Sure, your organization may touch on all 17 of the Sustainable Development Goals, but you're only 20 people, so is it realistic that you can spread your focus so thin? By honing in on the answer to this question, you can identify the actual crux of your mission.

With this in mind, these questions can be useful to define your mission statement:

- Why should your company exist?
- What is the meaning of life in which your company believes?
- What is the ideal role your company will play in this life?

- What kind of world would we live in without your solution?

And why should anyone care? Once you have answered these three questions, your brand purpose should sit somewhere in the middle. I suggest making a short list and testing them with your employees, investors and customers. See which one they like, ask why. It's important that these three groups resonate with it because it serves as a common thread which ties you all together. Make it aspirational.

BRAND VISION

A brand's vision is the future your business is ultimately working towards building. It's is the "where" of the equation. It's a specific and tangible end destination that focuses on the future. But not your future. You are not the protagonist, your customer is. In this way, your vision should reflect their end destination. What's life like once your solution has solved their problems?

The greatest mistake that many make when creating a brand vision, however, is thinking that a a brand vision is about you. (i.e., "We want to be the biggest provider of X by 2030" in Europe."). It's not. It's the end destination for your customer (By 2030, we will live in a world without plastic). It's where your business will take them if they choose to work with you.

A strong brand vision statement is spurred on by the knowledge of either technological development or knowledge of where the industry is going to go in the future. It's proposing a promised land and offering a route there.

There are two key elements to a brand vision:

- **The status quo.** The status quo is the where your customer is at right now. It's Planet A. How are they currently solving their problems? What's the problem with this strategy?
- **The destination.** Where does the customer want to go? Let's call this Planet B. What is life like on Planet B for your customer (once they've solved their problems using your product or service? What are the benefits of being on Planet B versus Planet A?

What transformation is needed to get from planet A (the status quo) to Planet B (the promised land)? This transformation is the core of a strong vision: It should offer your customers, investors and partners an opportunity to join you on a journey to that destination.

SUSTAINABILITY NARRATIVE

A strategic sustainability narrative is a high-level story. Stories humanize your brand and give both colour and context to your product or service. And no matter whether you're telling your brand's narrative to an investor, a room full of potential clients or your family over a Christmas dinner, it will help you explain what you to and why you do it.

The fact is that it takes just eight seconds to form a first impression. Just about the same time as it takes to say the following sentence: "Our technology is the most sustainable innovation on the market, driven by our systemic, circular approach to creating an inclusive economy". Blah. Did you feel anything? When you lead with your technology or your methodology, there's a large chance that you fail to capture the attention of your audience. And if that person is an investor or a potential customer, then you've just wasted an opportunity to realize your potential impact. Instead, set the stage. Create conflict. Tell a story. The honest truth is that there are many messages flying around out there. Just like numbers, no matter how impressive, products and features tend to get lost without context. Brand storytelling can increase the effectiveness of a message by 22x — and in today's attention-deficit environment, that can make a big difference.

Before we go on, let's look at why people make decisions in the way they do according to a new form of marketing called "neuromarketing". Neuromarketing is a commercial communication field that a applies neuroscience and cognitive science to marketing. Essentially, it studies why some messages move us and others are igonerd. The main challenge which neuromarketing identifies for us is that facts and figures target the part of the brain which does not evoke action: The rational brain.

- Our rational brain was developed later in our evolution. It's what gives us the ability to make decisions based on rational facts. For instance: A monkey would never leave a banana uneaten just because you tell him that he can have unlimited bananas in monkey heaven. But with our developed rational brain, humans can listen to facts and figures, crunch the numbers and come to a conclusion that while you could eat the banana, it may be more rational to leave that banana there, if there is a good chance that monkey heaven exists on the other side of the door.
- Our primal brain on the other hand— similar to that of other mammals — makes decisions based on instincts. It interprets

> the world around us and analyses whether something is a threat, whether something is tasty or whether it's attractive without us processing it. We feel it and react. For instance, if you saw a lion in the wild, before you realise you're scared the hairs on the back of your neck would already be standing up. This is the part of the brain that reacts to stories.

A strategic sustainability narrative leverages storytelling to get the facts your business wants to present across in an engaging way. As Climate Tech professionals, we are prone to talk in facts and numbers instead of telling stories. Yet facts and numbers appeal to people's rational mind and the rational mind is not where decisions are made. In fact, rationality only represents about 20% of human decision-making. Plus, facts without concext are essentially just useless numbers. For instance, what's the difference between 50m tons and 500m tons of CO2, without knowing what you're talking about and why you should care? To avoid this common trap in Climate Tech, it's important that we frame our facts in stories that our audience can connect with emotionally.

People are impulsive, they make emotional judgements, and then use rational facts to justify their decision. That's why stories are so beneficial in business: Because stories appeal to our emotional, not our rational mind. Emotions are the driving force behind decision-making. Research shows that messages delivered as stories can be up to 22x more memorable than just facts — because they engage our emotions and our emotions drive us to take action. If you're a sustainability professional you're likely to be a fact-teller, than a storyteller... and that's a problem. When we continue to speak in numbers, rather than tell stories, we're hurting our own cause.

Let's take the existance of climate change as an example. At the moment, it's like bringing a knife to a gunfight. On one side — the side that relies on science — we talk about the hottest year on record, the weight of plastic in the ocean, and the amount of CO2 being released into the atmosphere. On the other side, they tell stories. Stories about the negative impact of actions on peoples lives. Stories about the dangers of wind turbines. And stories about the danger to the global economic system if we pivot from fossil fuels. For too long, this negative narrative has been weaponized by proponents of the status quo. And we keep trying to counter it by throwing facts against the wall. We've known the science for over 30 years, we can't keep relying on facts to achieve our climate goals. We need to start framing our solutions in a better narratives. We have to tell stories of the opportunities that come with change, not the challenges.

Those building a sustainable future can't rely on numbers anymore, we have to tell stories. A strategic narrative is your brand's foundations told in the form of a story. It's the basis of the commercial side of your brand and it intends to harness the same narratives that both Greek mythology and Hollywood has used for centuries. How? By introducing the context first and setting the scene, then introducing characters, creating conflict and showing the journey — not telling. Only once these parameters have been set do you introduce your product's features. When you begin your sales deck or investment pitch with a product's features, you're likely to bore your audience to no avail.

Andy Raskin, a leader in creating strategic narratives in Silicon Valley believes that this form of storytelling is best way to align everything from website copy to investor pitches. "Conversations about messaging are really conversations about strategy... and ultimately, the only way to get strategic alignment is with a simple story." Raskin goes against the grain with the way that he brings the elements together, in a way that may feel uncomfortable in the Climate Tech industry. But there's a reason stories have been told the same way for thousands of years: Because we're hardwired to process information in this fashion. Raskin outlines five elements of a this simple story strategic narrative.[2]

THE FIVE ELEMENTS OF A STRATEGIC NARRATIVE

1. **Context and Setting: Name a Big, Relevant Change in the World.** Not a feature. Not a product. But a transformation occurring. "Don't kick off a sales presentation by talking about your product, your headquarters locations, your investors, your clients or anything about yourself," he says. This is demonstration of the "why" that Simon Sinek talks about. It's the point that says "do we agree" or not? If the audience agrees with your statement, then you're already half way towards hooking them in.
2. **Conflict: Show There'll Be Winners and Losers.** What are the stakes? If you (the audience) continue along on the status quo, this is what you'll have to lose if you miss the boat. "All prospects suffer from what economists call "loss aversion." That is, thcy tend to avoid a possible loss by sticking to the status quo, rather than risk a possible gain by opting for change. To combat loss aversion, you must demonstrate how the change you cited above will create big winners and big losers." This should evoke the need to change.

2 Andy Raskin, 2016.

Don't give the way to do so yet…that comes later. This section should just build angst and tie it all together with a common trend.

3. **Introduction of Resolution: Tease the Promised Land.** Instead of telling about your company, your products or your value proposition, this is where your vision comes into play. Raskin advises to resist the temptation to begin talking about yourself here. "Your Promised Land should be both desirable (obviously) and difficult for the prospect to achieve without outside help. Otherwise, why does your company exist?" This should be the mission statement from the customer's perspective. Getting to Graceland or destroying the death star. The promised land should be aspirational and hard to reach.
4. **Tools: Introduce Features as "Magic Gifts" for Overcoming Obstacles to the Promised Land.** Now it's time to show your product's features as "magic gifts" which will help overcome the obstacles on the way to the promised land. "If it's not clear by now, successful sales decks follow the same narrative structure as epic films and fairy tales. Your prospect is Luke and you're Obi Wan, furnishing a lightsaber to help him defeat the Empire. Your prospect is Frodo and you're Gandalf, wielding wizardry to help him destroy the ring. Your prospect is Cinderella and you're the fairy godmother, casting spells to get her to the ball." Ask yourself, what are the obstacles to the client's goal and frame your product's features in this way. Anticipate the challenges. What's stopping them getting there? Your features should be the answer to a problem.
5. **Validation and Conclusion: Present Evidence that You Can Make the Story Come True.** Proof that it's possible to get to the promised

land. That you're not just making it up and that you're the right person to take them there. "In telling the sales narrative this way, you're making a commitment to prospects: If they go with you, you'll get them to the Promised Land." This is where you can tackle a sceptical audience. Evidence should include stories of customer success and/or demos telling about their own personal experiences and what it took them to win. Evidence shows that the transformation took place.

WHAT CAN I USE MY BRAND STORY FOR?

A strong brand story can be used across multiple communications channels, including but not limited to the following:

- Investor pitches (investors invest in founders who can get people to join their journey. That takes a great story.).
- Team alignment (internal communications).
- Product positioning (go-to-market strategy to show how the world has changed and why it matters)
- Thought leadership (break up your tools and write an article about each).
- Public relations (pitch your narrative as a stand-alone story or break them up and submit them to industry publication.
- Sales decks (show your customer that the world is changing and they need to adapt).

HOW TO STRUCTURE YOUR STRATEGIC SUSTAINABILITY NARRATIVE

Now it's time to get your hands dirty and write your own brand story. There are two ways in which you can do this:

- In a deck
- As an article

Whichever you choose, this may be one of the most important exercises you do when building your business. It will go on to help you build a scalable brand and give you strong foundations for the future. To write your brand's story, consider the following structure:

1. Context and Setting: Name a big, relevant change in the world that directly affects the way your customer is doing business. The old world where the "old way of doing things" was normal and the new world where we have to do things differently. And guess what, the new way of doing things is the way you think they should be done. (200-300 words / 1-3 slides).
2. Conflict: Show there'll be winners and losers. This can be those in the field who are doing really well vs those who have already lost. Think for instance, Blockbuster and Netflix, Ford and Tesla. Find statistics and or different evidence that prove this change is occurring and don't be afraid to back them up. This is meant to capture the attention of your audience. We want them to think, "I'd better keep listening because I'm putting myself at risk if I don't." It's the what if scenario. "What if I don't act when I know

the path?".

3. Introduction of your vision: Tease the promised land or Planet B. Where you want to help your audience go. Also, think about where they don't want to go. The key here is to be as specific and as vivid as possible. The Promised Land is not having your solution, your help or your advice, but rather what life is like thanks to having it. For instance, it's not "having a strong and sustainable investment portfolio" but rather, "the ability to navigate an uncertain future due and increase returns whilst minimizing environmental impact."
4. Tools: Introduce the ways that you want to help your target audience from A - B as tools: "Magic Gifts" for overcoming obstacles to the Promised Land. Framed like this, your features are no longer benefits to your product, but value propositions (think back to the first week) positioned in the context of transitioning from an "old world" (the way things are done now) to a "new world," (the way you're proposing to do things).

   These tools are the foundation for an engaging conversation with prospects—technical and otherwise—about why it's so hard to reach the Promised Land with traditional solutions. They first require you to identify the obstacles (what's standing in the way of your target audience reaching the promised land) and then proposing a solution to overcome the obstacles.

   Ask yourself, what are the obstacles to the client's goal and frame your product's features in this way. Anticipate the challenges. What's stopping them from getting there? Your features should be the answer to a problem.

List 5 obstacles to reach a more attractive future. Rank them in order. For the top three, ask yourself, "what's the answer to this problem"? Is it something that you can provide? Then write one paragraph about how each solution helps them get around the obstacle standing in their way. If you've clearly stated your Planet B and the obstacles to it, prospects have the context they need to understand why your capabilities matter.

5. Validation and Conclusion: Present evidence that the story can come true. Proof that it's possible to get to the promised land. That you're not just making it up and that you're the right person to take them there. In telling the sales narrative this way, you're making a commitment to prospects: If they go with you, you'll get them to the Promised Land. This is where you can tackle a skeptical audience. Evidence could include success stories of those who've done it before to ways you've helped. Anything that shows that the transformation.

As the old Chinese proverb goes, "Tell me the facts and I'll learn. Tell me the truth and I'll believe. But tell me a story and it will live in my heart forever". Storytelling has always been central to the human experience. The human brain is 22x more likely to remember stories rather than facts (I know I've said it before, but according to psychologists, it takes at least seven times before a message sinks in). And whilst the way that stories are told continues to change, our bandwidth for authentic, narrative-led stories is as high as ever.

Yet instead of telling stories, too many Climate Tech brands focus on a global problem or their product's features. And it holds us back as a collective industry. So instead we need to learn to tell stronger stories. A few final tips to improve your storytelling?

1. Have a focus on the audience.
2. Set the scene.
3. Have a clear structure.
4. Embrace conflict or develops tension.
5. Have a single message.
6. Base it in facts.
7. Let it come from personal experience.

MISTAKES TO WATCH OUT FOR

Unfortunately, many brands — especially in the sustainability industry — fall flat when they're telling their brand's story. Here are a few common mistakes to watch out for when your writing your own strategic sustainability narrative:

- **Talk About Ourselves First.** Because we're likely to be from a scientific or academic background, we're quite used to the common "problem > solution" framework of speaking. However, without introducing context or conflict, these facts seem meaningless, just like the difference between 100 tons and 200 tons of CO2.
- **Too Complex.** It's almost inevitable that you're going to be telling

your story to people outside of your industry. One of the quickest ways to kill interest in your product or service is by using industry-specific jargon.

- **Telling, Not Showing.** Stories are far more memorable than facts. Stories are made by bringing people along with the narrative. Showing someone the path will always work better than simply telling someone why they should walk along it.
- **Lack of Conflict.** Every good movie has conflict. A strategic narrative should tap in to that source of conflict — ideally from the client's perspective — and show vulnerability.

By following this narrative, you can present the why, what and how of your business in a way that actively captures your audience. I would wholeheartedly recommend putting this book down here and opening up Powerpoint immediately. Take 15 slides and make the bare bones of your strategic narrative. If you need any guidance, check out Raskin's blog on Medium called *The Greatest Sales Deck I've Ever Seen* or his analysis of Elon Musk introducing the Powerwall in his blog titled *Want a Better Pitch? Watch This.* Once you've written your strategic narrative, use it as the basis for your investor pitch, your website copy and your explinations about what you do. I guarentee it will increase the interest in and retention of facts about your product or service.

EXERCISE 01

BRAND PURPOSE

A brand's purpose is it's reason to exist beyond making money. It's your why. It's what people connect to emotionally, not rationally, when considering joining your journey. So make sure it's different from every other Climate Tech startup out there!

Step 1. What are you passionate about?

...Write Your Answer Here

Step 2. What is your startup good at?

...Write Your Answer Here

Step 3. What does the world need?

...Write Your Answer Here

Purpose Statement (long)

...Write Your Answer Here

Purpose Statement (one sentence)

...Write Your Answer Here

EXERCISE 02

BRAND VISION

A brand's vision is a short phrase describing the future your brand is ultimately working towards. A brand's vision portrays this by outlining the future position of the marketplace. It reflects and supports the business strategy: It's the promised land. An essential and pivotal role in every story.

Step 1. What is the status quo (Planet A)?

...Write Your Answer Here

Step 2. Where does the customer want to go (Planet B)?

...Write Your Answer Here

Vision Statement: What transformation is needed to get from A to B?

...Write Your Answer Here

EXERCISE 03

BRAND STORY

A band story leverages key elements of storytelling to present facts in an engaging way. As Climate Tech founders, you are prone to talk in facts and numbers instead of telling stories. Yet these numbers, without context or conflict, mean very little. Stories can make a world of difference when explaining what you do and for who.

Step 1. Name a Big, Relevant Change in the World

...Write Your Answer Here

Step 2. Show There'll Be Winners and Losers

...Write Your Answer Here

Step 3. Tease the Promised Land

...Write Your Answer Here

Step 4. Introduce Features as "Magic Gifts" for Overcoming Obstacles to the Promised Land

...Write Your Answer Here

Step 5. Present Evidence that You Can Make the Story Come True

...Write Your Answer Here

5.

TARGET AUDIENCE: CRAFTING YOUR NICHE

Once you've got a clear idea who you are as a brand and what you stand for, the next step is to gain a greater understanding of your target audience. To successfully communicate, you've got to know whom you're talking to. Why? Because not everyone wants what you're selling. And nor should they. Market segmentation is the process of dividing all of your potential customers into smaller groups, based on certain characteristics. I.e., industry, company size, annual revenue or challenge. This is undeniably important when it comes to communicating your position in the market and your value proposition. If you don't have a clear target audience in mind when you begin to communicate, your value is going to be spread too thin. Simply put, communicating with everyone is a waste of valuable resources. By doubling down on your ideal customer, you can actively craft a message which speaks directly to them.

An essential pillar of brand building, market segmentation follows a 3-step chronological framework often referred to as segmenting, targeting and positioning (STP).

1. The segmentation process identifies the market to be divided into customer profiles; identification, selection and application of bases.
2. Targeting is the process of selecting the most attractive segments from the segmentation stage which usually amount to the best economic potential.
3. Positioning is the final step in the process, where the business must assess its competitive advantage and position itself in the consumer's minds to be the more attractive option in these categories.

By understanding the needs of your most valuable customers, you can tailor your communications to address these pain points and offer your solution. But it all starts with knowing your ideal customer.

Why not target multiple audiences at once?

At first, it may be appealing to believe that you can sell directly to anyone and everyone. It's especially a common misconception within the sustainability industry, that because our solution is solving global issues, that everyone will want our solution. Many of my clients often tell me that their target audience includes governments and multinationals, NGOs and startups. As a Climate Tech brand, it's just impossible to target such a large demographic with such little resources. Within this belief comes an even larger issue. We're selling a product not solving a problem. People buy products and services to solve their problems. For instance, no one wakes up in the morning and says, "Today, I'm going to invest in an electric vehicle". No, they've got existing problems: "My car won't be allowed in the city centre in 5 years" or "My car doesn't reflect my green identity" or "The price of petrol is unstable" and they're going to solve those problems with that new vehicle. Customer segmentation lets startups create personalized messages which focus on solving these problems, which their ideal customers usually respond better to than generic and impersonal marketing.

As a startup, you have limited money and manpower to execute your communications efforts. By focusing on a small market segment, you're able to allocate your precious resources and focus on the audience that has the highest probability of purchasing your solution. If you successfully target multiple customers within the same segment, you can build early momentum as a problem solver within that specific niche and build a cache of success stories. The fact is that it's easier and cheaper to narrow down your target audience and communicate with your ideal clients directly. That narrower your audience becomes, the quicker you're likely to gain market traction and cement your reputation with your early adopters. They are the people who are more likely to turn into evangelists, spreading the news of your solution to their market peers, because it solved their specific problem so well. By niching down and focusing your efforts on a small segment of your entire market, you can quickly build a small but enthusiastic crowd of brand ambassadors to spread your message.

I recently spoke to startup marketing mentor and market segmentation expert Csaba Dudas from Climate KIC to ask him how to do just that. Csaba works with sustainability startups based in the European Union to help them attract their first customers and build their brand. "For impact startups, it's a life or death to invest in marketing," he says. "I always encourage the startups I work with to self-educate in marketing and communications because their impact is not going to be realized if they're not communicating properly."

When I asked Csaba about his initial process, he said that their basic need is to look credible and reliable. "I check if they have their foundations in place and I don't talk about any communications without having the proper digital assets." Then he says his approach is to find the shortest, easiest and most cost-efficient way to their initial clients. "When we're talking about the way to market for startups, there's always going to be a very small niche that's waiting for the solution with open arms. This is especially true for B2B brands. For a startup, it can mean wonderful early traction if they find the easiest way to these clients. It's much easier to build trust with these clients — who are innovators and early adapters themselves — rather than in the early or late majorities."

Csaba has his clients brainstorm every possible category of market that these early adopters could exist in. For instance, he gives an example of a client of his creating a high-end acoustic panel made from waste materials from the fashion industry. "While they know their product can be sold to many people around the world, for a startup that's not feasible. It would require a marketing budget that's huge compared to their current stage and no investor would give them this kind of money until they generate early traction." Instead, he had them write down each market that may be interested — from hotels to the music industry to interior designers — and then do outreach to potential clients within each industry itself.

Once he has identified his early adopters and innovators, he suggests to reach out to them directly. "Cold reaching out usually works because we — impact-driven and sustainability entrepreneurs — usually have the advantage of being those who "do good". We're the ones who are working towards a better future. So for us it's much easier to have this type of market research than our for-profit peers who usually need to pay participants. It's typical to have between 15-20 interviews. I usually encourage them to do the interviews until they begin to see the same patterns, which means that they're reaching some kind of statistical significance."

At first, he says they compile a list of hypotheses that they assume is true for their market segment. Then they create a list of interview questions that they would like to ask potential customers or industry experts. "They actually compile a questionnaire which they use during the interview but they also have an open-ended dialogue, we encourage them to get these people for an hour of conversation. Not like a survey, because this way, they might get unexpected hints and advice from these peoples. A lot of the time, they get back from the interviews, the best potential market segment could be different than they initially thought."

Once his clients end up finding their certain niche, they get back to their labs and workshops and start working to integrate the findings into their product. "By this time, we usually have some companies from this research group showing interest as future clients and we encourage the teams to befriend these companies because they're the innovators in the space. Then they can get a foothold in the market through these clients. If everything goes well, then they're bringing a product to these clients that they're really happy about, they'll become their first references. Then new teams will be ready to go and target the wider audience in the segments."

For impact businesses in a growing marketplace for purposeful companies, it's essential to find their first customers and solve their problems. It's just so important to find the gap in the market, a pain point or opening where consumers and businesses are craving solutions. The main word in that sentence is "solutions". Every single time we purchase anything for our business, it's because we need to solve a problem. On an office scale, it's a printer that works better than the last one. On a consumer scale, it's using an app rather than standing in a taxi rank. The best and biggest problems that our planet faces all have solutions, but whether people are willing to pay for them or not is another question.

When it comes to real sustainability-orientated companies, this concept holds its weight. Our impact can only be scaled if our solution not only takes on a global problem but also a consumer or customer issue. We must consider what problems our business solves and then create value surrounding that concept. As this value begins to hold its weight, that's when your business can start to scale and your impact will scale accordingly.

MARKET SEGMENTATION

Market segmentation lets brands create personalized messages which focus on solving these problems, which their ideal customers usually respond better to than generic and impersonal marketing. As a Climate Tech brand, you have limited money and manpower to execute your communications efforts. By focusing on a small market segment, you're able to allocate your precious resources and focus on the audience that has the highest probability of purchasing your solution.

If you successfully target multiple customers within the same segment, you can build early momentum as a problem solver within that specific niche and build a cache of success stories. It's easier and cheaper to narrow down your target audience and communicate with your ideal clients directly. The narrower your audience becomes, the quicker you're likely to gain market traction and cement your reputation with your early adopters.

They are the people who are more likely to turn into evangelists, spreading the news of your solution to their market peers, because it solved their specific problem so well. By niching down and focusing your efforts on a small segment of your entire market, you can quickly build a small but enthusiastic crowd of brand ambassadors to spread your message.

In the next section, we'll look at how you can define your ideal target market with market segmentation.

HOW TO SEGMENT YOUR MARKET

In the first stage of the MTP process, you'll gain the ability to get outside your predetermined assumptions and explore new opportunities. By dividing the total market into segments, brands can acquire a better understanding of the needs and wants of multiple customers, and begin to distinguish between them. This ultimately enables you to tailor your company's communications — and your solution itself — towards a customer's problem, rather than simply present your innovation as a a stand-alone solution.

Step 1. Market brainstorm

Start by coming up with all of the markets, sectors or industries that would possibly get value out of your product. Write ten or more down. Anything and everything that comes into your mind, write it down. Be it as farfetched or impossible as you want. The important thing is to get specific and brainstorm. For example, a smart city tool that measures carbon output from buildings could put any of the following options:

- Business Parks
- Universities
- Airports
- Conference Centers
- Self-Managed Towers
- Private Building Construction
- Public Schools
- Government Infrastructure Buildings
- New Residential Constructions
- Hotels

By putting everything on the table, you avoid the classic tunnel vision trap and open yourself up to a whole lot of different opportunities that you may not have considered.

Step 2. Narrow it down

The next step is to add further criteria to each of your target segment as identified in Step 1, including geography, demographic, behavior or psychographic segmentation:

- **Demographic segmentation.** The most popular and commonly used types of market segmentation referring to statistical data about a group of people including revenue, location, size, etc. (i.e., How big is the company you want to work for? How much did they earn last year? Are they public or private? What stage of funding round are they?)
- **Psychographic segmentation.** Categories audiences and customers by factors that relate to their personalities and characteristics including values, motivations, priorities and jobs-to-be-done. I.e., Are they concerned with other sustainability issues (plastic pollution) which could help you influence them? Are they equal opportunity employers? Do they all want to become BREAAM certified?
- **Behavioral segmentation.** How a customer acts and what patterns they display including their purchasing habits, spending history and how they interacted with products in the past. (i.e., Have all the executives just purchased an EV? Does the company only have vegetarian lunches? Are they (aspirational) B Corps?)
- **Geographic segmentation.** The most straightforward segment based on locational borders, which includes data like postcode, city, and country. I.e., Do they live in Amsterdam? Are they European? Do they all speak English as a first language?

Demographic segmentation	Psychographic segmentation
Behavioral segmentation	Geographic segmentation

When you put it all together, one response might look something like this: I want to work with:

- Enterprise Business Parks in Northern Europe with 20+ buildings, *or*
- Airports in North American Cities with over 1m people that also have Smart City projects.

See how much they can vary?

Step 3. Ask the hard questions

Whilst you may have already decided your product or service will fit, it's in your best interest to identify any untapped needs in the marketplace itself. Are your potential customers being underserved by competitors? Can your potential customers afford your solution?

HOW TO CHOOSE A TARGET MARKET

Targeting is the process of selecting the most attractive segments from the segmentation stage which usually have the best economic potential. Once you have a list of between five and 10 main market segments, it's time to start getting specific and targeting.

Serial entrepreneur Bill Aulet suggests filtering your potential segments by asking several questions in his book, Disciplined Entrepreneurship. [1]

1. Is the target segment well funded? — I.e. Do they have the spending power to purchase your product?
2. Is the target customer readily accessible to you? I.e. Is the distribution channel to reach your target customer feasible for you to execute?
3. Can you enter adjacent markets from this segment to scale? I.e. Does gaining a stronghold in this market allow you to springboard into other markets quickly?
4. Does the target customer have a compelling reason to buy? Find out if the customer is happy with what currently exists. Are they doing workaround or perhaps they're doing nothing about the problem at all?
5. Can you deliver a complete product? Based on what your customers' needs are, can you deliver a product which satisfies those needs fully, not just partially?
6. Is there an incumbent competitor that could block you? Are you going against a market leader head to head which you can't compete against?
7. Is the market consistent with your passion and goals? Are you willing to commit years of your life to this market segment and will

1 Bill Aulet, 2013

this give you the satisfaction of achieving your individual goals?

How niche do I go?

At the end of this process, you should be left with only a few segments which are viable, assessable and attractive. The next step is to figure out how those markets will respond to you and your solution and find your ideal target market, often referred to as a beachhead market.[2]

A beachhead market can be defined as a small market with specific characteristics that make it an ideal target to sell a new product or service. A beachhead market comes from a well defined military strategy wherein the protagonist wins a small border area that becomes a stronghold from which to advance their campaign further. In business, this term represents the smallest market that you can own from which to advance into the broader market itself. The term itself references the 1944 invasion of Normandy, where allied troops focused their attention on taking Normandy, their beachhead from which they used to stage a counter-invasion of Europe.[3]

To find your beachhead market, "the answer lies in doing primary customer research," Aulet says. By going out and talking to real customers, finding out what problems are and walking in their shoes is essential to creating a product that they will pay for. "Don't trust what you see on the internet, go out and see for yourself because the answer lies with the customer." Ask them about their problems and their challenges, tailor your solution to fully solve these problems and demonstrate expertise in the market itself. Don't worry about going too small, once you have a

2 Corporate Finance Institute.

3 Geoffrey Moore, 1991.

stronghold in your beachhead market, you can always grow from there.

BRAND POSITIONING

Brand positioning is the final stage for successful market segmentation for your Climate Tech business. It's where you determine where your brand sits concerning similar brands in the same market. You've defined your total market as well as your ideal target audience. Now it's time to determine what sets your company apart from the competition and creates a defined place in your customer's mind for your brand.

To create a defined brand position means you have to study the playing field and carve out a little chunk that you can call your own. A unique for place for yourself. Then, when the time comes to communicate that position, you already know which tone to take and what angle.

Remember: Sustainability is a business value, not your value proposition.

Sustainability may be the reason your business exists, but in your customer's eyes, it's one of multiple value propositions. Don't compete solely with this because — as we've seen in multiple markets over the past five years — you're not the only player doing so. And if you are, it won't be long until you have competition. Simply put, don't position your brand as the "sustainable alternative" because it won't be long until you have company.

HOW TO POSITION MY BRAND?

Brand positioning is an important exercise to demonstrate your understanding of your own industry, and to be able to tell customers and investors, "what's different about your business?" and "why you?". It helps you go beyond the answer, "we're more innovative and our technology is better", which literally makes almost everyone roll their eyes. But how can you get there? The following six steps are a good way to start:

Step 1. Competitor research. Go across to the websites of the ten closest competitors in your niche and try to find words that define each brand. Are they trying to be "eco-friendly" or "impact-driven"? Are they "green thumbs" or "cleantech"? What sets them aside from each other?

Step 2. Competitor terminology research. What terms do they use to describe: Their technology's Reasons to Believe (RBTs are statements which show the most compelling evidence that a product delivers on its promise) and their sustainability pledges? Make a keyword list and mark each time you see a word.

Step 3. Choose matrix dimensions. Choose comparative dimensions on each side of a 2x2 matrix. They should be words or terms that have come up in your competitor research which are the opposite of one another. For example: Simple + Complex, Timeless + On trend, EcoGreen + Cleantech, Luxury + Economy, Convenient + Prestige.

Step 4. Place your competitors. Once you've decided on the comparative dimensions for your matrix, put each of your competitors on there. Then once you've done so, look where there is blank space, and where the crowd is. Chances are, this is a strong option to position your brand.

Step 5. Write a brand positioning statement. Once you have identified the free space, it's time to write it down. The sentence should look like this:

"I want to work with _________________ that _________ rather than those who _____________________________."

Make sure it brief, simple and memorable. No more than one paragraph. Focus on what differentiates your brand from your nearest competitors.

Step 6. Test it. As with almost everything in branding, testing is key. Go out and ask five people in your target market what sets you apart from your competitors. As well as what sets them apart from each other. Test your assumptions and iterate until your happy with the result.

The benefits of a brand positioning may not seem obvious in the beginning. Down the road, however, a solid brand position makes the entire communications process smoother and easier. By holding a certain position in your target audience's mind (ie. value for money/organic or innovative/traditional), you can begin to differentiate your brand in the market, show your customer your unique value and attract the right ecosystem.

This is especially true when it comes to Climate Tech brands. As entrepreneurs, we often think that there is no product out there like ours. Why else would we put such time and effort into making a company? As impact entrepreneurs, it's even worse. We tend to imagine our target audience exists of everyone on the planet. Or at least a large chunk of it, because everyone needs our product. However, when it comes down to selling, it's back to the drawing board. For example, imagine that your company is a technology provider. You have, after years of hard work, created a unique methodology which backs up your innovative technology and as a result, you have a product that has a high level of sustainability and applicability in your field; say, cities. It's going to be a game-changer. Whilst you may think that there is no competition because no one has a similar product or outlook, the truth is that there are thousands of methodologies out there and thousands of technologies. If your brand position is "unique" and "sustainable" then it doesn't really say anything, does it?

This mentality — the idea that your product is truly unique and as a result, everyone will buy what your selling — is counter-productive to growth. By narrowing this down and creating a specific and recognisable position for your brand, you can give your start-up a better chance to scale in the growing sustainability landscape.

BUYER PERSONA

To help you market more effectively, and help you sell more personally, it's important to hone in on who you're actually selling to. So what is a buyer persona? A buyer persona is fictional character created to represent a user type that will typically be the ones who interact with your brand. The CEO or the CFO. The Sustainability Officer or Innovation Manager. Your Buyer Persona is the one who you'll actually have to target at the organization you want to work with. The ones who'll be the point of contact in the buying cycle. By undertaking research, it's possible to find out who they are and what kind of language they use. In my case, I want to work with founders and CMOs of venture-backed Climate Tech brands that have raised at least Series A capital in Europe.

Step 1. Interview your target audience. Your buyer personas need to be based on real-world data, not gut instinct. I suggest asking five companies that you want to work about their buying process. Learn about your audience, from your audience! Some of the questions that are commonly asked are:

- What are their job responsibilities?
- What is their age & position at the company?
- What industries are they present in?
- What are they interested in outside of work?
- What is their annual revenue?
- What level of experience do they have?
- What are their goals?
- What are their challenges?
- What are their favourite brands?

Step 2. Define their challenges and jobs to be done. The next step of the process is to ask yourself "What are the challenges they face and how does your product or service solve that problem?" Some possible answers could be:

- What are their major pain points that drive them towards your solution or product?

- What are their career/life goals? For instance, if they're an entrepreneur, it might be getting VC funding or going to IPO, whereas an employee might care more about a promotion.
- What are their business goals?

How can you find out more about your buyer persona?

- Google research. How would my customers find me online? What are they searching for?
- Ecosystem. Create a list of all the solutions which your target audience may already be using. How are they communicating? Look at your competitors and see whom they've partnered with. Analyse their ecosystem and see if you can find any similar companies to strike up a conversation with.
- Ask them. Ask your potential target audiences where they get their information, what publications they read and what would convince them to work with you over someone else.
- SEO research. Write a list of your keywords. What are your customers are using to search for your product? Find out with a product like SEMRush or Ubersuggest.

Step 3. Compile the research. Gather all of your research and start looking for common characteristics. Give your buyer persona a name, a job title, a home, and other defining characteristics. They should seem like a real person. For example, if your selling impact measurement technology to mid-size NGOs, your target audience might be COOs.

They may all well be at the end of their career and working with NGOs after a for-profit career. Or potentially they've spent their entire career in the non-profit sector. Knowing these differences is important. Either way, they also might like to go camping regularly, all own electric vehicles, and have limited experience with impact measurement. Based on research, you'll give them representative characteristics that make them a real person:

- More likely to be a woman.
- She is 50 years old.
- She has two grown up kids.
- She lives in London.
- She works as a COO.
- She owns a Tesla.
- She likes to camp in Devon.
- She has a few years left and wants to set the organization up for success.
- She doesn't have much experience measuring impact
- She is technology-focused.

Step 4. Give them a name. To align your team around a common character in your brand's story, I suggest that it's imporant to give your buyer persona a name. For instance, in the example above, I'd call her Electric Lizzie. This gives a somewhat metaphorical concept a real depth of meaning and identity. After all, the purpose of a buyer persona is to sell more personally. This process, of creating a buyer persona, is important for the next step in branding — Strategic Messaging — because it's

Electric Lizzie's pain points we're going to be solving. It will also save a lot of time and money if and when you begin to use paid advertising, you already know a lot about the habits of the person who will be in charge of buying your product.

EXERCISE 01

MARKET SEGMENTATION

Start by coming up with all of the markets, sectors or industries that would possibly get value out of your product.

Step 1. Market brainstorm

1.
2.
3.
4.
5.
6.
7.
8.
9.
10.

Step 2. Further segmentation data: Market segment no. 1

Demographic segmentation

Psychographic segmentation

Behavioral segmentation

Geographic segmentation

Step 3. Further segmentation data - Market segment no. 2

Demographic segmentation	Psychographic segmentation
Behavioral segmentation	Geographic segmentation

Step 4. Further segmentation data - Market segment no. 3

Demographic segmentation	Psychographic segmentation
Behavioral segmentation	Geographic segmentation

Step 5. Further segmentation data - Market segment no. 4

Demographic segmentation	Psychographic segmentation

Behavioral segmentation	Geographic segmentation

Step 6. Further segmentation data - Market segment no. 5

Demographic segmentation	Psychographic segmentation

Behavioral segmentation	Geographic segmentation

EXERCISE 02

TARGETING

Targeting is the process of selecting the most attractive segments from the segmentation stage which usually amount to the best economic potential.

Step 1. Targeting checklist

Market viability questions	Market segment 1.	2.	3.	4.	5.
Is the target segment well funded?	☐	☐	☐	☐	☐
Is the target customer readily accessible to you?	☐	☐	☐	☐	☐
Can you enter adjacent markets from this segment to scale?	☐	☐	☐	☐	☐
Does the target customer have a compelling reason to buy?	☐	☐	☐	☐	☐
Can you deliver a complete product to this audience?	☐	☐	☐	☐	☐
Is there an incumbent competitor that could block you?	☐	☐	☐	☐	☐
Is the market consistent with your passion and goals?	☐	☐	☐	☐	☐

EXERCISE 03

POSITIONING

Your positioning statement essentially conveys the main value proposition of your brand to the brand's ideal customers.

Step 1. Competitor brainstorm

1.
2.
3.
4.
5.
6.
7.
8.
9.
10.

Step 2. Competitor terminology research

Sustainability terms/pledges	Technology USPs

Step 3. Create a brand positioning matrix

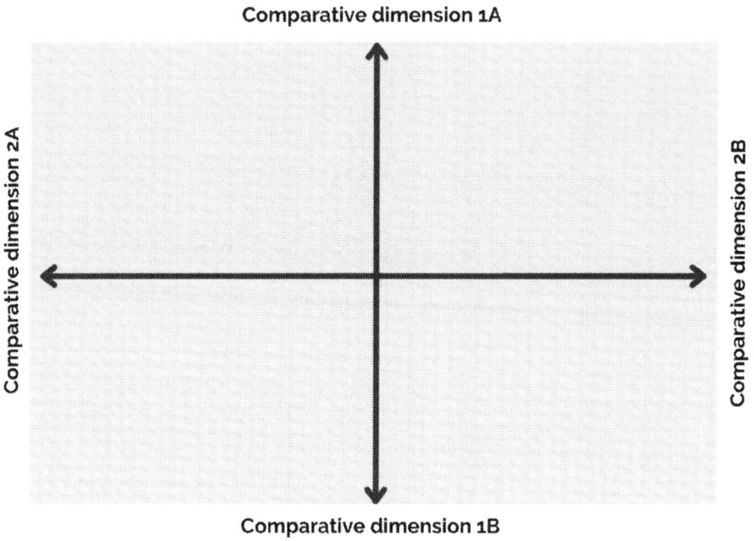

Step 4. Place your competitors on the matrix
USPs

Choose comparative dimensions on each side of the matrix. They should be words or terms that have come up in your competitor research.

Step 5. Write your brand position & polarize it

I want to work with ____________________ that _________ rather than those who _____________________________________.

EXERCISE 04

BUYER PERSONA

Your buyer personas need to be based on real-world data, not gut instinct. I suggest asking five companies in your target audience that you want to work about their buying process.

Step 1. Define your ideal buyer's character traits

What are their job responsibilities?

What is their age & position at the company?

What industries are they present in?

What are they interested in outside of work?

What is their annual salary and what level of experience do they have?

Step 2. Define their challenges

What are their major pain points that drive them towards your solution or product?

1.
2.
3.

Step 3. Identify their business's goals

What are their business objectives? What about their individual career goals?

1.
2.
3.

TARGET AUDIENCE

6.

STRATEGIC MESSAGING: COMMUNICATING VALUE

Whenever you communicate as a brand or an individual, how you framed your message will determine whether it will be successful. When a message is framed well, it carves out a piece of your target audience's mind and lives there. If you've just started your business, then you'll essentially be targeting a problem which your Beachhead Market holds. You want to become known in your position as an expert and be able to get your market proposition across as value-driven. That's your first aim. Once you have a foothold in their mind, you want to give them stories — or strategic messages — that empower them to share that value proposition with their immediate network. In this way, you can rely on those who you've served well and those who stand behind you to share your message for you.

All great movements started with an idea. When ideas spread they create movements because they evoke emotion and they tell a story. Religions, political movements and social awakenings were all started with an idea and those fanatic enough about it to spread the gospel and convert others. Brands are no different. Tesla, BrewDog, Nike, Apple and Patagonia have all leveraged strategic messaging to become household names the world over. But a message only spreads if it's strategic. Strategic messaging is a value-based communication framework that communicates product value to the target audience by describing the solution to a problem they have.[1] However, we as impact entrepreneurs usually believe that as we're doing something positive for the planet, its inhabitants and our society, we don't have to bring value to the table. We just ask for it instead.

Impact entrepreneurs and climate tech startups go one of two ways when it comes to framing: Overly complex or incredibly broad. Scientific or social. Why? As we've covered, on one hand, you're more likely to be an academic or scientist and on the other, you're an inherently social human being.

The scientific or academic route is a classic Climate Tech entrepreneur character trait: It's a complex subject and you want to show that you're qualified. However, this often drives us to speak to our peers, not our target audience. Effective messages are both simple and consistent. When you communicate as a climate tech startup or entrepreneur, you should ask yourself before you communicate externally, if what you're sending out checks both of those boxes. It's common for founders with a technical background to describe the product itself, the features and the techstack which empowers both. They often believe that this will

1 Myk Pono, 2016.

get the audience excited. However, because decision-makers in your target audience don't usually relate to these kinds of messages, they're often rendered redundant. For instance, if you're a cleantech startup selling energy-producing glass to the construction sector, the person who actually buys your product won't have the same technical background as you. What they do have however, is a problem that needs solving. "I need my building to generate X amount of energy to be carbon neutral and for that technology to integrate into the existing framework our buildings use." Getting into the benefits that your product brings and the problems that that specific buyer has will make your message far more effective.

The social side is another story: Sustainability professionals are often generalists who want to help educate everyone on the planet. They don't want to offend or exclude. But the thing is, if you catch too wide a net, you'll end up catching nothing.

Both are a problem because if you can't communicate what you do effectively, you'll struggle to bring clients, partners or investors along on your journey. The answer? Niche down your target audience, ask them about their problems and then address them in their own words. Only then will you be able to really fine-tune your startup's branding efforts and communicate strategically.

For this group, the main thing which hinders their communications is their goal. When I ask the question, "What's your goal in communicating" to my clients, far too often do I get the same response: "We want to educate the society/the world/our community on climate change/plastic pollution/overconsumption/any other social issue." There are two main problems with this sentence.

1. It's not demonstrating your ability to solve a problem.
2. It's not targeted to a market segment that you're looking to serve.

As a result, many sustainability-driven businesses end up spreading their message too thin. Creating content that only "informs" or "educates" the general public, but only reaches those who already believe what they believe. It achieves nothing more than rallying those who already believe in your cause and excluding those who don't. Essentially, it's preaching to the chior. And if your goal is to increase sustainable actions — like purchasing your product — then this doesn't get you too far. Your goal should only be to educate an audience if they're interested in what you have to sell. And then, they probably don't need to know about the global problems — climate change, etc — but rather, as an awareness tactic, what that means for their particular business and what they can do about it. A surefire way to make your comms more effective is to focus on identifying and solving their problems rather than educating the public.

As we have seen with the Diffusion of Innovations theory by Evert Rodgers, adoption of new technology, ideas or change to the status quo goes through five sections of society before it becomes widespread. An innovation, for Rogers, is an idea, practice or project that is perceived as new by an individual or other unit of adoption. Diffusion analyses the conditions that increase or decrease the likelihood that an innovation — a new idea, product or practice — will be adopted by a group. Your service, product or idea, no matter have advantageous it seems to you, is not going to be automatically adopted by wider society. It's going to go through the same process as other ideas and technologies. First via the innovators, then by the early adopters, etc. In this case, the innovators already want action on sustainability — they just don't have the ability to make it happen.

We spend far to much time on convincing a wider society of the benefits of our product or service. We lecture to a general audience. In terms of Roger's theory ... we end up lecturing the early majority to try and turn them into innovators. And it simply doesn't work.

It's the equivalent of trying to convince your uncle at a BBQ to go vegan. He might have sympathies towards the challenge — that he eats way to much meat, but it's already ingrained in his identity. And if we've seen anything from American politics over the past few years, identity is engrained in the sense of self. But then imagine one of his best mates offers him if he wants a Beyond Meat burger, saying it's not only delicious but it solves his health issues at the same time. Your uncle is much more receptive to the latter than the former.

In simple words: YOUR TARGET AUDIENCE ALREADY WANT IMPACT!

It's your job to help them achieve it. And you do that through delivering value. Solving their problems. Helping them achieve their impact goals — not by telling them that their impact goals should be bigger. If your product is as great as you say it is, then they will help spread the benefits through to the naysayers. You've just got to arm them with the benefits and the stories to do so.

Getting over these major challenges is essential for communicating your brand's potential to grow (it's equity). As the number of impact-driven startups grows and the sustainability space becomes more saturated, your message is going to be key in setting your business apart. By now, you should have a defined vision and mission and you know who your target audience is. This chapter is going to look extensively on how to define your messages and relay them to your target audience. We're first going to look at the idea of creating something of value and giving it away for free. Value-driven messaging flips the traditional communications mindset on its head by introducing one key element: You're buying your audience's attention. Without providing something valuable, they aren't going to get their imaginary mind-wallets out and purchase whatever you're selling. When your message is valuable to that specific person however, you're far more likely to capture their attention: the first stage of engaging a new customer.

THE FOUR STAGES OF ENGAGEMENT

In essence, you'll have the first choice advantage over your competition. So how do you become and stay, top of mind of your marketplace whilst you're waiting for them to become ready to buy? There's a four step process to do so which includes engagement, qualification, nurturing and management.

1. **Attention.** Lead status: They're just discovering that you exist, but they may not know what you do or how you do it. When a customer first engages with your brand, it's more than likely that they won't need your help initially. This is typically known in marketing terms as the top of the sales funnel. It's where you put your best foot forward and tell your audience about the niche that you've carved. Show with action how you are embarking on your mission and reserve the spot in their mind that you exist in. The first step is to understand your client. Speak to their life and their world and

think about what problems they have and create value around solving them. Turn them into a story. One of the best ways that you can do this is by simply asking them. What was the job-to-be-done when they approached you? Or what jobs do they still need to do? One piece of advice here would be to create an Excel sheet here and literally put the answers in there. They can be as specific or arbitrary as you want, but understanding exactly what their problems are will help you solve them in the future. Once you have filled in a few answers to your questions, you can then move on to creating content which answers them. These can be in the form of:

- **Social Media Posts.** The biggest change in marketing over the last twenty years is undoubtedly the way that we consume news and media. Social media gives us the chance to put content tailored to someone's needs right into their lap. When it comes to content, there are two things that are important. You need to create content that speaks to your audience and you need your audience to see it.
- **Blogs.** Blogs are one of the best ways to have the right people find your content. Your website's blog should do the best to provide answers to your target audience's pain points. You have many tools at your disposal to do this and they include, but are not limited to the following posts:
    - How to's
    - Why you need to
    - 5 reasons why
    - How we use X to power X

    - The complete guide to
    - A cheat sheet to X
    - The ultimate glossary
    - How to craft a successful X
    - Mistakes to avoid when doing X
    - 10 X best practices

- **Free Resources.** As discussed in the previous chapter, content which provides the target audience with free digestible resources is a key pillar to generating demand. These can be anything from a whitepaper or eBook to a slideshow shared on LinkedIn. One of my favourite examples is Gary Vee's content strategy slideshow where he provides the insight on how to turn an one hour long interview into over 80 bits of content.
- **Events.** Online events and webinars are great ways to digitally distribute content without a sales pitch. What's more, each event can be turned into multiple pieces of short-form content afterwards making these events pay off again and again.
- **Outbound & Cold Reach Email.** Ask an illumination question; what does your client not know that can help them. Don't ask about problems, find them. Find a problem that you KNOW your client has. A big problem. Find out something that's going to hurt the client or something that's possible: "Did you know that whilst your sifting through emails for two hours each morning, your prospective clients

are 45% less likely to respond".

- **Pay-Per-Click Advertising.** As Google begins to ramp up it's advertising platform organic searches are getting lost further into the depths of the internet. That's not to say you can't rank highly in Google's search, but pay-per-click lets you get there a hell of a lot sooner.

  All of these techniques are the first step in becoming a customer. They're leads or as some call them "potential prospects". By engaging leads with non-sales tactics but rather focusing on the problems that they face on the day-to-day, you can build a reputation in their head as a problem solver in that specific niche.[2]

2. **Interest.** Lead's status: You've got their attention and they want to know if your product may be a good fit for them. Qualification is the process to determine if your lead has the potential to turn into a prospect or not. Traditionally, the qualification process would happen manually, usually by phone or email. Whilst that's not necessarily an issue, the idea of demand generation is that by the time you interact with your customer, you know they're qualified. That's why it's important that your content speaks to people's needs and asks them these questions in advance within your content. Before they enter into the nurturing stage, they should already know what problems they have that you can solve and that you're the right person/team for the job.

2 Wendy Connick, 2020.

For example, if you're selling a solution for drivers, a question that you may ask is if your leads have a car or if they plan on buying one. If the answer is no, then they are not a prospect. Another example in a B2B context could be focused on selling sustainability consulting services. Your question might be something along the lines of "Does your company want to become more sustainable and future-proof in 2020?" Obviously if the answer is no — either because they don't have a company or because they're not interested in becoming more sustainable — then they're not a prospect. The qualification process begins as soon as you receive someone's contact details.

As impact entrepreneurs, we often focus on people who aren't leads, asking "Why you should make your company more sustainable in 2020" rather than engage people who already think that they should make their company more sustainable in 2020. "How to make your company more sustainable in 2020". We spend too much time convincing people to make sustainable decisions and not enough time helping people make them. Tactics include:

- Community building & offline events.
- Exclusive content.
- Conversational email marketing.

3. **Desire.** Lead status: Keen to know more. Once you have determined whether your lead is the right fit for your business or not, the next step is to nurture them from a prospect into a sale. Here you have to introduce your product as a solution to the problems that you've identified further up the funnel. This is where most businesses start the process and whilst it's an important step, it's useless to start

here. You need to first have prospects discover your brand and then transition into a lead before you can nurture them into a customer. They include:

- Educational content. Product-Specific emails, playbooks, & sales decks
- Social proof. i.e., customer reviews, case studies, testimonials. If someone comes close to your CTA, but doesn't manage to make it, email them with a customer review or social proof that your brand follows through for clients.
- Inspirational content. Almost all quarters of B2B businesses are using video today to provide inspirational content and nearly three quarters report positive results to their ROI.
- Free trials, free introduction calls, free report or work done.

4. **Action.** Lead status: Ready to commit. Here you want to make sure that you make it as easy as possible for this prospect to become a customer. The key is to eliminate all hiccups they may have in the buying process. This stage is all about focusing on building meaningful relationships with the customer. Customers who have already purchased from you are 60 to 70% more likely to purchase from you again. Furthermore, they're likely to refer you to their mates. So maintaining these relationships is crucial to building your brand. Remember, your brand is how people experience your brand and that's just as relevant for today's customers as it is for tomorrow's. Tactics include having good refund policies or money back guarantees and not spamming people with emails when they're already ready to buy.

DIRECT & INDIRECT MESSAGING

Since the beginning and certainly since the turn of the century, B2B businesses have been sales driven. "Hey, this thing is going to make your life significantly better. Do you want to buy it?" The era was pre-internet and it was hard to reach people. To get your name or brand out there, you had to be physical and loud. Have a great business to get word of mouth sales. Do something radical or it took a very long time to get started. Now, there's not necessarily a problem with that but when you try and force a sale, you end up with your back against a wall. And with such an explosion in advertising that we're exposed to and so many pop-ups etc, people really don't want to be sold to.

Over the past five to ten years, that all changed. Marketing and especially marketing through social media, has become more important. But the tactics and techniques used didn't change. They stayed the same. People took their traditional sales-oriented techniques and just adapted them to social media. You'll recognise it from a lot of companies that have been around for more than 20 years. They legitimately just push out adverts on their companies LinkedIn, Facebook and Twitter. "Come buy our stuff, it's the best" or "come to our event".

Direct pushes don't work in the current climate. Why? Only 3% of people are in buy-mode. Out of your entire market, only 3% who are proactively looking to your product or services. And if only 3% of your market is buying at any given time, then 97% of your market is not. Author and brand strategist Jeremy Miller calls this The 3% Rule which he outlines in his book Sticky Branding. It's a model to segment your marketplace — including anyone who can buy your services: prospects, current customers, past customers — into buying groups. The 3% Rule divides your marketplace into five buying segments:

- **3% are active buyers.** These are the people and companies that have a need and are actively shopping for vendors. They want to make a purchase in the next thirty to ninety days. These are sales leads.
- **7% intend to change.** These prospects have a need, but aren't proactively searching for options. A well timed cold call or marketing campaign can be very effective on this segment, because they are receptive to new ideas.
- **30% have a need, but not enough to act.** This group is not buying. They may look like and act like prospects, but they won't make a commitment. They have other priorities. Until the need becomes more pressing, they won't make a purchase.
- **30% do not have a need.** This segment of the market does not have a need for your products and services and are not receptive to any marketing messages. They may have just made a purchase, they may be too small or they may not be ready for your services.
- **30% are not interested in your company.** There is a segment of the market that does not fit your brand. Basically, these companies are never going to choose you. They may be loyal to the competition. They may have had a bad experience with your firm. They may use alternative options. Don't sweat it. Just recognize that this dynamic occurs and your brand can't be all things to all people.

According to The 3% Rule, the bottom 90% aren't actively looking for your product, but they may buy at some stage. The top 10% are actively looking, albeit at different velocities. Miller says that this leads us to believe that there are two different types of marketing. Inbound and outbound.[3]

- **Direct.** The top 10%. Marketing to people and companies who have a need for your services right now, typically described as "inbound marketing."
- **Indirect.** The lower 90%. Marketing to people who don't have a need for your services, but will some day.

Before the internet, brands simply marketed to the top section. They used direct messaging to target those who were ready and looking to buy. But when brands are in buy-mode, they don't want to be sold to. They want to be understood and have their hand held through the process. They want the process to be as smooth and simple as possible. But they don't want a salesman, they want someone they already trust and know.

Most brands are great with direct marketing to the top 3% who are actively looking for your service. They're comfortable talking to the top 10%. But the opportunity lies in the remaining 90% who are so often ignored because there is no direct and immediate benefit.

This is the crux of demand generation, a new vision for digital marketing that goes beyond KPIs and other direct lead generation metrics and focuses more on brand. Targeting people who you know are in your market, before they are ready to buy. Build a rapport. So when it comes time to start looking, you are front and centre of mind. Miller says "Create an opportunity where your customers know, like and trust your company long before they have a need. That way they'll skip right over the inbound marketing messages and call your company first when they

---

3 Jeremy Miller, 2015.

have a need."

Indirect marketing, when done correctly, puts the 3% of your marketplace who are actively looking to buy your product or service on your doorstep. Instead of targeting the leads who are looking to buy, you create a funnel of them to your service or product. The business benefits of this are twofold: You reduce the time it takes to close deals, reduce cost per lead, receive better qualified and higher quality leads for sales to work on, increased deal size and experience less lead leakage.

HOW TO CREATE VALUE-DRIVEN MESSAGES

For any brand, leading with values creates broad points of agreement and shared goals that will resonate with your target audience. It shows that you understand their challenges and can provide solutions. To deliver value, you first have to know what that potential customer will find valuable. Simple right? Right. In this lesson, we're going to look at how you can dive deeper into your customer research, understand their challenges and create value propositions (the basis of value-driven messaging).

A value proposition is something that automatically brings your customer into focus and allows you to propose solutions to their problem from their own perspective. And to get there, we have to start with their pain points. In this process, it is very easy to make assumptions. Whether you realize it or not, your preconceived notions influence your interaction with clients. I strongly recommend that you avoid doing so and actually go out and discuss these pain points with potential customers.

Step 1. Make a list. Make a list of companies and people in your ideal target audience who might be interested in your product or technology.
Step 2. Interview your audience. Interview at least five of these organizations and ask them the following questions to identify what they care about, how they define their challenges, and the words they use. Record the conversations and compile a list of the top responses of pain points, gains and opportunities, and jobs-to-be-done.

1. **Discover the pain points:** Pain points are simply: Problems. And because they're problems for our customers, they are opportunities for our brand — if we can solve them, that is. But first, we have to identify them. A pain point is "an issue or problem causing 'pain' in an organization and requiring a solution. True business pain isn't a problem where the solution is a nice-to-have. It's a budgeted, pull-your-hair-out, have-to-get-it-solved, discussed-at-the-board-level kind of problem. Because they affect the bottom line, they must be solved in order for the organization to grow and function successfully." These five questions are the ones I usually use for my clients:

- **What is the biggest challenge you're currently facing?**
- What effect does this challenge have on your current business?
- What has prevented you from relieving the pain?
- What has prevented you from relieving the pain?
- What happens if the pain is left unchecked?
- Does this challenge lead to bigger problems in the future?

Make sure that you record the conversation so that you can listen back to their response. The words they use may prove invaluable.

2. **Seek out gains and opportunities.** Once you're finished asking your ideal clients their pains, let's flip it and ask them about their gains.

- What is the greatest desires your ideal target audience currently has (i.e., reduce costs, raise capital, hire more top tier candidates)?
- What effect could this have on their current business if achieved?
- Are these desires a nice to have (like candy) or a essential to achieving a goal (like going to the dentist)?

3. **Jobs-to-be-done.** What jobs do your ideal target market need done? Jobs to be Done is a theory of consumer action: It describes the mechanisms that cause a consumer to adopt an innovation. The theory states that markets grow, evolve, and renew whenever customers have a Job to be Done, and then buy a product to complete it (get the Job Done).

- What are the functional, emotional or social jobs or tasks that your target audience must complete on a daily basis?
- What tools could help your target audience achieve these jobs?

Step 3. Analyse the responses. While certain pain points will be unique to specific clients, many will be more universal. In this step of the process, you'll want to identify these trends. Ask yourself: "What are the most common pain points for all of your customers, what do they have in common?"

Create a list of between 10+ major pain points which multiple clients experience. Rank them from most common to least common. As a bonus, make a list of the common terminology that they use; this will come in hand later in the process when you're writing your value proposition.

Step 4. Product features. Next, make a list of all of your product's features. This step is important in creating your value proposition; by connecting your product's features with your target audience's pains, you can create strategic messages to solve these challenges.

Step 5. Write your value propositions. Once you have a interviewed multiple people in your ideal target audience, review the responses to create the basis of your value propositions. What do they care about? What collective challenges to they have? These will help you develop a strategic message that adds value to their live. Take all the pains, gains and JTBD and arrange them under three broad categories. These are your value proposition categories:

Value proposition 1	Value proposition 2	Value proposition 3
• • •	• • •	• • •

Then ask yourself, why does my buyer persona care about this category?

Step 5. Turn them into value statements. A value proposition is a promise of value to be delivered, communicated, and acknowledged. It is also a belief from the customer about how value will be delivered, experienced and acquired. Once you have a clear understanding of your customer's pain points, it's time to turn them into value propositions.For example:

- Pain Point: We are losing millennial customers due to environmental concerns. Value Statement: Minimize revenue at risk from losing millennial customers due to environmental concerns
- Pain Point: We don't know to measure our impact according to the SDGs properly and it's holding back our growth. Value Statement: Adequately measuring your impact in line with the SDGs.
- Pain Point: We are afraid our business is contributing to plastic waste issues abroad. Value Statement: Ensure that your business doesn't contribute to plastic waste issues in developing countries.

It's important that you take your VP category from negative to positive. For instance, if your category is to "reduce carbon consumption from transport" and your, your value proposition could be "zero emission delivery". Write multiple versions of this to iterate, use the vocabulary of your target audience, and test each.

Step 5. From value statement to strategic message. Create three different forms for each of your value propositions statements. These will be key in the process for writing everything from your brand's website copy, to product features, and awareness campaigns.

1. Tagline (5 words max)

2. One sentence statement (25 words): "Our company _____[value proposition] helps ________ [ideal target audience] with __________ [pain/gain/job-to-be-done]."

3. One paragraph statement (100 words max): "For ____________ [ideal customer] who ___________[has this pain] that __________

[wants to achieve/gain] to with our __________[what your company is] that provides_______________[your value proposition]. With ______ [your brand name], you can ___X_Y_and_Z___[list your main USPs]."

HOW TO START CREATING VALUABLE CONTENT

If attention is the greatest currency of today and people are giving your content their attention, then they are actually paying for your content. They're paying for it by reading it, watching it, digesting it, or acknowledging it. If you make them fill in a form to access it, they may consider this too expensive for the value that they're getting. If you hold back on giving away your insights, people will potentially feel like they're being short-changed. With so much information floating around, we don't live in a world where we can hesitate on this. If you want your content to really succeed, you need to focus on providing value to your ideal clients.

In my experience in this sector, content that gives something valuable for free converts better than gated content or content that holds back. Most start-ups are great at self-fiving. Some are great at bringing people along on their brand's journey. Only a few are great at creating content that gives value away for free. Creating content that provides value means that you have to step out of your own skin and insert yourself into your target audience's. You have to actually understand the problems that they encounter on a daily basis and provide them with a solution. Sure, your product may be one solution, but your knowledge and your experience may also help ease their pains. It takes time but it also takes emotional investment from the founder's side. But only then will you begin to see a payoff from your content strategy.

GIVE SOMETHING OF VALUE AWAY FOR FREE

Strategic messaging is another name for giving value away for free in exchange for the right person's attention. So often we, as entrepreneurs, have spent so long crafting our solution and are so proud of the features we offer, that it is all we want to talk about. Strategic messaging is literally the exact opposite. When crafting a strategic message, you have to start with the customer and work your way backwards. What do they need? What questions do they have? And what resolution does your solution afford them? It's all about the result rather than how you are going to achieve it.

When you start with your target audience in mind, you develop the ability to step into their shoes and understand what they're struggling with. As you have probably gathered by now, this form of communication is all about making sure that the story you tell is a) delivered to the right person, b) adds value to their lives and c) gets them to act in line with your goals; including following your company, sharing your story and reaching out to you for new business.

As we have discussed, every day, the average European sees between

4,000 and 10,000 advertisements per day. That's just insane. And what do they all do? The majority all do nothing other than self promotion and sales. We are currently living in a world full of information and void of value.

Before you share your next LinkedIn post or Instagram story, ask yourself; what is this piece of information going to bring to my target audience's life? Is it going to make it easier for them to achieve their goals? Is it going to help them make the right choice in a business situation? Or is it going to go past them like another advertisement for a new formula for toothpaste?

If there's one thing that you take away from this book, it needs to be this: GIVE YOUR AUDIENCE SOMETHING OF VALUE. It's not such a hard concept in theory, but it took me years to figure out what this means in practice. The fact is that really giving something away that is valuable is hard. But it goes hand in hand with crafting out your niche.

There is just so much crap out there, so much content, that to get any real estate in your target audience's mind, you have to actually provide them with something of value. ACTUAL value for your audience in order to engage them. Serial entrepreneur, investor and author Gary Vaynerchuk brings this concept into perspective. "If you provide so much up front value to an individual, you can actually guilt them into buying shit?

Especially if all your actions are predicated on not expecting them to buy it. That's the big part. When the energy of your tactics is to convert, you will lose. When your energy is to disproportionately bring value and let the chips fall where they may, you will win."[4] Vaynerchuk also highlights that all while all relationships in business need to be a two way

4 Gary Vaynerchuk, 2016.

street to be functional, before you get to this point, you need to give away value for free. It establishes the relationship. "Because the truth is, people like people. We're wired for it. And people do business with other people. So when you learn to generally give to those people without expecting them to do something in return, you win."[5]

With sustainability or impact in mind, however, we often get caught up in providing value for ourselves.

We like to brag about the impact we're making or challenge others, bring them down, harp on about how one company isn't doing enough or celebrate another that's doing better. Whilst this is all fine in small portions, it should not make up the majority of content you are putting into the world.

It provides little-to-no value for your target audience, but rather only engages others deeply embedded in the sustainability field who already have the same views. Kind of like an echo-chamber.

For instance, when you post something on LinkedIn saying, "Donald Trump's latest policy is the exact kind of climate denialism that we fight at our company, join us in our battle to save the climate", you're sugarcoating a sales pitch by attaching it to a trending topic.

Another example is a post that says "We are determined to make the sustainable economy a reality. Last year we grew our impact by x5. Want to be a part of our journey?."

As a viewer, neither of these posts bring any value to me. They're practically a self-five for your business.

---

5 Gary Vaynerchuk, 2015.

EXERCISE 01

IDEAL CUSTOMER INTERVIEWS

The first step in creating strategic messages for your brand is interviewing your ideal target customers (prospects) and validating your assumptions.

Step 1. Make a list of companies and people in your ideal target audience who might be interested in your product or technology.

1.
2.
3.
4.
5.
6.
7.
8.
9.
10.

Step 2. Interview at least five of these organizations and ask them the following questions to identify what they care about, how they define their challenges, and the words they use. Record the conversations and compile a list of the top responses.

Interviewee 1:

Interviewee 2:

Interviewee 3:

Interviewee 4:

Interviewee 5:

EXERCISE 02

VALUE PROPOSITION INTERVIEW QUESTIONS

The next step in creating strategic messages for your brand and communications strategy is to identify your target audience's pain points.

Step 3. What are the biggest challenges your ideal target audience is currently facing? List the 3 greatest pains:

1.
2.
3.

What effect does this challenge have on their current business?

Write your answer here...

What has prevented them from relieving the pain?

Write your answer here...

What happens if the pain is left unchecked?

Write your answer here...

Does this challenge lead to bigger problems in the future?

Write your answer here...

STEP 4. GAINS

What is the greatest desires your ideal target audience currently has (i.e., reduce costs, raise capital, hire more top tier candidates)?

1.
2.
3.

What effect could this have on their current business if achieved?

Write your answer here...

Are these desires a nice to have (like candy) or a essential to achieving a goal (like going to the dentist)?

Write your answer here...

STEP 3. JOBS-TO-BE-DONE

What are the functional, emotional or social jobs or tasks that your target audience must complete on a daily basis?

1.
2.
3.

What tools could help your target audience achieve these jobs?

Write your answer here...

STEP 4. COMMON TERMINOLOGY

As a bonus, make a list of the common terminology that they use; this will come in hand later in the process when you're writing your value proposition.

STEP 5. PRODUCT FEATURES

Next, make a list of all of your product's features. This step is important in creating your value proposition; by connecting your product's features with your target audience's pains, you can create strategic messages to solve these challenges.

EXERCISE 03

RESPONSE ANALYSIS

Once you have a interviewed multiple people in your ideal target audience, review the responses to create the basis of your value propositions. What do they care about? What collective challenges to they have? These will help you develop a strategic message that adds value to their live.

Take all the pains, gains and JTBD and arrange them under three broad categories. These are your value proposition categories:

VP Category 1	VP Category 2	VP Category 3
•	•	•
•	•	•
•	•	•
•	•	•

VP Category 1: Reasons why customers care about this VP category.

1.
2.
3.

VP Category 2: Reasons why customers care about this VP category.

1.
2.
3.

VP Category 3: Reasons why customers care about this VP category.

1.
2.
3.

Next, take your VP category and reverse it; from negative to positive. For instance, if your category is to "reduce carbon consumption from transport" and your, your value proposition could be "zero emission delivery". TIP: Write multiple versions of this to iterate, use the vocabulary of your target audience, and test each.

VP Category 1	→	Value Proposition 1
VP Category 2	→	Value Proposition 2
VP Category 3	→	Value Proposition 3

VP Category 1: What features of your product aligns with this VP category?

1.
2.
3.

VP Category 2: What features of your product aligns with this VP category?

1.
2.
3.

VP Category 3: What features of your product aligns with this VP category?

1.
2.
3.

EXERCISE 04

DEVELOP VALUE PROPOSITIONS

Create three different forms for each of your value propositions statements. These will be key in the process for writing everything from your brand's website copy, to product features, and awareness campaigns.

1. Tagline (5 words max)
2. One sentence statement (25 words)
3. One paragraph statement (100 words max)

Tagline: A 5-word description that defines your key value proposition.

_____[your value proposition]_____

One sentence value proposition statement.

Our company _____[value proposition] helps ________ [ideal target audience] with __________[pain/gain/job-to-be-done].

One paragraph statement (100 words max)

For ____________ [ideal customer] who ___________[has this pain] that __________[wants to achieve/gain] to with our __________[what your company is] that provides______________[your value proposition]. With ______[your brand name], you can ___X_Y_and_Z___[list your main USPs].

EXERCISE 05

VALUE-DRIVEN MESSAGES

Strategic messages are messages that deliver value to your ideal target audience about topics they actually care about (i.e., help your target audience solve their pain point). When you have determined their values, you can address to them & their attributing pain points with content. What's important is that you're actually solving these challenges, rather than promoting/selling your own product.

CONTENT IDEAS

Content ideas: Value Proposition 1

1. How to achieve/develop/secure VP
2. X things (pain points) stopping you from achieving VP
3. Why you're approaching VP1 wrong
4. The X steps to achieve VP
5. VP is changing; Here's what you need to know

Content ideas: Value Proposition 2

1. How to achieve/develop/secure VP
2. X things (pain points) stopping you from achieving VP
3. Why you're approaching VP1 wrong
4. The X steps to achieve VP
5. VP is changing; Here's what you need to know

Content ideas: Value Proposition 3

1. How to achieve/develop/secure VP
2. X things (pain points) stopping you from achieving VP
3. Why you're approaching VP1 wrong
4. The X steps to achieve VP
5. VP is changing; Here's what you need to know

"The mistake people make is thinking the story is just about marketing. No, the story is the strategy. If you make your story better, you make the strategy better."

- Ben Horowitz

7.

BRAND PLATFORM: CRAFTING YOUR BRAND

The first step to building a successful product is coming up with an idea. The first step towards creating a successful business is building your brand. Once you have your brand foundations and your strategic narratve down on paper, and you know exactly who your targeting and how, it's time to focus on building your brand's identity. There is a logic to having all of these pieces in place before you begin on your brand's platform. For instance, your narrative feeds into your website copy and your manifesto into your "About Page". The same goes for your customer funnel: How can you create content which captures your beachhead market if you don't know who your target audience is? This step is, for most entrepreneurs, something that they just do. They don't think so much about it because they don't have time or it isn't considered a priority. What usually happens is that an entrepreneur has an idea, they build an MVP, then they build a website and fill it with information about the MVP. It's classic and it's understandable. But later down the line, when you go to start raising capital, pitching your solution to accelerators or apply for a grant, a platform without any of these elements integrated will hold you back. Then in a last minute scramble, they realize that they're already two steps behind and they revisit their brand platform and reconsider whether it represents them. You can recognise this by the following sentence, "We'll get to it once we get some capital." Whether this is the case for you or if you're starting from scratch, having those elements in place is going to make building a strong brand much easier. This is especially true if you decide to have a designer to build your identity and website because the core information already exists and can be handed over without a thought.

Why is this important?

Every time anyone has an interaction with your company, it leaves an impression. The only thing in your hands is whether you take ownership or leave it up to chance. Whether the impression is "they seem like they're passionate and in control of their future" or "they're inconsistent and they'll never get anywhere", is up to you.

By taking control of the interactions which your brand has with the public, you can communicate your worth – and potential impact – subconsciously as well as consciously. This is especially necessary when you're interacting with potential partners or investors. When a decision is being made on whether to work with your company, branding can be a differentiating factor. Your brand is the perception of your company to the world.

A brand identity is how your brand presents itself. It's the channels you choose to use to communicate, it's your business cards and the design of your office. And it all stems from your visual identity, your tone of voice and your brand's character.

If your solution is the most forward-thinking and innovative X that there is, but if two other companies are offering similar services, how does the purchaser choose? What if your website looks like it comes from 2010? How can you then present yourself as forward-thinking or innovative? This kind of disconnect is especially a problem when it comes to impact entrepreneurs who think their methodology or their innovation will carry them further than the way that they present themselves.

People fall ill to an inherently human trait; they make choices based on gut instinct. This is especially when the metrics and price are similar. If you define that you're both on the same path, then it's a simple choice, but if your brand subconsciously communicates something that puts doubt into the head of the customer — perhaps something as simple as the fact that you haven't put much pride into your branding — then it can kill the transaction before it begins along with any future transactions and any goodwill that customer might have spread. In the long run, your customers are only human and they have the power to change the direction of your entrepreneurial journey.

Crafting a distinct and memorable brand identity stems from the other foundation elements. Your logo, your website, your business cards. They all project a certain image of you. The message is intrinsic but it's real whether you like it or not. By taking this into your own hands, you have the potential to influence all of your future business endeavours solely by the creation of an image which clearly shows how your brand fits the scene.

In this section, we're going to look how you can do just that by creating an authentic Climate Tech brand's identity as well as its digital footprint.

GREEN IS GOOD, RIGHT?

Too many Climate Tech businesses build brands that are fit for the past, not the future. In the Climate Tech era, making your brand visually distinguishable from your competitors is essential. Yet far the majority of sustainable brands still only compete on being "more sustainable" than the competition. With a green logo and images of nature. The fact is that sustainability is a competitive advantage that will always erode. It's a fact of modern economics.

Climate tech brands are prone to believe their methodology or their solution can compete because it's "more sustainable" or "more innovative" than anything else out there. We believe that we stand out from the crowd. And maybe it's true...for a while. But it doesn't last forever. Every solution can be replicated. Every innovative business model can be copied. You might have the solution to solve a specific problem now, but what happens when someone solves it for cheaper? Or is backed by a bigger company? So what sets you apart in this new landscape?

The fact is that the Climate Tech brand ecosystem is exploding.

Every day there are new sustainability and impact-driven brands being built. As a result, the ecosystem is exploding. This means that we simply can't continue being the one "green" solution on offer. We have to go deeper than this: Especially with our visual identity.

Imagine you're in the market for a non-plastic straw. Ten years ago, this market was a niche. Today, there are so many Instagram accounts selling "sustainable" straws, you couldn't count them on the feet of millipedes. So what differentiates them from one another?

The short answer? Nothing?

They all sell long, round bits of metal, bamboo or recycled plastic that you can drink through "guilt-free". They're all claiming to be sustainable. They all solve the consumer's problem: Not wanting to waste single-use plastic.

The sustainability of their product isn't their defining feature anymore. So how do can they compete for market share?

Now I know that there are some people out there thinking: "They shouldn't have to compete...there should be enough people out there that don't want to use plastic straws and they all should survive."

Competing on sustainability alone is a fool's game.

We so often think that our solution shouldn't have to compete because our solution stands alone; the only sustainable option on the market. That our solution's survival is guaranteed by humanity's humanity. In reality, however, the truth is much less secure.

People buy solutions. Sustainability isn't quantifiable for consumers; something is or it isn't. They're not looking for the most sustainable X on the market and they don't have time to check the specifics of a product against your competitors.

They have a problem and they value sustainability. If you're in the market of solving a sustainability pain point, all your competitors will be too. As that problem becomes more mainstream, more people will see value in solving it.

Just like plastic straws, reusable water bottles and packaging-free soaps were niche a decade ago, there are hundreds of unique solutions today that will grow into profitable markets. You might think you own the problem you're solving. But if you succeed in making a profitable business from solving it, it's only a matter of time until you have company.

VISUAL IDENTITY

There are five steps to define your brand's visual identity:

1. Personality (or brand attributes)
2. The colours your brand uses
3. Your logo (or logos)
4. Typography or fonts
5. The imagery you use

Below we're going to give an in depth look at how to build each.

1. **Personality.** Customers are more likely to purchase a brand if its personality is similar to their own. Your brand's personality is the human component of your brand and it's the basis of your visual identity, made up of the emotional traits and behaviours which you would like to exhibit. Most brand personalities can fit into five broad categories, or "dimensions," as they've been coined by social psychologist Jennifer Aaker (and have since become the industry

standard). Each dimension has its own personality traits and strengths:

Competence	Reliable, successful, intelligent. Customers are attracted to brands like this because they believe they will get the job done. Think brands like Microsoft or Volkswagen.
Ruggedness	Thick-skinned, outdoorsy, tough. These brands make customers feel powerful, and remind them of nature. Think brands like Woodland and Harley Davidson.
Sophistication	Charming, refined, high-class. It usually takes time to exude sophistication as a brand, but once they get there, these brands are poised, polished, and make their customers feel classy and elegant. Think brands like Tiffany or Armani.

Excitement	Daring, intriguing, imaginative, up-to-date. Maybe they push limits, but in a playful way. These brands are good at creating a lot of hype and building excitement in their audience, like Mountain Dew or Virgin Atlantic.
Sincerity	Wholesome, genuine, honest, warm. Customers love brands like this because they are believable and trustworthy. These brands keep to their promises and meet expectations. Think brands like Cadbury or Hallmark.

2. **Colours.** Research shows that the vast majority of consumers believe colour is the biggest motivator when choosing a particular product, and almost all of us acknowledge visual appearance as the most persuasive marketing factor overall. Yet it's one of the most overlooked opportunities in Climate Tech. "Like a carefully chosen brand name, colour carries an intrinsic meaning that becomes central to the brand's identity, contributes to brand recognition and communicates the desired image," states the Journal of the Academy of Marketing Science. According to Canva, "Colours elicit emotions and feelings, plus they convey certain information.

This enables customers to form an initial impression without even knowing what your product is about. Put simply, brand colors are powerful in helping customers decide whether or not they want to engage." A brief overview of the feelings which each colour elicites, according to the graphic design platform:

- Red is associated with danger, excitement, and energy. It's also known for being the color of love and passion.
- Pink is feminine, it's sentimental and romantic. Different shades, like hot pink, can be youthful and bold.
- Orange, like it's namesake, is fresh and full of vitality. It's also creative, adventurous, and associated with being cost-effective.
- Yellow is optimistic. It's a color associated with being playful and happy.
- Green is natural, often used to demonstrate sustainability. But it can also align with prestige and wealth.
- Blue is trustworthy and reliable. It's calming or often associated with depression.
- Purple is royalty and majesty. It can be spiritual and mysterious.
- Brown is down-to-earth and honest, often used for organic wholesome products.
- White is pure. It conveys simplicity and innocence, often with a minimalistic feel.
- Black is both sophisticated and elegant. It can be formal and luxurious, but also sorrowful.
- Multicolor is great for capturing the spirit of diversity.

If you've decided that your brand's personality is explorative, independent and non-conforming, then according to the wheel (shown above), your predominant colour maybe green. Not, however, because you're "more sustainable" than your competition. Choosing one colour based on this list is a good way to start and then complement it with a second, less intense colour. Choose branding colours that complement each other. I would recommend choosing two or three colours; one primary and one or two secondary to use in your communications.

3. **Logo.** Your logo is the face of your business. It's usually the first visual interaction anyone has with your business and a cleverly designed logo can edge itself into someone's mind, but a poorly designed one can be a stain on your company. Even worse than a poorly designed logo is the logo that fails to differentiate. I consistently come across "eco-friendly" logos with a brand name and a green tree in the background. If you want your logo to help you stand apart from the competition, it's only common sense to make something different. Thus, I would suggest splashing out on a logo. With your brand story and ingredients, you should be able to track one down for a small fee. If you're not a designer and you can afford it, don't consider trying to make one yourself. What are some characteristics of a good logo? Once you have made your choice, ask yourself the following questions:

- Simplicity: Is the design easily identifiable? Is it not too busy, confusing, or distracting?
- Memorability: Is it quickly recognizable?
- Timelessness: Will it still be a great logo in 10, 20, or even 50 years?

- Functionality: Does it work across a range of mediums?
- Appropriateness: Does it resonate with your ideal target audience and their industry?

4. **Typography.** Typography, or the fonts that you use and the way those fonts are laid out, is hugely important to the branding process. Fonts send a message to your audience about who you are as a brand. Are you old fashioned or modern and quirky? What's it going to be like working with you? How open to innovation are you? Your font can tell a story every time someone interacts with it, about who you are as a brand and what they can expect from working with you. Typography is important to knuckle down in the beginning because the last thing you want to be doing is chopping and changing fonts. Just like using Times New Roman or Comic Sans will send a different approach to if you choose to go with Helvetica for instance. If you're an early-stage Climate Tech start-up, you probably don't have the time or the inclination to think that much about fonts.

- **Step 1.** To choose your primary font, ask yourself which of the following describe your brand? Make a list from 1-6.
    1. Classic, traditional, educational, and trustworthy?
    2. Modern, clean, innovative, minimalistic, and approachable?
    3. Bold, confident, and authoritative?
    4. Stylish, elegant, and unique?
    5. Quirky, distinctive, and dramatic?
    6. Stylized, distinctive, and dramatic?

- **Step 2.** Each number above correlates to a group of fonts on the next page, including Serif, San Serif, etc. As the fonts you choose will nonverbally communicate your company's identity, consider which character traits you want to lead with in your communications. For instance, if your brand is "stylish" and "elegant," you may want to choose a script typeface for your primary font. If you're "innovative" or "mordern," a san serif font might be for you. If you're more "traditional" consider choosing a serif font.
    1. Serif
    2. San-serif
    3. Slab serif
    4. Script
    5. Handwritten
    6. Decorative
- **Step 3.** Choose two fonts which represent your brand to be your Primary Font and your Secondary Font. Consider choosing two different types of fonts (i.e., Slab serif for your Primary Font and San-serif for your Secondary Font), but don't be afraid to choose one font for both. Keep in mind, you can also use just one typeface across your entire brand or have one font in ALL CAPS for your title, and in paragraph for your Secondary Font.
- **Step 4.** Choose how you want to write your titles — ALL CAPS, Title Caps, or Sentence caps — and stick with it across your brand identity. For instance, with my branding connsultancy, in official documents, I always write the brand name in All Caps and have all headlines in Title Case (e.g., Compete on Brand, Not on Features).

5. **Imagery.** What images should you use in your communications?

   I've worked with brands before that didn't have a style guideline for imagery and as a result, there was no continuity in their communications. There were high-res black and white images, next to cartoons, next to cropped landscapes. It made no sense. This reflected badly not only on their design skills – they presented themselves as a design firm – but also made others question their ability to deliver. Choosing how you present images, the shapes that you use frequently and your form will keep you in check when it comes to communicating. Ask yourself "does this image represent us" and if the answer is no, then why are we using it? The best way to do this is to pick a single style and stick with it. For example, in all the images on my website, I've taken most of the colour out and put the contrast up. Others may use only images of nature or aerial shots. Whatever you choose, play with the colours a bit to make everything look continuous.

- **Step 1.** Align your imagery with your brand's persona. Just like your fonts and your colours, consider the characteristics you want to get across with your imagery. Do you want to be known for your unique design or do you want to be known as traditional or innovative? Each has a particular style of imagery. Think about the reputation you want to create for your business — what do you want your target audience to think when they interact with your business?
- **Step 2.** Create a mood board. Make a mood board on Pinterest of images which align with your brand's values and which are in similar colors to the ones you have chosen. A mood board is a

canvas where you collect imagery you like so that you can then go on and narrow it down. It will help you select the themes, colors, and tones and is an efficient way to begin. I recommend doing this by creating an account with Pinterest and making a board there.

Step 3. Define your imagery. The best way to do this is to pick a single style and stick with it. Examples of different styles of imagery which you could choose are:

- High resolution
- Low/high contrast
- Aerials of nature, cityscapes, buildings...
- Black & white portraits
- Granulated & high ISO
- Only cartoons or illustrations
- Journalistic features: Storytelling as a visual medium

You should be able to write down your brand style imagery in a single sentence. For instance, in all the images on the Impact Brand Building, we've taken most of the colour out, put the contrast up, and feature traditional cityscapes and photojournalistic images with people.

All in all, don't be afraid to get creative here and keep in mind that consistency is key. Every time you post something, ask yourself, is this right? Does this live up to my brand's imagery guidelines? If not, it might be best to reconsider.

YOUR DIGITAL ASSETS

Once you have the foundations of your brand marked out and have solidified your brand's identity, it's time to create the assets which underpin your startup. Likely, you've already got a LinkedIn profile, a Twitter profile and Facebook profile and you've probably even written something on all of them. Perhaps you've even posted the same link to a Guardian Environment article on all three. Copy. Paste. So why hasn't Fast Company called yet? I don't think you'll be surprised to hear; it doesn't work like that. Without the proper assets in place, it's unlikely that you're going to get far in your communication strategy. One thing at a time, as they say. In this section, I'm going to give you an overview of the strategy that I usually go through with my clients.

So many entrepreneurs jump the gun on this entirely. They begin to communicate without having the basic structure in place to make that communication effective. If you're one of them, you're not alone. Actually, the majority of impact entrepreneurs struggle with the same issues. And as an impact entrepreneur, you're more likely to be a scientist, an academic or a Delft University genius than a marketeer. But getting your online footprint right is one of the single biggest advantages you can give your startup.

Your digital footprint comprises of three main components; your website, your social feeds and external links. Each carries a certain weight and all must exist in equilibrium to build a trusted brand. But there's an order in which you should build that follows a similar pattern.

THE WEBSITE

Your website is the best salesperson you have. It's a 21st Century business card, office and storefront rolled into one. It should be where the selling happens, not in your content beyond. If your customer or target audience has arrived there, it's because you caught their attention. But will you leave an impression? Or will they stroll past and move along in their purchasing journey?

Having a website that is in line with your business' values and both visual and verbal identity is a key pillar to success in building your brand. To do so, you need to display information relevant to your guest and let them know they're in the right place. For every website, there is a distinct order in which you should display information. When you follow this order, you're following a logical narrative which people expect to find information. But before diving into what that is, let's go back to psychology.

You have on average, eight seconds to capture someone's attention. That's roughly the same attention span of a goldfish. And we live in a world where attention is the greatest currency there is. We earn it. We spend it. We value it. And sometimes, we lose it. And that's a problem for impact entrepreneurs. You don't have the luxury to go into details about your circularity methodology or your technology stack. People simply don't have enough attention span to care. They care about themselves, their needs and their problems. So to reduce how quickly someone encounters and then leaves your site, design, comprehensibility and a focus on problem-solving are key.

Your website visitor should be able to figure out what your website is about within the first few seconds of landing on the page. In this first glance, they will see your design, logo, slogan and one sentence of text on the homepage of your site. This is the equivalent of a digital elevator pitch. If the prospect browsing your site doesn't know within the first eight seconds exactly what they can expect from you, then they will almost certainly leave.

Going back to the two common hang-ups which impact entrepreneurs can have when communicationg — scientific or social — we can see how each has a negative effect specifically in the context of our website.

1. The scientific or academic route is a classic impact entrepreneur character trait. Because those tackling some of the world's greatest problems head on are generally pretty damn intelligent, they tend to think their target audience is the same. Unfortunately, when overtly scientific language confuses your website's visitor, they simply leave and go somewhere less overwhelming. Industry-specific jargon has no place on your website, especially if your target audience comes from outside the sustainability bubble.

2. In a business context, social justice warriors also turn the audience off. "Save the whales...buy our product" is an all to common mantra that doesn't tend to convert customers so well. And your website is essentially useless if it's not helping you convert customers. Socialites also struggle to niche down. They use open language, broad branding and stock imagery as it appeals to a wider audience. However, as we really need to get across — within an incredibly short time frame —what we can do for our target audience. Our opinion on the latest IPCC report or a Guardian Environment

article unfortunately don't get that message across.

Your website is there to help you convert clients, showcase your case studies and elevate your thought leadership. When you create content for your website, always ask yourself if this content is contributing to a two-way dialogue. Content should always add value and solve problems for your audience. It's not a one-way monologue. It's a conversation. So when your audience — the person on the other side of the screen — doesn't understand you or doesn't see themself in the receiving role, they'll switch off from your message. After all, you're trying to hold their attention and talk to them; not talk at them. You must make it as easy as humanly possible for your target audience to get their hands on the information that will convince them to use your solution. To flip both of these concepts you need to know what language your customer speaks and what problems they have. It is incredibly important here that you don't talk about your brand from your perspective, but rather focus on what the customer needs to hear. Answer their pain points. Let them know that you have a solution.

There is a simple criterion here: The Golden Circle format. Start with why you do what you do, then consider how you solve your target audience's (call them out) pain point and then simply state what you do. These three things must be seen in the first eight seconds of someone landing on your website. To hold attention and convert visitors into leads, it's up to you to make sure that your user has the best experience possible on your website. But keep in mind that websites are scanned and not read. As a result, you should keep the overly complex language and industry jargon to the minimum. A website must be:

- **Usable.** Site must be easy to navigate, easily approachable and logical

- **Informative.** User must be getting something of value on your site
- **Findable.** Content needs to be locatable and navigable offsite and onsite
- **Useful.** Content should be original and fulfil a need
- **Credible.** Users must believe and trust what you tell them
- **Actionable.** When a potential customer comes to your site, give them a way to take action to solve their pain points.
- **Open.** Reduce barriers to entry as much as possible

To plan out the structure of your website, you should focus on keeping a three-phase structure of content. The typical tri-layered website structure is as follows:

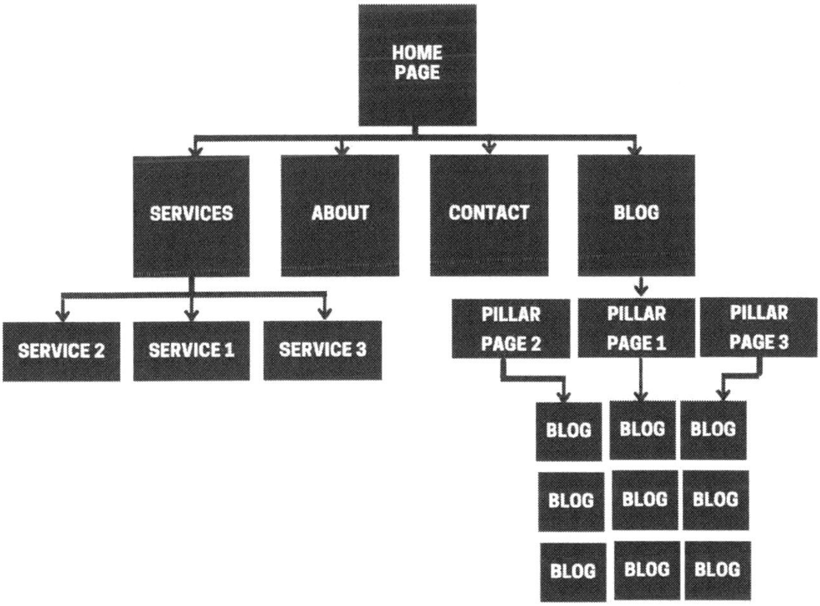

Home Page.

The first layer should be simple and easy to understand for your target audience. It should answer their needs and address thei r pain points whilst giving them social proof that you're up to the job. This is an example of a high converting UX designed home page:

1. **Above the fold.** Before you scroll down, you should see either a Hero Image or a full-page video banner with Text over it. The text should address the prospect and tell them that they are in the right place. You have three main goals in this section:
    - Call our your target audience.
    - Make sure they know what you offer.
    - Additionally, a nice to have is to know the benefit of your product.

   Following this concept, the following page shows the way that you can order your website so your text builds a story for itself.

And this one last.

YOU WILL READ THIS FIRST.

And then you will read this,

Then this one,

2. **Description.** Create a description that's a bit more in-depth than your tagline that shows how you're solving a problem for your target market.
    - **Purpose.** (WHY) written concisely.
    - **Tagline.** (HOW) strongly worded which shows the benefits your target users will get.
    - **Product.** (WHAT) Outline your product so that the visitor knows what you're talking about.
3. **Visuals.** A video between 30 – 120 seconds can take place of a description. This can be also placed higher in the website to replace your company's description.
4. **Call to Action.** Sign up to email list, join the platform, get a free trial, download your latest whitepaper.
5. **Testimonials for Social Proof.** You should ideally be posting three testimonials with photographs of the individuals giving them and a link to their company or organization. Having testimonials provides social proof that what you're offering, works.
6. **Client or Partner Banner:** Further displaying social proof.
7. **Thought Leadership: Seen in the Press section/Blog articles.** Here you can put either article from your most impressive blog content or a section linking to your most recent press articles. Press is valued as social proof above your blog, so if you have

finally got that interview with Fast Company, this is where it should live.

8. **Footer.** Add social media links & contact details.

About, Services, Blog, Contact.

The second layer should provide an extra layer of complexity. You should assume that if your visitor has made it there from the home page, they are at least intrigued by your solution. This is where you can get more specific about the industry that you're active in, expand on your purpose and the greater societal trends which are driving your existence. Here you can go in-depth on WHAT you do. Outline your services, define your product. Chances are when someone is on this page, they're here to find out if they can use your product. To make it as easy and actionable as possible, give prices, show videos, add personality.

Services/ Technology	About	Blog	Contact
• Service 1 • Service 2 • Service 3	• Mission • Story • Team	• Pillar 1 • Pillar 2 • Pillar 3	• Email • Contact • Calendly

Long-Form Content.

The third layer is where you can get into your in depth analysis of your subject matter. This layer consists of knowledge and insights in the form of articles, blogs and news.

I suggest beginning with a pillar page strategy to help boost your SEO from the get go. A pillar page is a high-level piece of content that broadly overviews a main topic and links out to in-depth articles (or blogs) about specific subtopics. People want quality information when they're searching and by providing your target audience with quality content for free, you're building trust with them and helping them solve their business challenges. A pillar page strategy does just that. It's not the easiest option, but today, it certainly is the most effective. Remember: Strong foundations are the basis of a brand that can grow tall.

A pillar page is an in depth, long-form guide that helps your target audience achieve their goals. For example, if your business helps companies measure their carbon footprint, you might write a pillar page called The Ulimtate Guide to Carbon Measurement for Business — a vast topic in itself — and have multiple pieces of topic specific cluster content about how to reduce Scope 1 emissions, Scope 2 emissions and Scope 3 within the article. Then each could be broken up into stand alone blogs with the title, How Businesses can Measure Scope 3 Carbon Emissions. Whatever your product or service helps your target audience achieve, this is where you get into it the details of "how" and "why".

I usually recommend my smaller clients to build a strategy around their value propositions or for larger clients, around each of their market segments (i.e., Carbon measuring for financial institutions). As a rule of thumb, each article should be 2,000 plus words with the ideal target being around 4,000 words to help your content rank in Google search engines.

Headlines and content for blogs.

Blog content should be titled with clickable headlines (not clickbait, but not sciency stuff that your target audience might not understand). This is simply because that's how people search on the internet. For example, say you've written a great piece of long-form content about bees in cities. For instance: If your headline reads "Why Bees Are Important for Smart Cities" then it's more likely to show up in search engines over "Apoidea Ointment: Lo-Fi Smart City Natural Capital". Whilst the second may be more intriguing for a magazine article, it's going to be lost in the deep blue depths of Google's search algorithm and certainly, unless your target audience is a bee-keeping fanatic, it's going to go straight past them.

Consider how they ask search engines about their pain points. For instance, when a customer wants help becoming circular in their waste streams, they search for "how to create a circular waste stream" rather than a brand name "CE Consultancy". To give your results the best chance to top the list, it's important to make sure you've got content that answers these questions.This is the basic principle of Search Engine Optimisation. It asks, what are your customers searching for and where you fit into that? Often if you're selling something new, you may believe that people are going to use new words to find us. This is not true at all. We must find the words which our customers are using to look for our solutions and own them, rather than creating a whole new way to describe our solution.

That doesn't mean you have to make your articles boring, just that the titles have to appease the search engine gods and your target audience, not your ego. The article can be whatever you want it to be. It simply means that there is no point in creating something that is purely for yourself to enjoy. And by utilizing SEO, you can make sure that your content actually brings value to people out there.

THE CUSTOMER FUNNEL

In the last section, we introduced the idea of the customer acquisition journey and the buyer's journey. Now we're going to look at the content which populates the latter stages of the funnel. In this section, I want you to map our the useful pieces of content which will live on your website as well as on your social channels. In the next section, we will go further into top-of-funnel content (value-driven content that solves customer's problems and positions you as a leader). Keep in mind that without both in place, your marketing and lead generation efforts will be less-than optimal.

"Content is King," they say. And it's true. Once you've made and optimised your home page, unfortunately, it's not time to sit back and relax. It's time to produce. Content appears at all three stages of the sales cycle.

- Top of funnel content is what you're likely to find on social media channels. It attempts to amplify your reach, to entertain, be informative and answer your customer's questions about a particular pain point. It's the "ah-ha" moment that we have when we're scrolling through our social feeds.
- Middle-of-funnel content is more in-depth. It can be anything from a whitepaper to email marketing, webinars or live events. The purpose of middle-of-funnel content is to nurture your leads until they're ready to buy.
- Bottom of funnel content is more serious business. It's the type of content that a potential buyer would show to their boss during a

pitch on why they should work with you. It's your portfolio and it's case studies which help the buyer feel empowered to make the right decision.

This next section is going to focus on the types of content you will need to host on your website.

Top of Funnel Assets

The idea of a funnel is quite simple. It's the entire customer journey from the introduction, to how you nurture those leads to closing a deal. Top-of-Funnel content helps introduce your brand to the marketplace. It's the awareness phase. At the top-of-funnel, your content should aim to inform your target audience that you exist and about topics related to your brand. Its primary goal is not focused on selling. You should focus on understanding what type of content your target audience responds to and create a constant stream of it. This is not the place to create something and let it fall to the back of your website. Instead, it should be a rolling machine. For example, if you're a company that focuses on measuring impact, you could create content that relates to the impact ecosystem, how to measure impact and why investors must see impact measurement. One of the most classic examples of this type of content is the research paper in exchange for an email address. As soon as the stranger enters their email address, they transform into a lead. The following is a list of top-of-funnel content which can be hosted on your website:

- **Guides.** Guides are essentially step-by-step long-form articles which help your potential clients solve their pain points. Usually hosted on a company's blog page, they're a valuable asset for organic search. You can usually identify a guide online by the title "The Ultimate Guide to X" or "How To Develop Your Sustainability

Strategy: A Start To Finish Guide" or "Ten Steps To Transform Your Business". When writing a guide, consider how you go about your business and write it out for a customer who wants to do the same. For instance, if you have an online 3D printing business, your guide could be The Ultimate Guide To 3D Printing Your First Product and then name each step in the process.

- **Events & Webinars.** Events and webinars are fantastic ways to engage your target audience in a non-sales environment. Whilst they are relatively different in practice, the theory behind why they work is fundamentally the same. They put a name and a personality to a face; and we're much more likely to trust a person than a company. What's more, we're programmed to trust the recommendations of people much more than a brand itself. An event can influence, inspire and impact people's lives. It can be a talking point or a point of assertion for people. In turn, they'll likely begin to believe in your brand and share their experience with their trusted peers. More on this in Chapter 10.
- **Research Studies.** One of the best ways to have your content promoted for you — and earn you backlinks from other websites at the same time — are research studies. This is arguably one of the most powerful approaches to drive traffic to your website through both press and organic channels. Research can include a survey of your potential clients and report or their client and focus on a number of topics including pain points, opinions and forward-looking objectives. Consultancies use this tactic a lot and you can recognize them in headlines like "90% of CEOs believe in X". Research studies are not only a great way to establish your business

as a thought leader, they are also fantastic ways to engage your potential clients in a valuable and non-sales manner.

To optimize the content that you have created for your top-of-funnel, you must consider your target audience's pain points. Consider how they ask search engines about them. For instance, when a customer wants help becoming circular in their waste streams, they search for "how to create a circular waste stream" rather than a brand name "CE Consultancy". To give your results the best chance to top the list, it's important to make sure you've got content that answers these questions.

That's the basic principle of Search Engine Optimisation or SEO for short. It asks, what are your customers searching for and where you fit into that? Often if you're selling something new, we believe that people are going to use new words to find us. This is not true at all. We must find the words which our customers are using to look for our solutions and own them, rather than creating a whole new way to describe our solution.

To make a start on this, all blog content should align with your keywords. Make a list of the words which you believe your target customers will use to search for you. For some help use; Scrape suggested keywords from multiple sources, Google Trends is another great free option to explore. Another good way is to go to the websites of your most successful competitors and see what words they're using to start you off. Incorporate these keywords naturally (about 1-3% of your written content) to maximize your keyword search results.

For your website's blog, you should be directly answering the issues that your customers have. Save the more conceptual stuff for your personal blog. Remember — it's about the customer. I'm going to keep on saying that until it sinks in because it took me far too long to wrap my head around it. Hopefully, I can convey the importance of the message to you so that it sinks in a bit easier.

Middle of Funnel Assets

Middle-of-funnel content nurtures your leads until they're ready to buy. They've been introduced to your brand. They're leads. But they're not ready to purchase yet? This is the type of content that is made to entertain, to build confidence in your brand and to improve the client's perception of your solution. In short, it should build the lead's intent to buy. Middle-of-funnel content is educational and entertaining. This form of content marketing can also include email, but in this section, we're just focusing on assets for your website. We'll get into email marketing later. The following are three examples of middle-of-funnel assets:

- **Whitepapers & eBooks.** A whitepaper or eBook is usually hosted on a website and promoted through both native and paid channels on social media and search engines. They aim to help a prospective client solve a particular pain point in exchange for client information. They'll often be sent in the form of a PDF to your email address after signing up. You'll want to package your solution in a way that your buyer persona will actively be looking for on the web.
- **Case Studies.** Case studies are an in-depth look at your portfolio. Before buying, 9 out of 10 people are looking for proof before making a purchasing decision. For instance, I recently signed up for a free trial with Mighty Networks to build an online community. Every few weeks, I receive an email from them with a link to an article. The article goes into detail about the strategy one of

their clients used to create an online community. As I've not yet become a paying customer, these are relevant for me because I want to achieve the same results as those who they're featuring. Each email I receive, I grow one step closer to becoming a customer. A case study should follow the structure of 1) Introduction — where you identify the client's key problems, 2) background information — where you set the scene, 3) evaluation of the case at hand, 4) the solutions which your business implemented, 5) and the direct result this had on your client's business challenges. They should be accompanied by personal anecdotes from your clients and outside statistics to support your argument along the way. I always recommend that my clients' host case studies on the front page along with client testimonials (in addition to having a dedicated page for them in your portfolio).

- **Social Storytelling.** When someone has already been introduced to your brand, a great tactic is to let them into the inside life of the business. This can mean interviewing your clients or employees and asking them about things that matter to them. Hosted on your website's blog and cut into short form for social media, this can be powerful content to engage during the nurturing stage. It gives personality to a brand. Social storytelling can be either raw and unedited content or a short-form documentary. The main thing is that it lets the viewer in behind the scenes of your business, vision or mission and gives them a feeling of being part of the story. You can also ask your employees to contribute to creating this content which boosts their personal brands as well as giving them a feeling of being valued in their positions.

Bottom of Funnel Assets

Bottom-of-funnel content increases transparency in the buying process. It helps your buyers feel like they are making the right choice by choosing your solution or innovation. The role of this type of content is to nurture prospects and customers to aid in sales conversion. Without it, you may attract prospective clients to your website but they may leave empty-handed. One of the main reasons your website fails to retain the convincing elements of the sale is inconsistency in the message flow, insufficient proof of concepts or insufficient social proof. Providing the following type of content will help your startup increase its chances of conversion at a crucial stage in the sales cycle:

- **Portfolio.** A product portfolio is a crucial element of your bottom-of-funnel strategy as it helps the company determine the types of projects you've done in the past and whether you'll be able to fulfil their specific needs. I like to group my client's portfolios into sections which satisfy some clients needs and get more specific the deeper you go through them.
- **Customer Testimonials and Reviews.** Potential prospects want to see what your previous clients have said about you. Having a set ready can help them in their buyer journey, but they should be quantitative where possible. When you've finished a project, ask your clients for a review and you can always offer to make the process easier by writing it yourself. Just make sure you get it checked off. Alternatively, you can always reuse the reviews and testimonials from your LinkedIn and your case studies to be stand alone quotes.

- **Impact Measurement.** This is an important function in any sustainability or impact-driven business. Yet it's also one of the most elusive. Measuring your impact as a startup is a difficult and complex concept and one that can cost more than most startups can afford. Yet tools are popping up like Climate Impact Forecast — used by several Climate KIC startups — which can help entrepreneurs measure their projected impact.
- **Pricing Guidelines & Estimates.** Pricing is about knowing your customer. It can be one of the determining factors of your business and it can also lock you into less-than-desirable contracts when you get it wrong. It's normal then that entrepreneurs don't want to put prices on their website. However, the fact is that visitors want to know — or at least have a ballpark idea — on whether or not they can afford to use your solution. The key here is confidence in your brand; if you believe that you should be charging what you charge and believe that you've demonstrated that with value to your prospective clients, then you should have either a pricing guideline or at least an estimate of how much they will spend on your website. Ultimately, it saves time, avoids the awkward budget questions later on down the line and shows that you're confident in your ability to sell for that price.
- **Tutorials & Live Demonstrations.** Lastly, tutorials and live demonstrations are a great way to help your new clients see what they'll get by engaging with you. By taking them through your product or service at an execution level, you can smooth out or directly address any of their concerns in real-time. A product demo shows your customer how the product works visually and enables

them to experience a more expensive product at no cost.

As with all content, you can always be creative when making bottom-of-funnel content. For example, take SodaStream's 3D product demos which are located around the world including Tel Aviv airport. The demos include a cage which holds 10,657 used plastic bottles; the equivalent of one family's plastic consumption over a five year period. The installations are so successful because they show the huge amount of waste produced graphically, strengthening SodaStream's overall value proposition.

All of these forms of content can also be reused and repurposed across the entire customer journey. For instance, you can turn a product tutorial into a YouTube video or cut it up into shorter clips with highlights for Instagram. You can also turn each case study into a press release or a blog. By repurposing this content, you can save yourself a lot of time and effort in the creation process.

Repurposing Content.

All of these forms of content can also be reused and repurposed across the entire customer journey. For instance, you can turn a product tutorial into a YouTube video or cut it up into shorter clips with highlights for Instagram. You can also turn each case study into a press release or a blog. By repurposing this content, you can save yourself a lot of time and effort in the creation process.

SOCIAL MEDIA CHANNELS

I'm asked by impact entrepreneurs if they should be using Facebook or Instagram, LinkedIn or Twitter. But then there's TikTok and there's email marketing and Medium and your blog and then what? And what about Facebook? Isn't Facebook dying? Honestly, I have no idea what the right answer is. There is no one right answer. All I can say is this, as a mostly B2B business, you probably have at least three target audiences. Your customer, your peers and investors. If you're a B2B company, all three hang out on LinkedIn. If you're B2C, then it's more likely that you'll find your audience on Instagram, TikTok and Facebook or other more casual social media sites. If you're into journalism, your peers are more likely to be on Twitter and Medium.

For individual professionals and B2B brands, I believe LinkedIn is the most useful social network. It has the largest network of professionals on the channel and they're active. This creates a unique and unparalleled way to directly contact your target audience. People are there for work and they're engaged and open to seeing direct marketing from businesses, whereas on Twitter and Facebook and to a lesser extent Instagram, that seems like an intrusion of privacy.

One thing is for sure, whereas traditional marketing is a drain on your funds, social media marketing is a low-cost alternative that gives you a direct line to current and prospective customers. And each channel has its particular benefits. Facebook has close to 2 billion monthly active users, YouTube has over 1 billion users, Instagram and LinkedIn have nearly half a billion and Twitter has just over 300 million users each month. In the following section, we will look into more specific stats of each site.

- **Facebook.** Facebook is the most used social media platform. The average Facebook user spends nearly an hour every day on the platform. Whilst the social network has made Facebook advertising solutions an increasingly valuable business tool organic reach is at a minimum. That means if you want someone who likes your page to see your posts, you'll have to pay. That's not to say it's not a useful tool, but if you're just in the beginning of your journey, it's not worth spending your dollars on "boosting" a post. However, Facebook is the number one site for testing your content to a wide audience. Now when you scroll through the platform, you're likely to see one advertisement out of every five or so posts. This content comes from those outside your network who want to introduce you to their business. A/B Testing is a way that you can run multiple pieces of similar content to see where it performs better (ie. demographic, region or interest) or variations of the same content (different ads, videos or images), to see which is consumed or converts at a higher rate. This alone can be useful when considering how to target your audience and what message resonates with them.
- **LinkedIn.** Early on, LinkedIn was seen as a digital CV. Today, however, that's changed and LinkedIn is now one of the most widely used social networks. LinkedIn members range from upper management and founders to students who are trying to expand their network in the early years of their career. It can be an incredibly useful tool when marketing in B2B circumstances, attracting talent and connecting with clients. LinkedIn is especially powerful for building a personal brand and establishing yourself as a founder or entrepreneur or an expert in your field. But a detailed

Company Page also helps you grow your audience, establish your brand's credibility and drive business results. Whilst the price you'll pay for advertising on LinkedIn is quite high in comparison to Facebook or Instagram, your organic reach goes a long way on this platform, unlike other social media networks. Ultimately, LinkedIn is the perfect place for someone who wants a brief introduction of what your company does and what it stands for.

- **Instagram.** Instagram is essentially a storefront which allows you to show off your products and services visually. Building a following on Instagram is hard work and it takes a lot of dedication and time. For businesses not interested in gaining a big following, Instagram can be a platform which detracts from a brand's reputation. For instance, an account which says it's at the forefront of innovation and only has 200 followers doesn't exactly show authority. That being said, those that leverage Instagram from the beginning can highlight the technical and people aspects of their brand. But unless you're selling a product directly to consumers, this is not the place to post promotional content about your service. Successful Instagram accounts post-native-mobile content multiple times per day and they leverage user content, raw content and short-form stories. If you're going to commit to Instagram as a founder, make sure that you're willing to put in the work and understand what your audience wants to see...chances are, it's not a product review.
- **Twitter.** Twitter is a fantastic tool and yet incredibly misunderstood by most businesses. First of all, let's start off with what Twitter is NOT for; promotions, vacancies, link-only content and company self-fives. Your followers don't want to be inundated with content

that has no value to them. They want tidbit bites of stories that have real meaning behind them. That being said, if you're targeting early adopters, Twitter is worth considering: 61% of users regularly use Twitter to follow and interact with small businesses. This becomes even more apparent when you take into account how journalists use Twitter. Journalists are highly active on Twitter so if your ambition is to receive press coverage, it's a great tool to interact with a journalist before reaching out to them and asking them to write about you.

- **YouTube.** YouTube is not the most obvious star when it comes to social media, but if your business is in B2B, then it can be a powerful tool for your clients to connect with you. With YouTube, consistency is key. To use this network successfully, you'll want to be uploading long-form content (above 10 minutes) at regular intervals. The types of content that perform well on these channels are: Product videos, tutorial videos, animated videos, interviews and how to's. Most entrepreneurs, however, are terrified of posting non-polished content and will, instead of shooting for quantity, only produce one or two videos a year. Whilst these can be great introductions for your brand (on your homepage for instance) they won't open your startup up to a new audience. If you're going to use YouTube to its full potential and you don't have a fully-fledged video production team, you have to become OK with imperfection. That's not to say you have to produce sub-par quality content, but there will always be a difference in quality between an iPhone and a full camera crew.

Ultimately, it comes down to who your target audience is and whether you'll be able to hold yourself accountable when it comes to creating content for these channels. As with all marketing, social media success doesn't come overnight. It takes time, consistent messaging and content that engages your audience to build a following. Whatever you choose, remember this. Don't spread yourself too thin in the beginning because you want to be everywhere. It's not a case of build it and they will come. Choose your channels and own them.

EXERCISE 01

VISUAL IDENTITY

A brand's internal identity (its mission, vision and story) comes to life in its visual identity. And every brand needs a clearly defined and distinct visual identity. Your startup's visual identity is based on four distinct factors: Colours, logo, typography, and imagery. In this section, we will give you a basic overview of each, but we wholeheartedly recommend getting professional help if you're not a designer.

BRAND CHARACTER

Step 1. Ask yourself: Which of these archetypes best represents my ideal target audience and their own personalities?

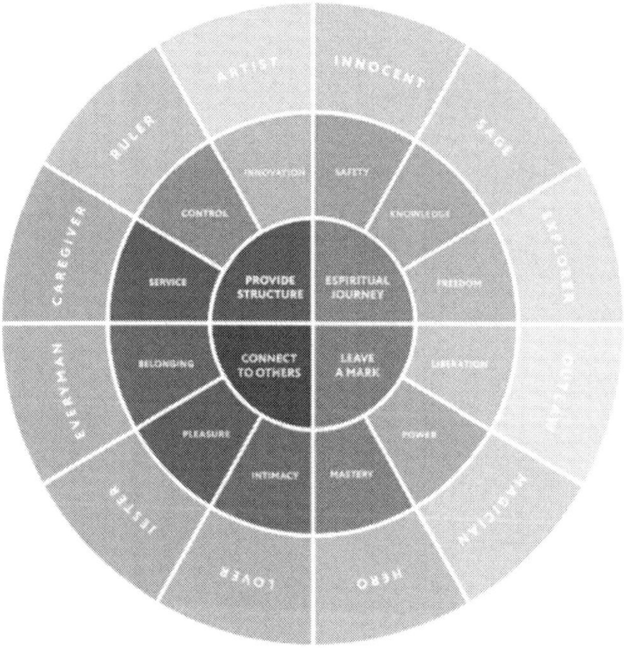

Step 2. Decide which of the following defines your brand and number them 1 - 5 below.

	1 - 5
Competence: Reliable, successful, intelligent. Customers are attracted to brands like this because they believe they will get the job done.	☐
Ruggedness. Thick-skinned, outdoorsy, tough. These brands make customers feel powerful, and remind them of nature.	☐
Sophistication. Charming, refined, high-class. It usually takes time to exude sophistication as a brand, but once they get there, these brands are poised, polished, and make their customers feel classy and elegant.	☐
Excitement. Daring, intriguing, imaginative, up-to-date. Maybe they push limits, but in a playful way. These brands are good at building hype and making their target audience's hearts race.	☐
Sincerity. Wholesome, genuine, honest, warm. Customers love brands like this because they are believable and trustworthy. These brands keep to their promises and meet expectations.	☐

Step 2. Decide which of the following defines your brand and number them 1 - 5 below.

	1 - 5
Competence: Reliable, successful, intelligent. Customers are attracted to brands like this because they believe they will get the job done.	☐
Ruggedness. Thick-skinned, outdoorsy, tough. These brands make customers feel powerful, and remind them of nature.	☐
Sophistication. Charming, refined, high-class. It usually takes time to exude sophistication as a brand, but once they get there, these brands are poised, polished, and make their customers feel classy and elegant.	☐
Excitement. Daring, intriguing, imaginative, up-to-date. Maybe they push limits, but in a playful way. These brands are good at building hype and making their target audience's hearts race.	☐
Sincerity. Wholesome, genuine, honest, warm. Customers love brands like this because they are believable and trustworthy. These brands keep to their promises and meet expectations.	☐

Step 2. Decide which of the following defines your brand and number them 1 - 5 below.

	1 - 5
Competence: Reliable, successful, intelligent. Customers are attracted to brands like this because they believe they will get the job done.	☐
Ruggedness. Thick-skinned, outdoorsy, tough. These brands make customers feel powerful, and remind them of nature.	☐
Sophistication. Charming, refined, high-class. It usually takes time to exude sophistication as a brand, but once they get there, these brands are poised, polished, and make their customers feel classy and elegant.	☐
Excitement. Daring, intriguing, imaginative, up-to-date. Maybe they push limits, but in a playful way. These brands are good at building hype and making their target audience's hearts race.	☐
Sincerity. Wholesome, genuine, honest, warm. Customers love brands like this because they are believable and trustworthy. These brands keep to their promises and meet expectations.	☐

Step 3. Your brand can, just like any person on the planet, have multiple character traits. Once you've defined the main categories (above), it's time to dig deeper into the specific character traits that that category holds.

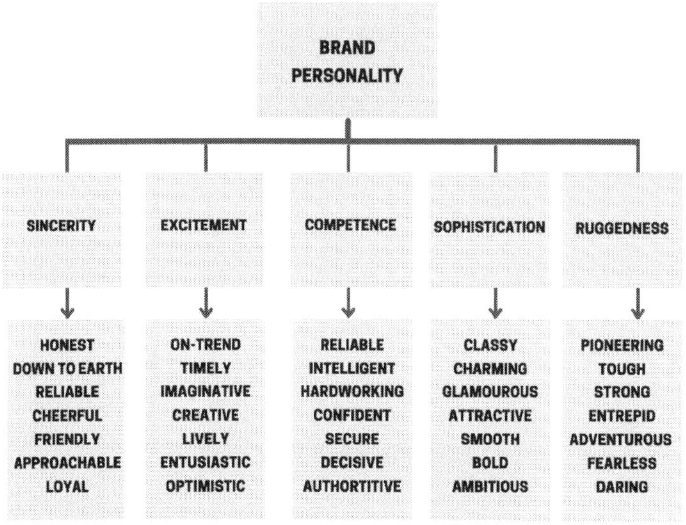

Step 4. Decide which of the following defines your brand and number them 1 - 5 below.

Competence: Reliable, successful, intelligent. Customers are attracted to brands like this because they believe they will get the job done.

- 3 -

BRAND COLOURS

Step 1. Pick your primary colour: Your brand's primary coluor is the one most associated with your startup. Think of the signature Tesla's red or Greenpeace's green. For your primary colour, look for something that best embodies your business based on the meanings which colour can bring.

HEX CODE:	CMYK:	RGB:
#______	0, 00, 00, 00	000, 00, 00

Step 2. Pick your secondary colour: Once you have chosen your primary colour, pick a secondary colour to support it. This colours will compliment your primary one, and can either appear next to it or exist independently from it.

HEX CODE:	CMYK:	RGB:
#______	0, 00, 00, 00	000, 00, 00

Step 3. Pick your supporting colours: After you've chosen the two key colours for your brand, choose at least two neutral tones (shades of grey, black, and white) which you can use to hold your colour pallet together. These neutral colours will define the colour of your text, your backgrounds, and everything between.

HEX CODE	CMYK:	RGB:
#DBOFOF	8 0, 93, 93, 15	216, 15, 15
#DBOFOF	8 0, 93, 93, 15	216, 15, 15
#DBOFOF	8 0, 93, 93, 15	216, 15, 15

TYPOGRAPHY

Fonts send a message to your audience about who you are as a brand. The fonts that you use, and the way those fonts are laid out, is important to the branding process. Below are six of the most common options and each is linked to a set of values.

Step 1. To choose your primary font, ask yourself which of the following describe your brand? Make a list from 1-6.

- **1. Classic, traditional, educational, and trustworthy?** ☐
- **2. Modern, clean, innovative, minimalistic, and approachable?** ☐
- **3. Bold, confident, and authoritative?** ☐
- **4. Stylish, elegant, and unique?** ☐
- **5. Quirky, distinctive, and dramatic?** ☐
- **6. Stylized, distinctive, and dramatic?** ☐

Step 2. Each number above correlates to a group of fonts on the next page, including Serif, San Serif, etc. As the fonts you choose will nonverbally communicate your company's identity, consider which character traits you want to lead with in your communications. For instance, if your startup is "stylish" and "elegant," you may want to choose a script typeface for your primary font. If you're "innovative" or "mordern," a san serif font might be for you. If you're more "traditional" consider choosing a serif font.

Step 3. Choose two fonts which represent your brand.

1. Primary font:

2. Secondary font:

Step 4. Case of titles? Choose one of the following:

ALL CAPS ☐ **Title Case** ☐ **Sentence case** ☐

BRAND PLATFORM

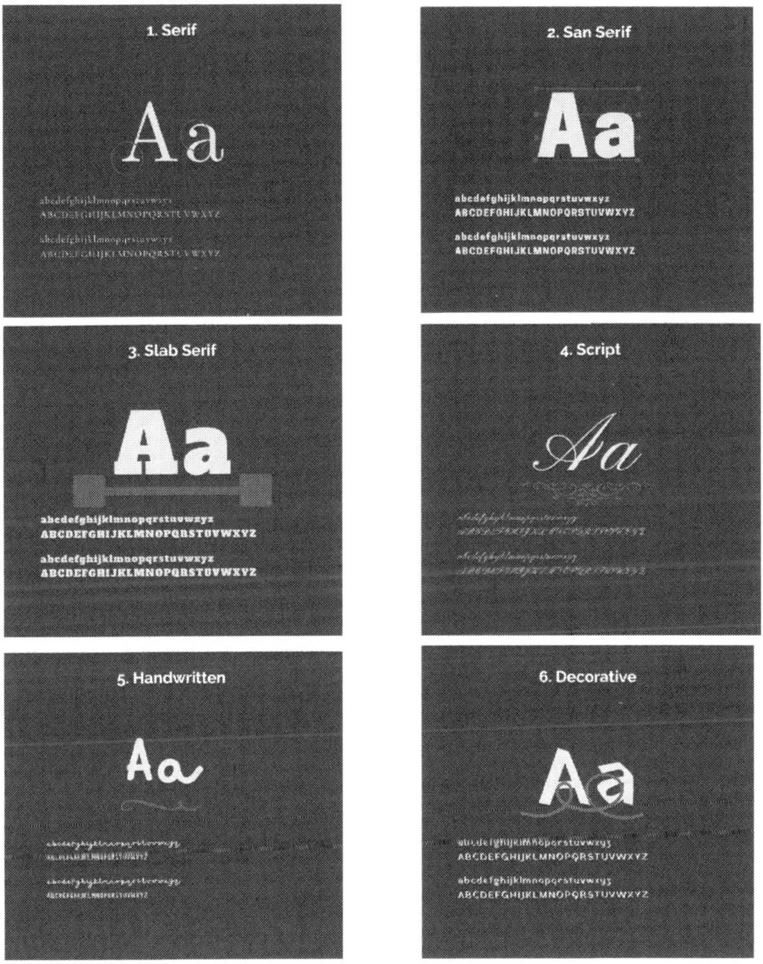

LOGO

A logo is meant to make your brand stand out. We get it: you're brand is sustainable. But choose something that's not a green tree for your logo... everyone else is already doing that.

In this section, I'm not going to tell you how to design your logo. That's entirely up to you. However I will say this: If you want your logo to help you stand apart from the competition, which is exactly what it's there to do, it's only common sense to make something different. Thus, I would suggest steering clear of falling into the "green" trap.

Once you have made your choice, ask yourself the following questions:

1. Simplicity: Is the design easily identifiable? Is it not too busy, confusing, or distracting?
2. Memorability: Is it quickly recognizable?
3. Timelessness: Will it still be a great logo in 10, 20, or even 50 years?
4. Functionality: Does it work across a range of mediums?
5. Appropriateness: Does it resonate with your ideal target audience and their industry?

IMAGERY

Step 1. Align your imagery with your brand's persona. What characteristics do you want to define your brand? Make a list of 3-5 traits which define your brand's identity.

1.
2.
3.
4.
5.

Step 2. Make a mood board on Pinterest of images which align with your brand's values and which are in similar colors to the ones you have chosen.

Step 3. Define your imagery. Write one sentence that explains the kind of image you will use and stick with it.

My brand will only use imagery that...

EXERCISE 02

WEBSITE

Your website is your modern-day business card. Having a website that is in line with your business' values and both visual and verbal identity is a key pillar to success in building your brand. To do so, you need to display information relevant to your guest and let them know they're in the right place. For every website, there is a distinct order in which you should display information. When you follow this order, you're following a logical narrative which people expect to find information.

WEBSITE LAYOUT

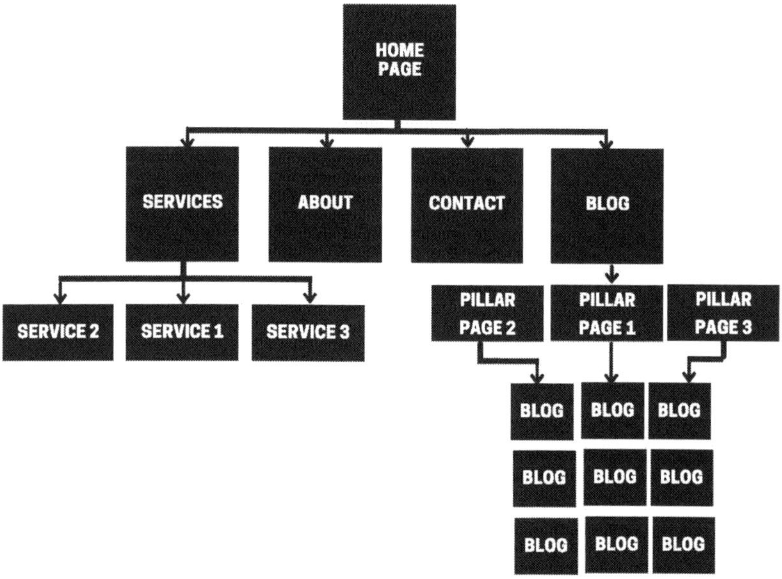

HOME PAGE

Step 1. The first layer should be simple and easy to understand for your target audience. It should answer their needs and address their pain points whilst giving them social proof that you're up to the job.

Above the fold. In most cases, you only have about seven seconds to capture someones attention on your website. Your tagline must be concise and intelligible enough to make sure that your visitor walks away with a comprehensive understanding of what you offer and for who. This copy should be accompanied by your hero image.

Tagline: Value proposition. Who for? And a call to action (CTA).

Descriptions. Create a description that's a bit more in-depth than your tagline that shows how you're solving a problem for your target market.

- WHY: What's your brand's mission?
- HOW: Strongly worded which shows how you do what you do.
- WHAT: Outline your product.

Visuals. Visuals on your website help to provide visitors with a more in depth introduction to your innovation, mission and team.

Add a video between 30 - 120 seconds can take place of a description — this can be also placed higher in the website to replace the your company's description — or a slide show with images which show what your technology does.

Call to action. Repeat the call to action from the hero image above the fold and give the visitor a way to take the next step.

Sign up to email list, join the platform, get a free trial, download your latest whitepaper...

Testimonials for social proof. You should ideally be posting three testimonials with photographs of the individuals giving them and a link to their company or organization. Having testimonials provides social proof that what you're offering, works.

Add between three and five testimonials from people who've used your product before. If your still in the development of the innovation or haven't gone to market yet, these testimonials can be about you as a founder and your competencies, drive to achieve your mission, etc.

Client or partner banner. Add a banner with the clients who you've worked for in the past to further display social proof.

Your client banner can be one , two, or three columns high. Who have you worked with in your target market's industry that's influential? Don't go overboard here: 12 clients is enough — it doesn't have to be everyone you've ever worked with!

Seen in the press section/blog articles. Press is valued as social proof above your blog, so if you have finally got that interview with Fast Company, this is where it should live.

Here you can put either articles from your most impressive blog content or a section linking to your most recent press articles.

Footer. Add social media links & contact details.

SECONDARY PAGES: SERVICES, ABOUT, CONTACT, BLOG

Step 2. The second layer of your website should go into what you do, how you do it, and who you do it for.

Services

- What you do...(see the lesson: "How to explain what you do to actual human beings" to see what not to do).

About

- Mission
- Vision
- Your brand's strategic narrative
- Team

Blog

- Feature your brand's top thought leadership pieces written by your founder/CEO

Contact

- Email address
- Contact form
- Calendly link

THIRD LAYER: LONG-FORM PILLAR CONTENT

Step 3. The third layer is where you can get into your in depth analysis of your subject matter. This layer consists of knowledge, insights and resources in the form of articles, blogs, and news.

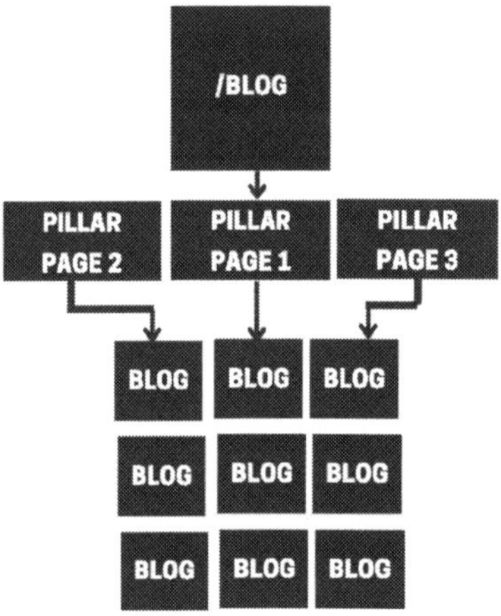

/Blog

- Featured: Turn your strategic narrative into an article, written by CEO/Founder
- Featured: Write an article about your vision of the future, predictions about the total addressable market backed up by evidence.
- Featured: The Why. Write an article about your mission, and what problem you exist to solve.

Pillar Pages

Take your three value core propositions and turn them into pillar pages which answer your ideal target audience's key questions on the subject matter.

1.
2.
3.

Individual Blogs

Turn each pillar page into individual blogs which succinctly (within 1,000 words) answers the individual questions your target audience may have about each pilar page topic?

-
-
-
-
-

9.

THOUGHT LEADERSHIP: GAINING INFLUENCE

Leadership is one of the attributes which we expect from CEOs, founders, investors and executives. Leadership can be defined as the capacity of a company's management to set and achieve challenging goals, take fast and decisive action when needed, outperform the competition, and inspire others to perform at the highest level they can. Leadership, without communication, is a trivial persuit. Many of these characteristics are impossible without a strong, unwaving vision of the future and a strategy of how to get there. What's worse, many of those we expect to be strong leaders struggle to articulate their vision for their company or their industry. As a result, much of the work that's gone into building their brand will undoubtably come undone. One way which you can demontrate strong leadership is by establishing your Climate Tech business as a thought leader in your field. In this chapter, I aim to give you a better understanding of exactly what a thought leader is, the first steps to becoming one and why this will be beneficial for your brand. Here, I particularly want to focus on individuals (founders, CEOs, leaders) as opposed to companies and I also want to hone in on LinkedIn as a platform, as sharing original content and connecting with your target audience is essential to gaining influence in your sphere. This chapter will solely focus on your personal brand, and how you can plan and distribute your strategic messages through on LinkedIn. I will also cover how to successfully set up your LinkedIn profile before you raise capital.

Thought leadership is one of the biggest up and coming concepts in marketing right now. But really it's just a new buzzword for an old concept: Building a personal brand but with modern content distribution methods. It's the digital equivalent of being an expert or the professional equivalent of being an Instagram influencer. Thought leadership is defined as "free deliverables (content) which organizations or individuals produce on a topic they know a lot about and feel others can benefit from having their perspective on. Thought leadership, in this context, does not include content primarily focused on describing an organization's products or services."[1] That's the practical answer to "what is thought leadership?". The emotive answer is that thought leadership, when used properly can be your smoking gun: According to 2020 research from Edelman, "companies with the best ability to produce timely, thought-provoking thought leadership content are much more adept than their competitors at capturing their customers' attention and turning that attention into positive results."

For the sake of this chapter, I am going to rein that in even more and remove the word organization. By focusing solely on individuals and

1 2020 B2B Thought Leadership Impact Study, Edelman.

personal brands, we can get the best use of LinkedIn's algorithm and have content shared at a high velocity.

Firstly, people inherently want to interact with other people. More often than not, we're more trustworthy of people than companies. But, besides this practical insight into human nature, LinkedIn's publishing system is only available for individuals and this is an integral element of a thought leadership strategy. LinkedIn is integral for thought leadership for two reasons. Firstly, if your company runs a blog on its website and you as an individual share that piece of content, it's much less likely to show up in your target audience's feed (i.e., where they consume content). This is due to LinkedIn's preference for content produced on its own platform vs. content that will take a user off the platform onto a third party site. Secondly, when you share that piece of content, it's much more difficult to use a personal voice over a more neutral company tone. Of course, it is possible to create thought leadership content from a company perspective, but when you're just starting, I would recommend focusing your efforts on engaging on your personal LinkedIn account.

In the previous chapters, I've already given a detailed analysis of each social media platform and which you should use. However, I didn't include my bias towards LinkedIn. I believe LinkedIn is the most effective marketing channel by far if you're targeting B2B businesses or looking to launch a funding round. In the UK, 96% of B2B marketers are using LinkedIn as a content marketing channel, with 61% saying they find it highly effective. And while people are spending time on other social channels, they're investing time on LinkedIn.[2] Furthermore, a whopping 80% of B2B leads come from LinkedIn over other platforms. Whilst I

2 LinkedIn, 2015.

can't be sure what the future will hold, all of this is true right now.

The Benefits of Thought Leadership Content

When used correctly, thought leadership, instead of product or sales-led communications can create a lead pipeline, shorten sales cycles, build trust and give your brand credibility with investors. Nearly all (89%) of B2B decision-makers say that thought leadership content has enhanced their perceptions of an organization and half believe Thought Leadership influences their purchasing decisions. There are three main reasons brand founders, especially those who put impact at the heart of their business should be looking to utilize a thought leadership strategy:

1. Investors are looking for founders with expertise: Most investors of early-stage companies don't just invest in the product but the team behind the product. They want to know that the founders have the industry experience to pull of the next big thing. Developing thought leadership allows potential investors to learn about your market knowledge and industry expertise as they do their due diligence on your company.
2. It provides low-cost marketing materials: Let's face it, most early founders are so busy building a product and building their team that they often leave marketing as a thing they focus on later down the line. Or worse, they put an intern on it. By building thought leadership — especially thought leadership content, which features the founder or CTO — in your early days, you are beginning your marketing efforts for next to nothing. Having a robust thought leadership and content strategy and featuring industry experts allows you to have some marketing material without heavy-hitting expenditures like SEM, advertising buys and tradeshows.

3. Sales needs tools to build trust: Today, customers refer to online content instead of seeking help from a salesperson. This creates a defined need for specific, accessible material to help with decision-making to buy a product. While no single prospect is going to close early on because you have a great thought leadership strategy, but they will use the content that you generate as a result to research your company and you.

LinkedIn is the only major platform at the moment that is in a content deficit, meaning that there is not enough good content to satisfy its users. As a result, LinkedIn's organic reach or how many people your post will reach without having to promote it by paying the platform is at its high point right now. LinkedIn is today, where Facebook was roughly 8 years ago. With over 500+ million active users, it's the destination for B2B entrepreneurs and start-ups. Whilst Facebook is still the largest social media network by far, its organic reach for brands has declined to almost nothing over the past few years. This happened almost immediately after they brought in the "Boost" button. If you post from your company's Facebook page and you want people inside your network of followers to see it, benefit from it and share it, you almost certainly will have to pay for it. If you want anyone outside to see it, you can damn sure forget about it. Paying for Facebook ads is a fantastic strategy if you have time to put into testing your content, promoting it and building your following with creative content. However, if you are anything like the majority of other entrepreneurs, you're probably low on time and funds. As a result, LinkedIn's current setup is a much better option. Building a following on LinkedIn comes down to networking and connecting. And the best way to do both of those things with those outside your network is by providing something of value…i.e., thought leadership.

For example, one of my biggest markets right now is ghostwriting content and guest blogs for clients. I'm guessing you wouldn't know this was a thing that people did, because to be honest, I didn't know it was such a big market until I saw the results. Creating content to share, be it on LinkedIn, Medium or external news publications is a great way to build authority and reach your target audience. It also reinforces the fact that you exist to your network. But so many founders don't have a lot of time to commit to this process. In this chapter I intend to convince you that a) you should definitely be taking the time to spend on this vital form of communications and b) you should be using LinkedIn as your main medium initially. But before we get into it, let's look at why you should invest time into your personal brand and the benefits of being a thought leader in your topic.

FOUNDER BRANDING

You're a founder, a CEO or an entrepreneur and you're busy building a company which will create systemic, lasting global impact. It's natural to think that your company, the company that you've put so much energy into builing, is your brand. Unfortunately, that's only half the story. You as a founder are an integral part of your start-up's brand. Whilst many founders like to hide behind their company's image, consumers, customers, partners and investors believe that leaders who are active on social media are more trustworthy than those who are not. One study by the Impact Learning Center found that although consumers are 82%

more likely to trust a company when the CEO is active on social media, only one in five CEOs are active on social media. And further, up to 49% of a company's reputation can be attributed to the leader or founder and up to 60% of a company's market value can be attibuted to a company's reputation.[3] This paints a picture founders and leaders simply can't afford to ignore.

As we've discussed, sustainability entrepreneurs are more likely to be an academic or an engineer than an internet personality. This leads to challenges surrounding quality, fear of retribution by our peers and not wanting to offend anyone. But when so much is at stake, leaving personal branding up to chance is not a long-distance tactic. Personal branding at its core is about building trust. With trust comes credibility and with credibility comes growth. As such a robust personal brand will not only help your company grow, but it will also allow you to grow your network and share your story with the outside world. Because whether you've invested time or effort into it, you have a personal brand. Google your name and see what comes up. What about on LinkedIn, Facebook and Instagram? Are they public? Do they represent you as a founder or an entrepreneur? This is the basis of personal branding and in a digital-first world, if you refuse to embrace this concept, you're in danger of being consumed by it. To put it plainly, because of the internet, whether you like it or not, you have a personal brand. That's now irrefutable. What you can control however is what it portrays. Luckily for some out there, it's possible to shape this online persona. By creating content that you strategically place across digital mediums, you can actively play a role in determining what anyone searching your name will come across.

---

3 Weber Shandwick, 2012.

When used correctly, thought leadership, instead of product or sales-led communications can create a lead pipeline, shorten sales cycles, build trust and give your brand credibility with investors.Nearly all (89%) of B2B decision-makers say that thought leadership content has enhanced their perceptions of an organization and half believe Thought Leadership influences their purchasing decisions.

There are three main reasons brand founders, especially those who put impact at the heart of their business should be looking to utilize a thought leadership strategy:

Investors are looking for founders with expertise: Most investors of early-stage companies don't just invest in the product but the team behind the product. They want to know that the founders have the industry experience to pull of the next big thing. Developing thought leadership allows potential investors to learn about your market knowledge and industry expertise as they do their due diligence on your company.

It provides low-cost marketing materials: Let's face it, most early founders are so busy building a product and building their team that they often leave marketing as a thing they focus on later down the line. Or worse, they put an intern on it. By building thought leadership — especially thought leadership content, which features the founder or CTO — in your early days, you are beginning your marketing efforts for next to nothing. Having a robust thought leadership and content strategy and featuring industry experts allows you to have some marketing material without heavy-hitting expenditures like SEM, advertising buys and tradeshows.

Sales needs tools to build trust: Today, customers refer to online content instead of seeking help from a salesperson. This creates a defined need for specific, accessible material to help with decision-making to buy a product. While no single prospect is going to close early on because you have a great thought leadership strategy, but they will use the content that you generate as a result to research your company and you.

Why is this important? Firstly, if you downplay the importance or existence of your personal brand, you fail to grasp a vital opportunity for growth. As a leader, you can inherently be more opinionated and personal than your company can. Putting that out into the world allows you to craft an authentic and genuine persona. You would never leave your business model or your accounting up to the internet. Taking the reins of your own digital identity can help you build credibility for your start-up, grow your network and present an authentic version of your company. Secondly, personal brands differentiate products in saturated markets. When you as an entrepreneur build a platform and get your voice out there into the world, it creates a wider awareness of a) your existence and b) your product. Whilst you may not believe it, you have competitors out there who are selling something similar to you. That's just the reality of business, every business has them: Copycats or lookalikes. What defines you usually may not always be your product or services. No matter how much you would like to believe that your product is superior if you're worse at getting this information in the hands of your customer, then perhaps it doesn't matter. By sharing stories and connecting with your customer through creating experiences and providing values, it's possible to inform them of you and your product in a subtle way that can, in turn, turn them into fans and eventually customers. Thirdly, journalists are far more likely to approach people than companies. Unless you're Tesla (and I don't think I'm going out on a limb to say that I doubt Elon Musk is reading this), journalists aren't very likely to approach your start-up and ask for a product rundown. Chances are, most people don't care about the specifics of your product or service. And strangers certainly don't care. As journalists are in tune with their readers and what they want, they're very unlikely to write a story that explains what your start-up does. However, your personal story about how you one a challenge at university which led to your start-up receiving funding is, however, much more likely to resonate with readers.

HOW TO BUILD YOUR THOUGHT LEADERSHIP STRATEGY

When considering what to actually write, consider the different touchpoints where your prospect's problems and your solution meet trending topics. Before we get there, there are a few more things to consider:

- The first step is to consider your goal: Do you want to showcase your ability to lead, warm up prospects or get in contact with investors?
- Are you B2B or B2C? If you're B2B, then you'll be able to use your thought leadership content to acquire new customers. If you're mainly B2C, then your strategy may well be more focused on investors and partnerships.
- What are the trending topics in your niche right now? For instance, in branding, there is demand generation, conversational marketing, and thought leadership. In impact investing, there is impact

measurement, climate finance and corporate impact. Hint: They're your value propositions or your "magic tools" as discussed in the narrative section earlier in the course.

Once you've determined the answers to these three questions, it's time to think about where they are (both online and offline), and deliver them your messages.

USE YOUR MAGIC GIFTS

When you're designing your thought leadership strategy, go back to your brand's story. The basis for your content will be the "change in the world" that you identified in the first module (Brand Story). Within this context, everything you say should be fundamentally different than your competitors. You can then take the Magic Gifts (old world vs. new world way of doing things) and expand on them as your subject matter.

For instance, my six-month thought leadership strategy looks like this:

Context: Today, entrepreneurship is society's main mechanism to create impact. Whereas impact used to be delivered by charities, non-profits, and philanthropy, today brands must be the ones to build the sustainable economy of tomorrow. However, sustainable brands still communicate like their peers of yesteryear, and it holds back their growth.

Solution: To overcome these challenges, Climate Tech brands need to approach entrepreneurship differently. They need to show their commercial acumen and their business prowess. And the best way to showcase both of these things is to build a brand (that tells stories, not just a product (that talks about features).

There are six "magic gifts" or tools which will help you build a strong brand and create an investible Climate Tech brand:

- Brand Foundations
- Target Audience
- Strategic Messaging
- Brand Platform
- Thought Leadership
- Public Relations

Sound familiar? It should. This course is based on this strategy. And so is my content strategy. That's because my content strategy always follows one of these six pillars of brand building within the context of "the new way to do things vs. the old way".

Step 1. Magic Gifts

What are the key areas in which you operate? If you think back to your brand story in Section 1, this will be the "magic gifts" which you're armed with to help you target audience. Name between three and six.

Step 2. For each topic, ask yourself the following five questions:

- What is it and what's the context? How does this subtopic tie into the greater brand story from Chapter 4?
- Why is it important for your ideal target audience?

- How does doing this wrong hold your audience back from success and what are the main mistakes they usually make?
- How to do it right? What's the forumula? What are the steps you usually take with your clients/customers?
- Give an example (or multiple of companies that have done it right. What about in your own experience? Or perhaps a famous case? Case studies build credibility in thought leadership.

Once you know your the answers to these five questions for each of your subtopics, create a long form piece of content surrounding one topic a month. This will potentially be the most important thing that you read in this book. If you've gotten this far, you've realized that whilst you may lay the foundations, if you don't communicate effectively you've wasted your time. Social media and in particular, LinkedIn and Instagram, let you connect with your audience. They give you a direct line of influence. Yet as impact entrepreneurs, we consistently under-leverage these platforms. Whether it's because we don't value them or simply because we don't have the resources to throw at them, it holds us back from scaling our influence and ultimately, our solution. To conclude this chapter, I will give you the code to cracking content creation. It's so simple and yet so effective. And employing this consistently is the code to turning you into a thought leader and LinkedIn into a lead generating machine.

"What could be so simple yet so effective?", I hear you asking. The answer is: Repurposing content. It all comes down to how we consume content today. Short-form video, audio and short, punchy text is what social media is about. Repurposing content is the one most effective way to turn an hour into a month creating each of these pieces. Each month, if you're posting between 3 and 5 times a week, you'll need roughly 20 pieces of short-form content, 1-4 blog posts depending on the length, plus quotes and images for Instagram. Throw in a couple of videos and you've got yourself a month's worth of quality and engaging content. That sounds like a lot if you have planned out each video, script everything, edit everything etc. However, it doesn't have to be perfect. Whilst your company may be striving for perfection, these snippets should be more "behind the scenes" than faultless reality TV. How can you create this much-unscripted content each month?

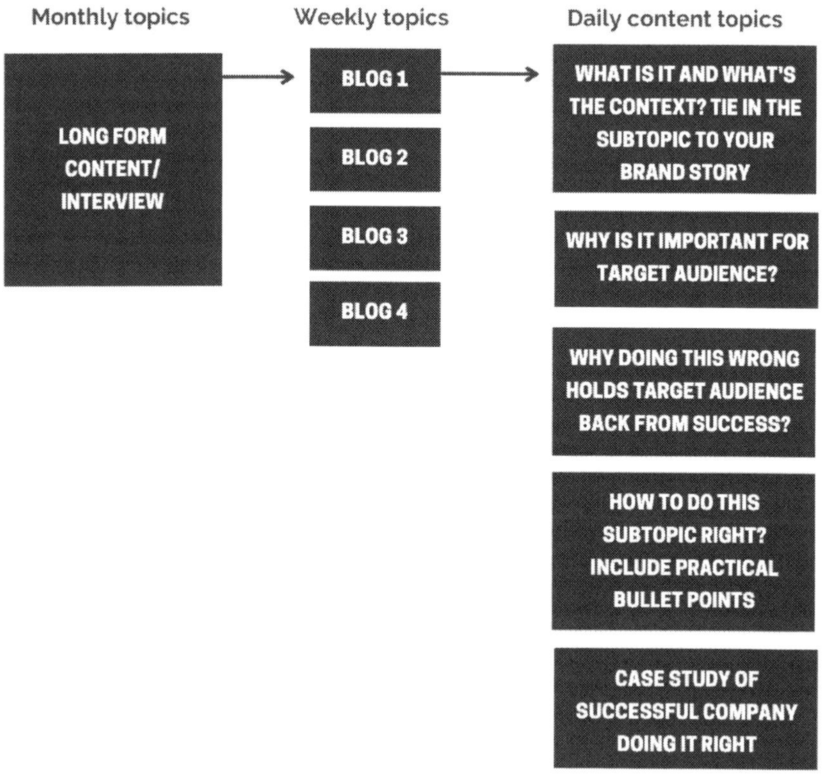

It all starts with having one podcast, webinar or piece to camera. Get someone to interview you about one of the subjects of above and recorded that interview. With that piece of content, you'll be able to cut it up into smaller videos, written into a blog and broken up into multiple social media posts. In practice, this is how small companies can create more content than most large companies. With the agility to move fast and the ability to create and distribute something that's not 100% perfect, this daily content strategy will help your brand build it's reputation and showcase it's brand.

Perfection prevents progress.

Keep in mind, your content doesn't have to be perfect. Whilst your company may be striving for perfection, these snippets should be more "behind the scenes" of your brand than faultless reality TV. Don't be too afraid to put yourself out there.

Social media and in particular, LinkedIn and Instagram, let you really connect with your audience. They give you a direct line of influence. Yet as sustainability professionals, we consistently under-leverage these platforms. Whether it's because we don't value them or simply because we don't have the resources to throw at them, it holds us back from scaling our influence and ultimately, our solution.

LINKEDIN PROFILE OPTIMIZATION

If roughly half of your business's reputation is built on the shoulders of it's founder or CEO, and as LinkedIn is the best place to build a personal brand, then LinkedIn instantly becomes the best route to establish yourself as a thought leader. To take this statistic literally, you should split your marketing efforts 50-50; work 50% on your brand and the other 50% in building your business' reach. Whilst this seems like a lot, you have to remember that when you're just starting out, your brand is linked to your name just like conjoined twins share the same skin. I understand that you want to focus on building your company's brand. It's not only important, it's necessary to grow your business.

However, in practice, you may only have a few hours a month to spend on communications. One of the most effective — and cost-effective ways — to make sure you utilise that time is to build your own connections and brand on LinkedIn. Ask anyone who's gone through this process before you and they will tell you, it's all about consistency. One of the most effective ways to do so is to establish yourself as an expert/thought leader/influencer on LinkedIn. Becoming known in your niche is not easy on LinkedIn, but with persistence and a smart strategy, you can build meaningful connections with your target audience in a way that's not possible on Facebook or Instagram. For this chapter and to ensure that I'm not boring anyone to death, I am going to presume that you already have some presence on the platform. If that's not the case, your first job is to fix this immediately. As I have just noted, LinkedIn is currently in the phase — right now — that Twitter, Facebook and Instagram were at at the start of last decade. This means that there are massive opportunities to gain influence and have your content reach your target audience without paid advertising. Another reason why I recommend working with LinkedIn is that it's hyper-tailored to sharing content. For instance, when you share something on LinkedIn — whether it's a post or an article — if somebody comments on it or likes it, it will show up in their newsfeeds for their contacts to view. This means that growth is exponential and curated to boost networking and content views. You can use this tool effectively to reach your contact's contacts and if they also like or comment, it will continue onwards and forwards. Lastly, if your content reaches LinkedIn's influencers or thought leaders and they interact with your content, then your content will get boosted by LinkedIn's algorithms and will have greater velocity. Whilst these features are available in Twitter, Instagram and Facebook, there's a greater chance that you have to pay and that your content will be taken out of a professional context.

The first obvious step which you should take to grow your influence on LinkedIn is your profile. Your profile is your landing page and it will be the first thing that people see when looking you up on the platform. As an entrepreneur, it's just as important as your resume or your website. An incomplete profile — whether it's your work history, your business's profile or your profile photo — is going to send messages to your target audience that your heads are not in the game. Here are the major downfalls that I see all the time when it comes to entrepreneur's profiles.

- **No profile photo/unprofessional profile photo.** It's honestly amazing how many times I come across founders with no profile photo. I don't care if you're camera shy or if you don't have any friends with a good camera, this is one fundamental concept which should not be glossed over.
- **Tagline that says nothing specific about how you do what you do and or your actual role or title.** For instance, "Growing sustainable ecosystems for your business" and not "Founder and Director of

Sustainable Ecosystems at X Start-Up". This boost's your searchability from the LinkedIn homepage and builds credibility for your profile.

- **About section is filled in with fluff.** Your About section should tell the reader, in concrete terms, that they're in the right place, that you understand their needs and what your business can do to help them solve those needs. This is also where you should use multiple keywords to help direct your profile to the right place. For example: My start-up, Company A, helps businesses in X, Y and Z sector. Name all the sectors that you're interested in working with and be specific so that your ideal target audience can identify themselves in there.
- **The ugly grey company tombstone logo.** In my opinion, one of the least professional things that you can do on LinkedIn is list multiple companies that you've worked for which don't have a logo. Each grey box subconsciously signifies that you haven't worked for any credible companies and it's not the message that you want to send on your profile. This is not the look you want to go for when investors are scouring your profile to decide whether to invest in your company or not.

Once your profile is up to date, I wholeheartedly recommend writing three articles and pinning them to your page. What articles you should feature depends on what your goal is — getting funded or getting customers. If your goal is to get funded, would put:

- One article which details why you started your business
- One article about the potential growth in the market in the future

- One article which shows that you are obsessed with the problem and not your solution

If however your goal is to use LinkedIn to get customers, I would add:

- One article about why you started your business and how that connects to their why as an innovator
- One articleabout the transformation which you give your clients
- One article which pinpoints the major problem or pain point you solve for your clients

For instance, I have three articles on my profile right now titled "These six steps will take your climate tech startup from MVP to investment ready", "Sustainability Is The New Digital" and "All Sustainable Start-Ups Struggle to Communicate Effectively Because of This Simple Concept", which show the the transformation I offer, why I do what I do and the problems that I solve, respectively.

CONTENT SCHEDULE

"But Joseph...how often should I post?" This is a question I get all the time. Below is a timeline that I try to follow and it's what I recommend anyone starting out on their personal brand to follow as well:

- 3x posts per week (the LinkedIn equivalent of a status update). Write in sentences, not paragraphs. Fill up the entire 1300 characters and always keep your target audience in mind. Say something personal, don't tell them about a global event that's happening or share another bloody Guardian Environment article on melting sea ice.

- 1x article per month (see below for what you should write about).
- Adding 20+ people in your target audience per week and always add a note. I use "Hey, My name is Joseph D. Simpson and I help impact entrepreneurs and climate tech startup founders build their brand. [insert something personal here about what you have in common]. Would you consider adding me to your LinkedIn network? Best, Joseph."
- Engage for at least 15 minutes per day and leave comments on your target audience's posts. You have to engage to see engagement. The LinkedIn algorithm punishes you for not engaging with your connections. This is an even bigger problem considering that only 1% of LinkedIn users post on a weekly basis. I have a list of 30+ people that I would LOVE to work with and I make sure that I say something thoughtful when they share something. Do it when you're on the toilet or having your morning coffee...It's far more effective than scrolling through the bullshit on Instagram or Facebook right now.

THE LINKEDIN ALGORITHM

Beating the LinkedIn algorithm is quite simply the best way to hack LinkedIn and grow your influence as a thought leader. And the first way to hack the algorithm is to understand it. The majority of us don't post from our own accounts on a daily basis. Usually small start-ups post once a day or perhaps a few times a week or month, hoping to directly gain clients as a result. Unfortunately, LinkedIn is not that simple and it requires a bit more creativity to get it going. The LinkedIn algorithm is however predictable and if you want to grow your presence on the platform, you need to understand what's happening under the hood of the platform.

LinkedIn is in a content deficiency. Rather, LinkedIn is in quality content deficiency. There is so much that is blatant advertising out there and the platform does not like to show advertising rather than organic or valuable content. But how does it decide what is an ad and what's authentic?

When you post a piece of content on LinkedIn, the platform goes through four stages to determine how valuable the content will be to your target audience. Your target audience is your followers, those who you're in a group with, the hashtags you use and your connections' connections. The piece of content will get graded as either clear, low-quality or spam and the outcome depends on the attributes of the text, the image or video and the influence of the member who posted it. If your post is counted as spam, it will end up in the bin and no one will see it. If it's considered low-quality (like content redirecting the user away from LinkedIn or considered self-promotional), it will be exposed to a small selection of your connections and if it is considered clear, then it will go directly to the next phase of the algorithm.

Phase two sees the content posted in the first hour or so be shown to a sample selection of your network. It is then ranked based on the amount of likes, comments and shares it receives. You can look at it like this: a like is worth one point, a share worth two and a comment is worth three points. The more points you get in this incubating session, the higher

LinkedIn will grade your post and the more likely it is to be shown to the rest of your connections and their connections. LinkedIn loves comments because it fuels discussion, keeps users on the platform and boosts their ability to collect crucial data.

If your post performs well in this initial test round, then it will be displayed to a wider audience. What's important to note is that the best authors on LinkedIn can create discussion in their posts or articles. They invite you to leave a comment by asking a question or triggering you to think about your own experiences. When you receive a comment, it's equally important for the algorithm that you reply. Some believe that it can bring up to 250% more views on the post as a whole.

The algorithm also finds posts valuable when:

- **You only post once a day.** If you post more than once a day, the algorithm will punish your second piece of content.
- **You don't link to external sources.** LinkedIn wants you to spend as much time on the platform itself as possible. So when you publish a link to an external source; your website, the New York Times or YouTube, your post will be ranked less and your content will be penalised. Alternatives include writing articles on LinkedIn about the news you are talking about and uploading your images or video directly to the platform.
- **You don't add a photo or video.** Whilst we may believe that adding an image doubles engagement with your post, LinkedIn considers text as valuable content. This is especially true in a world where the majority of posts just use random stock images.

TYPES OF CONTENT

Taking the potential to influence your target audience into account, you can optimize your content on LinkedIn for maximum impact. The dictionary definition of content is a digestible piece of digital data, be it video, voice, image text or any combination of the above to identify, forecast and satisfy the necessity of the customers. To become a thought leader, you must create thought-provoking content. And if you're not saying something that someone will disagree with, then you're not saying anything at all.

There are four major types of content that you can post on LinkedIn to become a thought leader. The first way is to create a post which will go out to all of your contacts — what on Facebook is called a status update — the second is to share someone else's post with your own specific take on it, thirdly you can create original content and upload it onto the site and the fourth way is to create and publish an original article on the platform.

Regardless of what you post, it's important that you follow one simple rule: give away all your best advice and secrets for free. You will grow by lifting others up. If people say "you're crazy, you should be charging for this kind of advice" that's when you know you're on the right track! A lot of people initially feel conflicted giving away this kind of advice for free. However, consider it from the audience's point of view. If you're not putting out your best then you're putting out something sub-par. There's no two ways about it. So as an audience member, if you're not giving me your best, why would I follow up? Experts must provide value to their audience; it just makes sense. If your audience values your content, they may turn into customers: It's a powerful way to build your expertise and create demand for your product and services. To succeed in creating valuable content, keep these things in mind:

- Speed wins in marketing. But companies artificially put up red tape that prevents them from going fast.
- Don't wait for perfection, this isn't a Superbowl ad. Put stuff out, test it
- Stop focusing on what your competitors are doing and focus on your own customers.
- Write content you wish the Younger You had found 3 years ago.
- Focus on how the buyer wants to buy a product, not on how you want to sell it.
- Let your website do the selling, you don't need to do it in your content.
- Start with the ideal end result in mind; the ultimate action you want to happen.
- When you give buyers good information, they feel empowered to make their own choices.

Some of the simplest ways to begin engaging with LinkedIn is to post one thing in the morning. I try to post between 10-11 am; when people are having their morning coffee. Topics which people are interested in vary as per the industry, but one thing that should always shine through is your personality. People prefer to know about you, your highs and lows and your experiences than the turnout of your company's latest event.

Consider LinkedIn's posts a professional long-form Twitter. It's a great place to:

- **Post relevant news that your audience will find valuable.** Sharing news is a great way to get your name out there and keep on top of the happenings in your industry. If you're struggling to find news on your topic, go to Google News and type in your subject, chances are that you're going to find something new and unique here. And remember, post your link in the first comment!
- **Ask questions.** One great way to attract responses from your audience is to ask a question. It's simple psychology that people want to be known as an expert. Enticing them to answer a question is one great way to play on that desire and to get your content to spread. Remember that if someone comments on your post, it's got a higher chance to be shared on their connections feeds as well, making the chances for others to see it and interact with it much higher.
- **Get recommendations or ask for advice.** When you ask your network for advice on how they did certain things — whether it's get something featured in the press or hire your first employee — you can create a post full of tips and resources that is not only valuable for you, but others in your place. This is also a great way to bring others along on your journey through entrepreneurship.
- **Post statistics that you've come across.** As much as we don't want to admit it, when it comes to facts and figures, there's always a bit of nerd in us. Sharing visuals or numbers creates for an interesting and memorable post that engaged the viewer.

- **Share news.** Be careful here because a common mistake is to only post news or links to only share negative news about the environment and climate change. Whilst this might be relevant information to your purpose and your journey, it doesn't inspire people to follow you. Always keep a balance of news that is shocking or depressing — the majority of news about the environment — and developments in your specific sector or industry (Smart Cities, Cleantech, etc.)

Here's a couple of examples of a successful posts that I shared so you can get an idea of what I'm talking about:

"What can you learn from Beyond or Impossible?

People always say to me: "I don't get it, why would vegans want to eat alternative meats? If you're a real vegan, you don't want to replicate the experience you've rejected."

Vegans and vegetarians aren't the target audience.

They're a small percentage of the population, making up between 1-4% of Western countries.

They already don't eat meat.

So if Impossible Foods and Beyond Meat aren't for vegans, who are they for?

Meat eaters. Or in other words...the other 96%.

Meat alternatives are a new technology and they're introduced to the population like any other innovation.

- First via the innovators, roughly 2.5% and in this case, the vegetarians and the vegans.

- Then the early adopters: The 12.5% of forward-thinking meat-eaters who feel guilt about the negative environmental or cruelty aspects of meat but still choose to eat it.

- Now they're looking to the early majority: the next 34%

Every new technology will be adopted in a similar way. The innovators first, to the early adopters and then on to the early majority.

So if you're building a #sustainable solution, don't assume that your target audience are only innovators.

#brandbuilding #impactinvesting #cleantech"

This post asks a question at the beginning and then explains to the audience the answer from my perspective. The perspective of a branding and communications expert. It evokes thought and it provides evidence to back up what I'm contending. This post was also trending on LinkedIn due to the hashtags I used, meaning that those outside my network, but who follow those hashtags saw it in their feeds.

"> LOOK. A speling misteak <

Did the world end? No.

Am I still employable? Yes.

Over the past few years working with #impact #entrepreneurs and #sustainability #innovators, I've seen this a hundred times.

We're so afraid to put a piece of content into the world

that's not 100% perfect. That's not worthy of an A+. That's not showing our intelligence. Showing the rest of the impact ecosystem how smart we are.

For fear of retribution from our peers, we check and check and check. And then, we delete.

We continuously ask ourselves, "what are the direct benefits of this post?" and if the answer is even slightly; "I don't know", we don't click Post.

Instead, we just copy links to an article by The Guardian Environment or promote our next event. It's easier this way.

Fear. We're scared of what our peers think about us. That they'll judge us for getting something wrong.

Better not to do anything than to get something wrong.

I understand because I've been there too. But the last-minute hovering dance that you have with the Post button is only costing you time and energy.

Click it, get feedback. Put yourself out there. Get stuff wrong. Learn what your audience likes. Test. And for god's sake, nobody cares about a spelling mistake.

#content #impactinvesting"

This post did quite well because it caught people's attention from the get go. It encouraged debate amongst those who commented and provoked my target audience into being more active on LinkedIn.

"Public Service Announcement for Sustainability

Communicators:

When you tell people not to do something, they switch off to your message.

Stop driving so much, it's bad for the planet. Stop eating meat, it's bad for the Amazon. Stop flying and take a train instead. Has it worked? No.

Research shows that when someone is told that they can't do something, it makes them want to do it even more. The Reactance Theory, a term from the field of psychology, states that people are convinced they possess certain freedoms to engage in so-called free behaviours.

"Reactance is an unpleasant motivational arousal that emerges when people experience a threat to or loss of their free behaviours. It serves as a motivator to restore one's freedom."

In layman's terms, it causes a knee jerk reaction to resist.

So when you're marketing to people outside of the "impact bubble", try to remember not to tell them what to do. Instead, give them a viable alternative and make it easy for them to understand, digest and spread.

Because telling people what not to do, never changed the world for the better.

#impact #sustainability #communications #impactinvesting #techforgood"

Another valuable form of interacting on LinkedIn is to comment on other people's posts. This may sound simple, but it's a key strategy to becoming a thought leader on LinkedIn. Because LinkedIn is a platform in a content deficit, when content that is meaningful and thoughtful is posted it goes further than it would on Instagram or Twitter. If you like or comment on a post, then the algorithm — that decides what you see on your feed — is likely to decide that this post is of high value (because of your interaction) and thus is likely to share it with your connections as well. In this way, a share is an endorsement of someone else's views or opinions so this comes with a heavyweight for LinkedIn's algorithm. Also, as we've discussed, people crave recommendations from their peers and are far more likely to trust someone when their content is liked by a friend or colleague. This is true far beyond the digital realm as well. When someone endorses your brand to their network, it comes with a lot more gravity than when you're advertising. There are three ways which you can interact with someone's content; liking, commenting and sharing and each is weighted differently by the LinkedIn algorithm. Think of it like this:

- Liking = 1 point
- Commenting = 2 points
- Sharing = 3 points

The more points a post receives, the more velocity it will have in the authors' network and in your own as well. By commenting on others' posts, you're essentially validating that you find it interesting.

EXERCISE 01

CONTENT STRATEGY

By now, the foundations of your brand should be strong enough to create a solid 6-12 month content strategy. You have your story. Your mission. Your vision. And you're armed with strategic messages to get your customers excited. Now it's time to turn that knowledge into content and get it in front of your ideal target audience.

Step 1. What are the key areas in which you operate? If you think back to your brand story in Section 1, this will be the "magic gifts" which you're armed with to help you target audience.

1.
2.
3.
4.
5.
6.

For each topic, ask yourself the following five questions:

1. What is it and what's the context? How does this subtopic tie into the greater brand story from Section 1?
2. Why is it important for the target audience?
3. How does doing this wrong hold your audience back from success and what are the main mistakes they usually make?
4. How to do it right? What's the forumula? What are the steps you usually take with your clients/customers?
5. Give an example (or multiple of companies that have done it right. What about in your own experience? Or perhaps a famous case? Case studies build credibility.

What about for no. 1?

What about for no. 2?

What about for no. 3?

What about for no. 4?

SIX MONTH DAILY CONTENT STRATEGY

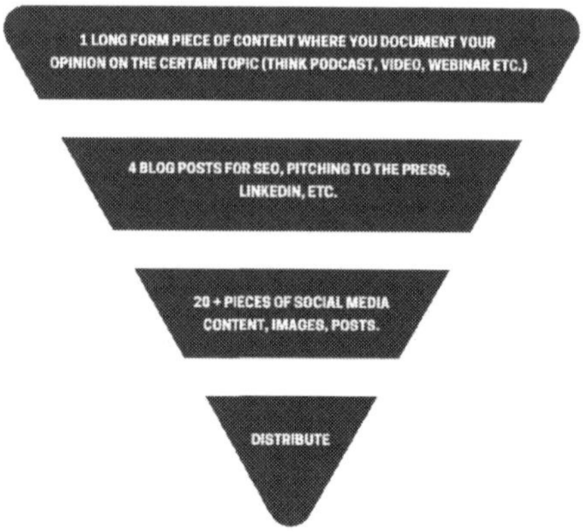

Once you know your the answers to these five questions for each of your subtopics, create a long form piece of content surrounding one topic a month. Once you've recorded that piece of content, you'll be able to cut it up into smaller blogs and content for social media.

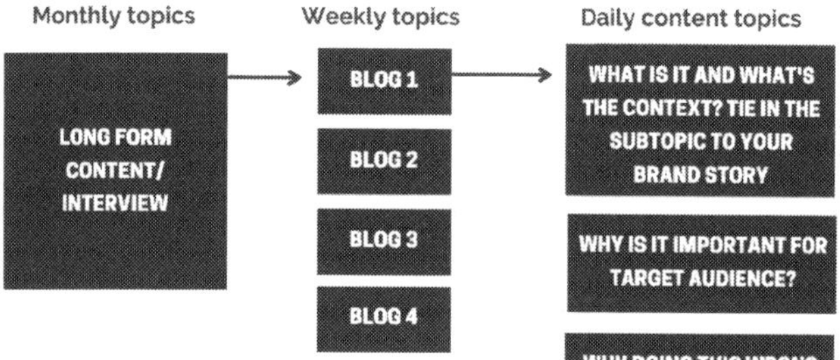

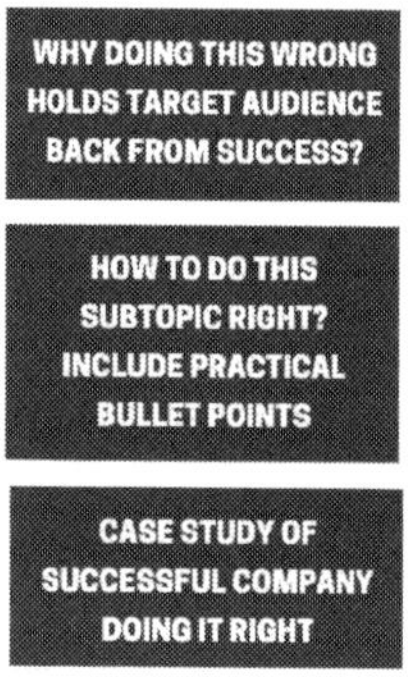

In practice, this is how small companies can create more content than most large companies. With the agility to move fast and the ability to create and distribute something that's not 100% perfect, this daily content strategy will help your startup build it's reputation and showcase it's brand.

EXERCISE 02

LINKEDIN PROFILE

If 50 percent of your business's reputation is built on that of it's founder and as LinkedIn is the best place to build a personal brand, then LinkedIn instantly becomes the best route to establish yourself as a thought leader. However, too many profiles of founders simply don't cut it, especially when they're asking to raise funding from investors with multiple zeros on the end. This is how to structure your LinkedIn profile so that you cut through the noise.

1. Professional photo
- Put your face in the center of the frame.
- Crop the picture from the top of your shoulder to just above your head.
- Avoid bright or contrasting colours.
- Don't forget to smile.

2. Background
- Your background is your digital billboard. What do you want someone to know as soon as they stumble across your profile?
- For me, I want people to know that I've written a book.

3. Your full name

4. Your title
- Call our your target audience by name (for me it's climate tech brands)
- Touch on your value proposition (for me it's helping them scale
- Use language which shows you know and understand them (for me, it's accelerating the transition towards a world because they always use this phrase)

5. Your startup's logo
- Showcase your startup's logo and name here.

6. Location
- An up-to-date location is vital for LinkedIn's algorythms.

About 7

Sustainability over the last few decades has been defined by three distinct eras—each a product of their time:

1. The Green Era: Defined by NGOs, charity, and philanthropy, the Green Era ran until the early 2000s.
2. The Social Era: Defined by CSR, eco-friendly, and social impact, the Social Era ran until about 2020.
3. The Climate Tech Era: Defined by Entrepreneurship and Technology, the Climate Tech Era has just begun.

The pivotal difference in the Climate Tech Era is that entrepreneurship is key. And as Blackrock CEO Larry Fink puts it: "The next 1,000 billion-dollar start-ups will be in climate tech".

To thrive in this new era, Climate Tech founders need to shed their product-driven mindsets, become true entrepreneurs, and embrace the commercial side of their business. Because technology is not going to do the job by itself. Or as Katie Rae, chief executive of Climate Tech-focused VC says, "Technology is important but only if you understand how to bring it to market and make money to scale it".

However, this transition has created three key problems for entrepreneurs in the Climate Tech Era:

• First, Climate tech founders give far more priority to their innovation than in their business's development.
• Second, business partners and investors aren't interested in founders or startups who don't prioritize growth.
• This leads to the third challenge: Too many Climate Tech founders still build their businesses using the outdated strategic playbook from the Social or the Green Era.

7. About
- Feature your brand's story or strategic narrative here.
- Don't sell, but inform.
- Show your audience that you know what you're talking about.
- Tailor it to your target audience's pain points.
- Tell a story.
- Add a **Call To Action:** What's the next step that you want a potential customer to take when they arrive on your profile? Get in contact? Read an article? Join your newsletter? View your website? The next step because it can increase your chances of generating leads from your profile.

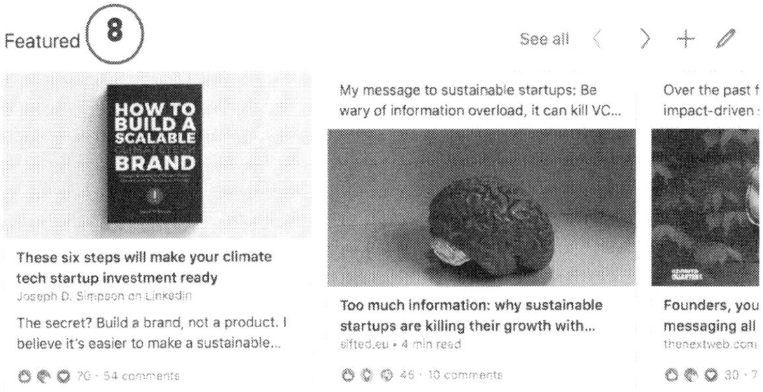

8. **Featured**
- 1 x Article which details why you started your business
- 1 x Article about the potential growth in the market in the future
- 1 x Article which shows that you are obsessed with the problem and not your solutions
- Add social proof if possible or articles you've written and submitted to known publications.

9. **Experience**
- Feature your startup's mission, logo and vision.
- Past experience: What makes you qualified to run this startup?

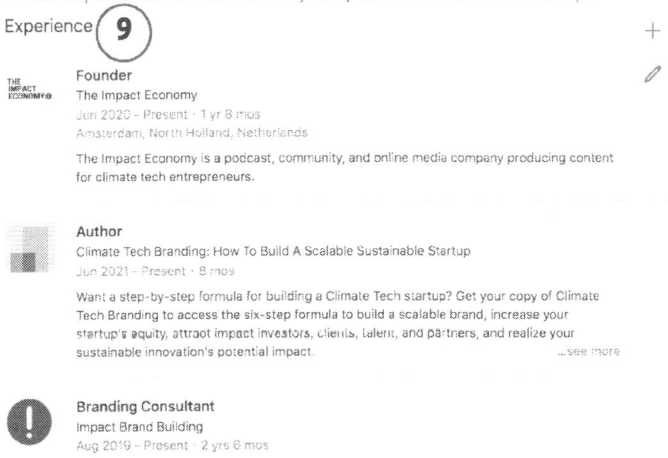

9.

PUBLIC RELATIONS: EARNING AUTHORITY

So you want to be in Forbes? What about Fast Company or Fortune? Would you settle for The Next Web or does it have to be Inc? You know your story, you can sell it. You've got a social media presence. But no one is buying. Why? Whether you're looking to raise capital, boost your public profile or launching a product, getting media coverage is one of the best ways to get your start-up noticed. But it's not that easy. Unfortunately, press coverage is more of an art than a science. But just like art, a well-informed strategy and ample practice can improve your chances of creating a masterpiece — or in this case, going viral. But before we get into it, let's touch on one important notion that you have to shake to be successful. Journalists are a tough cookie to crack.

Whereas gaining influence on social media and the time you put into building relationships are in your hands, publications have a mind of their own. They ask themselves, "who wants to know this story?", "why is this newsworthy?" and "who cares anyway?". If you can tick all three of these boxes, then there's a chance that you can get in the press. But before you do, you have to ask yourself what you want to gain from doing so.

I've worked with multiple clients over the past few years that told me "we want to get into Fast Company and we'll do anything to make it happen". Journalists can smell this kind of desperation from a mile away. You see, journalists have a bullshit radar. They can see when you're just making a story out of nothing. So, for the purpose of this chapter, we're going, to begin with the basics. We're going to go through exactly what journalists find interesting and what types of stories are out there. We'll then look at the intersection of public relations and guest blogging, how to pitch to journalists and we will lastly look at the press release. By the end of this chapter, you will not only be able to understand all the different methods that can get you featured in the press, but you'll hopefully have an idea on what journalists will find relevant. But first, let's start at the start.

PR is not a stamp of approval. If you only want to get into the Wall Street Journal so you can put their logo on your website, then there's a good chance that your efforts are going to be misguided. And probably unsuccessful. As useful as that credibility is, publications don't exist to give you a leg up. They're in the entertainment business. They're concerned about their own audience's attention. So instead of thinking about getting press for your benefit, you must flip this notion on its head. Your job is to tell a story that engages the reader. Brings them into a world in which you're a character, but not necessarily the protagonist. And when you take this out of the picture, you can truly ask yourself, if it's not for credibility, why do you want to target a certain publication?

This is where most startups go wrong. If their target audience is a) European, b) B2B and c) SMEs, then it's unlikely that your audience is going to frequent the New York Times. And you could spend your entire marketing budget for the whole year trying, but it's unlikely that you'll ever succeed to get your press release turned into a story by one of their journalists. Instead of wasting your time — especially at the beginning — consider going for lower hanging fruit. If you're launching a product or service, make a media list of where your audience actually consumes media (i.e., ask them!). Chances are they get their news on only a handful of mainstream media sites as well as smaller websites, blogs, influencers on social media as well as podcasts or short videos. By targeting these publications first, you're more likely to build influence with your actual target audience and when you finally get big enough news and publications like WST or NYT come knocking, you'll look legitimate enough to be featured.

WHY GET FEATURED?

Getting featured in the press is onc of the hardest forms of building a brand to master, but if done well, it can expose your message to a much wider sphere of influence. This book is all about building your climate tech startup's brand from MVP to investment-ready. When investors look into a startup , one of the first things that they will do is google you and your company's name. You're asking them for their hard-earned cash, so they're going to be as thorough as possible. They'll dig deep into your work history, your website and your social feeds. But they won't stop there. They'll look around for any interaction that your company has had with the outside world as well. And luckily for investors, Google basically acts as one big review. If your product or solution has been featured in the press then chances are that investors are going to view this favourably. Why?

1. Because it comes from a third party — media coverage demonstrates public interest in your company and shows legitimacy in your product.
2. Good press can put a face to your company's name which builds credibility beyond your product and can give important context to your start-up's story.
3. Press can show that you understand how the media game works and your ability to play along and thrive in an ecosystem outside of your own is a positive character trait in itself.
4. It can spread your message–your why–to investors outside your ecosystem and potentially expand your network by attracting like-minded professionals.

Getting featured in the press can turn a lot of heads. But you must know what your goal is in getting press in the first place. For instance, if you are trying to attract investors, then your eventual target publications will be those that investors read such as Fast Company, Forbes or TechCrunch. But if you're trying to attract top talent to your start-up, you're much more likely to be targeting local area (and language) publications. If you're trying to apply for government funds, then public servants are also more likely to read national newspapers than The Verge. Strategic messaging is always about starting at the end destination and working your way backwards through the medium and the message.

MESSAGING FOR PR

When it comes to getting media coverage, sustainable brands often fall into one of two traps: Jargon or sales. Firstly, our target audience may understand terms like "circular" or "systemic", but the press is another story. I've seen start-ups that, in their pitch to the media, literally have a list of their impact stack. "We're the world's most sustainable X because we use X, Y and Z technology and take a catalytic approach towards creating circular ecosystems. Blah blah blah." These types of long-winded explanations rarely captivate anyone's attention and if you're a journalist with over a hundred email pitches coming in every day, a jargon-full pitch is a short route to the recycling bin.

It's imperative to distil your message down to the core for journalists. I can't stress this enough. In the past 20 years since the Dot-com boom, the number of journalists has dropped dramatically. The majority of people now read their news online and a good portion of them don't pay for it. As a result, journalists today are very often overwhelmed with pitches by PR professionals and companies looking for free publicity. If you can't tell by now, this is not an easy form of communication. But it all comes down to making journalist's lives easier, giving them newsworthy and interesting information in a digestible manner.

The other pitfall which start-ups often encounter is trying to sell something directly through PR. There is nothing less attractive for a journalist than a sales pitch. They simply turn off and hit delete. If a journalist is going to write about your company, they are going to put their name next to your idea. That's a fair amount of credibility already. Getting them to do so whilst selling your product is as unlikely as getting you to sell their newspaper. It's always important to keep in mind that you are after publicity and they're after a good story. When you combine these two, sales is nowhere to be seen. If you're a founder, you must be agile enough to differentiate your publicity pitch from your sales pitch.

- **Be Newsworthy.** Whilst the goal for you may be to get the publication's logo on your website, journalists want news. They report on new, interesting, critical or entertaining information. So the key to getting press coverage is by giving journalists access to this information. This means that you have to go beyond the features of your product or service, what you offer or your opinion and give them something that is going to educate, inform or entertain their readers. It means drawing from the bigger picture. Drawing on the root causes. Talking about the effects of, rather than the process. Below are the seven elements that constitute newsworthiness.
- **Impact on the Audience.** The most important element of newsworthiness is whether or not the pitch is going to impact the publication's audience. The more people affected, the greater the news interest. Whenever you're writing a pitch, ask yourself, "how is this going to impact the journalist's audience?" The answer should easily front and centre for the journalist.
- **Proximity.** Journalists are interested in presenting stories that impact their communities. Proximity spans physical space as well

as concepts such as professions, sectors and industries. Journalists know exactly who their audience is, so when they receive an irrelevant pitch, they'll look past it without batting an eyelid. In a pitch, it's important to demonstrate that you know who their audience is. A great way to pitch a journalist is to help localise a global issue or provide insights on a local newsworthy matter.

- **Timeliness.** News consumers expect timely information and an event is more newsworthy the sooner it happens. News is precisely that; new information. Journalists don't want to report on your product or service. For something to capture their interest it has to be timely and journalists prefer to get time-sensitive news — that is, news before it happens that they have to act on. It triggers scarcity and fear-of-missing-out.
- **Prominence.** Events and announcements that involve high-profile or public figures are more likely to generate media coverage. In the start-up world, you can leverage this angle by collaborating or partnering with a bigger company or influential figure.
- **Conflict.** Interesting stories often involve some kind of conflict. By definition, these stories are almost always controversial to some degree. As they say, "if you're not offending someone, you're not saying anything".
- **Human Interest.** Often seen as "a story within a story" a human interest story tells the behind-the-scenes of people of interest and gives the audience a deeper level to which it can engage. Whilst many of the above news angles may feature human interest, a human interest story is a stand-alone feature. And the person of interest is usually the founder or investor. They aim to tap into the

emotional connection to an event or story, an insight into what you were feeling at the time and how it moved you.

- **Novelty/Shock Value.** The novelty of a situation can help influence whether or not a news outlet is likely to cover a story. To a certain extent, this is what you'd expect to see after the weather on prime time TV and it's also why we like cat stories so much on the internet. When you push novelty to the edge, you get shock value. Shock value stories are mostly negative and invoke feelings of distrust and fear. We usually associate shock value stories with the right-wing and tabloid newspapers, but environmental charities and NGOs are guilty of pushing shocking angels in the media as well. Think of images of starving children in East Africa during the famine in the early 2000s or skinny polar bears looking through bins for food. Whilst these may be causes closer to our heart, they still attempt to shock viewers into a response.

EARNED MEDIA

Your public relations game will only be a strong as your media list. It doesn't matter if you've got amazing content, a wonderful hook, or an exclusive interview you're willing to give, if you don't build up strong foundations for your list, your success in the PR department will be limited.

So what's a media list and how can it help? A media list is a document with the contact details of specific journalists, bloggers, writers, editors and influencers who write about your subject matter.

Mostly created in Google Sheets or Excel, a media list usually includes the name of the journalist, their email address, the name of the publication they work for, and a link to their recent article. Here's a full list of information you should include:

- Name of outlet
- First name
- Last name
- Job title
- Phone number
- Email
- Twitter account
- LinkedIn account
- Links to recent coverage
- A notes section for media pitching updates and reporter preferences

Just like with all brand building endeavours, the foundations you lay now will determine how fast you can scale. Doing this right is in your brands best interest. So how can you create one of the most useful CRMs for your startup?

Step 1. Brainstorm Media Outlets.

Brainstorm the potential publications which you know and would like to be featured in. This can include anything from the biggest names such as the New York Times to tiny tech blogs. Get creative.

Step 2. Ask your target audience

Once you've listed all the publications you know you'd like to be featured in, it's time to ask someone from your target audience what publications they read. Add them to the list.

Step 3. Google News Search

The next step in creating a media list is to go to Google News and type in the key words you'd like to be known for. For instance, at The Impact Economy, we would like to be known for terms like "Climate Tech" or "Sustainable brands". Find different and new publications which cover your industry and add them to your list.

Step 4. Assign A Media Tier

With most of the companies I work with, there are usually three or four different tiers of contacts — ranging from international publications to industry-specific bloggers.

- Tier 1: Top Tier — Top tier media consists of outlets with international reach and high circulation, including publications like The Guardian, The New York Times, The Washington Post etc.
- Tier 2: Regional/Local — Regional tier media contacts are usually specific to the country you operate in as well as the language. For instance, for a Dutch brand, national newspapers like Volkskrant or NOS would be considered 2nd tier media.
- Tier 3: Tech Blogs — The 3rd tier is usually overlooked as most brands want to be featured by the New York Times immediately. However, tech blogs are at times far more effective to deliver the

desired result. These could include publications like The Next Web, Sifted, or The Verve.

- Tier 4: Trade Magazines — Trade magazines and industry publications are valuable press contacts and often more open to featuring content from your brand. If you're in property technology, these could include publications like Propmodo, or Property Week. If you're in impact investing, it would be more Impakter, and Impact Alpha, etc.

Step 5. Create a spreadsheet

Create a spreadsheet with your desired publications, the ones where you would love to be featured, as well as the ones which your target audience reads for each of the above tiers.

Step 6. Look for recent articles and see who published them

For each of the publications on your media list, look through their recent publications and find articles which are similar to the one you'd like to be featured in. This can be in terms of the topic (i.e., they wrote about cleantech) or in terms of substance. Add each article to the row in your sheet, the author, and make a note of what you liked about it.

Step 7. Find the contact details of the author

Once you've identified your target authors, you have to find out how to get in contact. I usually do this for my clients via LinkedIn, Twitter, or old fashioned email. Try to avoid sending emails to addresses that are similar to info@publication.com — this is a one way ticket to waisting your time.

What we tend to do is go straight to Tier 1 publications with our stories, pitch them and never hear back. As a result, many founders and entrepreneurs believe PR is a waste of resources and they move on with other parts of their business. To put it in perspective, if you're a football team playing in the local league, imagine if you wrote to the Champions League asking to be involved in next year's cup. When you're small, you have to play with the small guys and grow together. Sure finding journalists that are willing to cover your topic may be difficult when it comes to the big publications but if you're offering a short-of-time, bootstrapping blogger an interesting scoop or newsworthy content, they're far more likely to take you upon it.

Targeting smaller publications in Tier 2 and Tier 3 is important because it also builds credibility around your brand. Journalists are wary of writing about a company who has never had any press before. This is especially true when that company claims to "revolutionise the industry" or "change the way that we do business". By building relationships with local publications or industry-specific publications, it's possible to grow your sphere of credibility and build up to Tier 1. This process will also help you perfect your pitches, understand how journalists and media outlets work and build your little black book of journalists.

PITCH IDEATION

Before it comes to pitching your ideas to a journalist, you need to understand the different types of articles that you can pitch. Firstly, there are guest blogs, secondly, there are feature story ideas and last of all there are press releases. Whilst there is no right or wrong answer for which form you should take, I usually suggest that pitching guest blogs should be a recurring thing, whilst pitching feature story ideas should be part of a greater campaign. Press releases are in their nature a more formal document, so they lend themselves to larger events or product launch.

- **Guest Blogs.** Guest blogs are by far the easiest type of content that you can get placed in publications so that is where I would recommend starting. This is mainly true because they don't require a lot of work from the journalist or editor of that specific publication. Guest blogs are exactly what they sound like. They're an article that you've written, to the specifics of the publication–typical article length, first or third person, that they will publish under your own name. In the media, they're technically called opinion editorials or OpEds and they're great if you want to comment on a recent event or share your experiences. Guest blogs should be considered as similar articles to your thought leadership articles on LinkedIn. They should, rather than advertise your product, add value to the audience. One of the simplest ways to do this is by commenting on recent developments in your industry or the way that a recent event will impact your business. It's integral to understand who the publication's audience is and what struggles they may have – they're likely to have a struggle that's similar to your own – and offer them information about how you are going about solving that problem. Guest blogs are also a great way of building the domain authority of your website. In return for getting your content featured in your target's publication, you will also get a backlink which helps you rank better in Google.

- **Feature Story Ideas.** A feature story has a long shelf life because it is not technically considered a news story. They generally range from between 2,000 and 4,000 words and are usually more creative, more descriptive and more subjective than news stories. For instance, a feature story may have the founder or CEO's name in the title of the article, it may have a large photo of the company or the subject embedded in the story. The front cover of a magazine is the most desirable and elusive feature story there is. Features are ideal for magazine publications, who tend to have their editorial calendar filled in months in advance, as well as industry publications and weekend newspapers. They are a chance to get in-depth and personal with an individual and see their take on life, written in the third person by the journalist. The basic structure of a feature is 20% context and 80% about you and your company. When pitching a feature, you will give a journalist or editor a package with all the information they need to decide whether they'll cover your story or not. The package will start the journalist's homework for them. In the pitch, you should include the unique angle, statistics or research which supports that angle and experts or customers who have agreed to be interviewed for the story. By giving them the information that they need to research the story effectively, you're making their job easier and improving your chance on a feature. Remember, features contain a human interest angle, which means they should also show your personal side, your experiences and your beliefs to the journalist.
- **Press Releases.** The press release is the most traditional format of public relations that we are going to cover. Press releases are

emailed out to media contacts to announce something newsworthy. Press releases are also the most common form of PR that journalists receive, so it's important to remember that if you want your story to get picked up, you have to make sure that the format and style conform to the standard. Press releases always begin with the most newsworthy information: who, what, when, where how and why. What follows next is supporting information that gives context to the story. This can be anything from an explanation of a global event, localization of a current affair to a history lesson. This context is then backed up by one or two sources who give a quote, adding additional context or backing up why the event happened. Quotes are the part of a press release that can add colour or flair to the article, so make sure you choose your words carefully. I always suggest that you read them aloud to make sure they sound authentic. I often ask myself"Is this something you would say?". A second outside source is a great way to build trust and credibility. For instance, if you're a tech company, then it can be a customer or a partner who's agreed to be quoted and can endorse what you're saying as truth. Lastly, a press release always ends with a synopsis of you or your company, which will be used by the journalist when they're writing an article about you. Always make sure you only include relevant information in this section, to avoid you having to follow up with the journalist later.

PITCHING TO PRESS

To start generating media coverage, you have to do the reaching out to the journalist. I say this specifically as to when I started out, I thought it was enough to just send a pitch to a general email address like info@fastcompany.com. Safe to say, this is not the case. The first step in the pitch process is to figure out exactly who you want to send your pitch to. As I've previously recommended, it's best to pull out your media list and select relevant journalists who you think would cover the story based on the articles they're interested in. Make sure that you're knowledgeable about what the journalist has written before and always keep an indexed list of articles that you would love to have been quoted in. When you see an article that you think would have benefited from having your opinion or angle in it, add it to your media list.

Whether you're pitching a guest blog, a press release or a feature article, the subject line is the most important factor in getting your story picked up. In a full email box, ask yourself "will this stand out? Will this line convey to the journalist that it's of interest to their readers?" Great subject lines often use words which convey urgency or are actionable, include numbers or statistics, ask a question or make the reader curious. Whilst editors are undecided on exactly what they want to see here, subject lines that include industry-specific jargon are unlikely to be opened. Remember, 85% of journalists and editors open an email based on the subject line, so the more time you spend here getting this right, the more chance you have of success. For the most part, try and keep your subject line between 40-50 characters. I like to include the type of PR content that the journalist is receiving in the subject line — e.g. "[GUEST POST PITCH]", "[PRESS RELEASE]" or "[FEATURE ARTICLE PITCH]" — after the subject line itself. The vast majority of email pitches are opened on a desktop computer, so the journalist is likely to see the content type if they are attracted to the subject.

Remember: Over 80% of journalists receive above ten pitches each day and only 20% finish reading an entire pitch. Don't give them any excuse to throw it in the trash can. Regardless of what type of content you are pitching, there are a few blanket rules to follow. The two main issues that will make editors click delete are that the email is, quite obviously, mass-produced or that it includes grammar mistakes. To avoid the latter, the mantra; write once, edit twice is important. Consider the format the publication writes in. Is it U.S. or British English? Do they have guidelines on submitting pitches and are you following them? Is the article the right length? Following these guidelines — written or unwritten — will make it easier for the journalist to digest your story without getting distracted by black flags. Secondly, the beginning of the email should specifically address the journalist or editor. Make it personal. Relationship building is key when it comes to pitching articles because value should never be a one-way street. And besides, there is a real person on the other side of the computer. Address them and personalize every email. Journalists hate thinking that you've gotten 100 email addresses together and given the same story to each of them. There is a word for this: Spam and if you received it, you would have the same reaction!

When the time comes to pitch your article and you have a list of journalists and a good subject line, what follows next is the core of your pitch. This differs for all three types of PR content so I will explain them separately.

For a guest blog, following your subject line and a personalized letter to the editor, you should include a short and sweet summary including a) an introduction of yourself, b) an explanation of why your writing would be relevant to their audience, c) the outcome that the reader will take away and d) if you've already written the article, a link to the Google Document like this: "You can read the full article here" and if you haven't already written the article yet, include a shortlist of topic ideas and a link to your previous articles.

The feature article pitch follows roughly the same structure as that for a guest post. Personalize it, introduce yourself and your story idea and tell the editor why the story is relevant for their audience. The biggest difference is that you will embed the pitch in the email as well. Don't bother with attachments, journalists prefer web links or Google Drive folders.

A press release email will also follow the same structure as the feature article, bar one important factor. With a press release, you should include whether your piece is time-sensitive or not. As such, before your press release begins, you should always begin with a full caps statement saying either: UNDER EMBARGO UNTIL [date & time] or FOR IMMEDIATE RELEASE. I also like to bullet point the three or four most important bits of newsworthy information in the release followed by a link to a google drive folder containing all relevant information: photos, videos and a Google Document containing the full press release.

An example of an email pitch would be the following text with the entire press release copied and pasted below:

Dutch start-up turns co2 into electricity [PRESS RELEASE]

UNDER EMBARGO UNTIL 00:01 21/01/2020

"Hey X

I've been following your series on carbon capture and storage and I thought that this would interest your readers for three reasons:

- Our cleantech startup [insert name] has recently finished a pilot project with the Dutch Government to turn carbon dioxide into electricity.
- In your recent article [insert article name], you wrote: "carbon capture will evolve in the future to be more than just storage, but will grow to become an economically viable solution." Our technology is proof that this is correct.
- The Dutch Ministry of Innovation believes that the technology will put The Netherlands at the forefront of sustainable innovation in the future (quote included).

Please find the press release attached here or view it below. If this story is of interest to you, feel free to reach out to me for any additional information.

Best, Joseph D. Simpson"

THE FOLLOW UP

Once you have clicked send, you may hope the process is over. If you're starting to get the gist of this public relations, it's not. Public relations is a long-term game and requires patience as well as relationship building. And the follow up is an important part of getting your pitch picked up. Journalists usually take up to one week to decide if they are interested in a story and it's OK to give them a nudge or two. Be firm, but don't be annoying. There's a chance that they're also busy but that they appreciate being in the know. After this initial week, if you don't hear back, it's likely that the journalist has passed on your story and that you should move onto the next option.

EXERCISE 01

MEDIA LIST BRAINSTORM

The first step to a successful public relations campaign is to create a list of possible publications that you would like to get featured in. A media list is a document with the contact details of specific journalists, bloggers, writers, editors and influencers who write about your subject matter. Mostly created in Google Sheets or Excel, a media list usually includes the name of the journalist, their email address, the name of the publication they work for, and a link to their recent article.

Step 1. Brainstorm the potential publications which you know and would like to be featured in. This can include anything from the biggest names such as the New York Times to tiny tech blogs. Get creative.

Step 2. Once you've listed all the publications you know you'd like to be featured in, it's time to ask someone from your target audience what publications they read. Add them to the list.

Step 3. The next step in creating a media list is to go to Google News and type in the key words you'd like to be known for. For instance, at The Impact Economy, we would like to be known for terms like "Climate Tech" or "Sustainable Startups". Find different and new publications which cover your industry and add them to your list.

Step 4. Categorize the selection from your brainstorm into a tiered media list. With most of the companies I work with, there are usually three or four different tiers of contacts — ranging from international publications to industry-specific bloggers.

International

-
-
-
-
-
-
-
-
-

Regional/Local

-
-
-
-
-
-
-
-
-

Industry Publication/Niche Blog

-
-
-
-
-
-
-
-
-

Trade Magazines

-
-
-
-
-
-
-
-
-

Step 5. Create a spread sheet. Create a spreadsheet with all the desired publications and fill in the names of each publication and a link to their website in the correct tier.

Tier	Publication Name	Website Link	Journalist/Contact	Email	Recent Article	Comments

Step 6. Look for recent articles and see who published them. For each of the publications on your media list, look through their recent publications and find articles which are similar to the one you'd like to be featured in. This can be in terms of the topic (i.e., they wrote about cleantech) or in terms of substance. Add each article to the row in your sheet, the author, and make a note of what you liked about it.

Step 7. Find the contact details of the author. Once you've identified your target authors, you have to find out how to get in contact. I usually do this for my clients via LinkedIn, Twitter, or old fashioned email. Try to avoid sending emails to addresses that are similar to info@publication.com — this is a one way ticket to waisting your time.

EXERCISE 02

PITCH IDEATION

There are three common types of content which you can pitch to journalists and publications: Guest blogs, feature articles, and press releases. Create a list of possible ideas for each below. (Hint: They should follow the value driven messages from Section 3).

Guest blogs. Create a list of possible stories for pitching which add value to your chosen publication's target audience, rather than advertise your product or service. These ideas should be timely (think: "Why [target audience] should change their strategy to succeed]" or "Three things you should to do win in 202X")

-
-
-
-
-
-
-
-
-

Feature articles. Create a list of possible stories for pitching which add value to your chosen publication's target audience, rather than advertise your product or service.

-
-
-
-
-
-

Press Releases. Create a timeline of expected milestones throughout the year (funding rounds, events, product releases, release of research, patent filing, etc.).

- January:
- February:
- March:
- April:
- May:
- June:
- July:
- August:
- September:
- October:
- November:
- December:

10.

CONCLUSION: SCALING UP YOUR BRAND

If you've made it this far then you're well prepared to take on the formidable feat of building your Climate Tech startup. I have given you all the information I could give to help you build the foundations of your brand, crafting your niche, creating content and scale the process upwards and onwards. However, you've still got a ways to go yet. Building a brand is not only a long-term strategy for success, but it likely takes a lot of time and dedication before you start to see any results. See ... branding is different from advertising in one main way. Advertising you can measure (I put X dollars in and I get Y dollars in return), branding isn't that simple. With branding, nothing is for certain. Well, OK, one thing is for certain: Success is not guaranteed. But when you take it into your own hands, branding can not only be an extremely successful mechanism to scale your business, it can be rewarding in the process itself. The process of truly getting to know yourself and how to tell your own story with meaning and passion.

By building strong foundations for your brand and communicating strategically to your niche, can increase the equity of your business. It's not the quick-and-easy marketing strategy that most founders want — the $1 in and $2 out scenario — but it is possible. And it takes equal parts creativity and determination to make it happen. But I'm guessing that if you're still reading this, then you've got a bit of both up your sleeve. The question is, do you want to change your growth trajectory and set yourself up for success? Or do you still want to base your growth on your product or service's features?

The goal should (obviously) be to turn your business into something more than a product and something that your target audience trusts to solve a problem. And there are so many tools at our disposal that can help you do just that. Perhaps you won't put all of the knowledge that you learn in this book to work. Perhaps it will only be a small part of it. But the knowledge in this book should give you the foundations to build something big.

Throughout this book, I have attempted to give you the most up-to-date information on why it's important and how to build your brand as an impact entrepreneur or climate tech startup. But, here's a confession: I'm just starting building mine. I've been working for a number of years across the marketing, communications and sustainability field and this book is an attempt to solidify my own position. I'm trying to assert my expertise in the best way I know-how. Honestly, this book is me taking the shortest route to be considered an expert in my field. I'm not telling you this because I want you to throw this book out in a rage. I'm telling you this because it's the truth. Books are great ways to assert your dominance in a certain field and in the long run, they're simply ultra long-form content marketing.

Here's another truth: I'm not an expert in everything that I've covered in this book. To be honest, I've spent many hours researching different theories from marketing and communications to the intersection of sustainability and psychology. I've read hundreds of articles, blogs and books on topics ranging from impact investing to PR best practices for startups. I've also reached out about a dozen entrepreneurs and professionals — some quoted herein and others behind the scenes — to beef up my knowledge on certain subjects. I'm not an expert, I'm a collector of knowledge. However, in doing so, I believe that I've amassed enough information that the value I'm providing justifies the time you've spent reading this. At least, I hope that's true. In saying that, I hope that (if you've made it this far) this book has at least made you challenge some of how you communicate impact. If it's helped you build your brand and create a positive impact, then it's been a success.

I would love this book to find its way into the hands of as many people as possible. I know that many impact entrepreneurs and climate tech startups don't have as much money as their peers in SaaS or FinTech. Whilst that's changing, it's still a fact of life. That being said, if you're reading this book, it's likely that you're in my target audience (aka, the people who I would love to work with). That's why I've written this book. Because whilst you may not be able to afford my services, right now, the information in this book is important to help you set yourself up for growth. And if you scale to a point where you can afford them, then hopefully I'll be top of mind. For me, it's a long term strategy. For you, I hope it services as both inspiration and practical advice to help you grow your impact-driven business. Let's scale together!

If you've downloaded Impact Brand Building, feel free to share it and if you have a paper copy in your hands, then give it away to someone who needs to read it. It's yours to do with as you wish. I only ask that you reach out to me on LinkedIn and tell me how you found it. Also, if you've come this far and you haven't done so yet, I'd love to invite you to join our community of Impact Brand Builders on Mighty Networks. I know that starting and growing a company can feel like a lonely journey. Especially so when you're in the impact sphere. That's why I've created this community for impact entrepreneurs and climate tech startups. I'd love for you to join us and we can all build our brands together.

In the rest of this chapter, I'm going to cover some of the basics of scaling your brand, what investors want and include a pre-funding round communications plan.

TYPES OF FUNDING AVAILABLE

The funding landscape has opened up over the past few years in a way that has changed the game for impact entrepreneurs. As we have discussed many times, impact entrepreneurs are more likely to be academics or engineers than seasoned business people. As a result, I've come across many impact entrepreneurs that don't quite understand the route which startups traditionally take to grow. The venture capital route. If you are familiar with this world, then I'm sorry for doubling up. But for those that aren't, understanding the differe phases of your startup and who you should be approaching at what stage is an integral component of raising capital and scaling your impact.

Access to capital has never been so readily available and even in the wake of the corona crisis, this trend is unlikely to change. What's more is that donors, philanthropists and governments are becoming increasingly critical about how their money is spent. Concerned over factors like transparency and competitiveness, many who were once handing out cash in exchange for impact, are now expecting a return on their investment. As such, business models are shifting to capitalize on this new impact ecosystem. Those who would have once started a non-profit are now looking towards impact entrepreneurship as the way forward. At the same time, traditional for-profit businesses have seen a substantial increase in benefits from being driven by purpose or impact. As a result of these two phenomena together, whilst there has never been more funds available for impact-driven companies, there has never been this much competition either. In this new reality, raising funds is a huge challenge. The rewards too, can be immense. But we have to play by their rules and speak their language. Below is an overview of the types of funds available and in what stage your startup should apply for each.

The Bootstrapping Phase ($10,000 to $100,000)

For impact entrepreneurs and startups with an idea, a MVP or who are exploring the feasibility of the concept and testing the market. This phase, also known as seed funding, gives you the ability to take your time and explore the ins-and-outs of developing your solution before approaching an investor. At this stage, access to capital can come in the form of:

- **The Bank of Friends and Family.** Asking your friends and family for money is probably one of the best ways to get your business off the ground.
- **Soft loans or grants from local, state or national governments.** Governments and municipalities are often interested in providing funds at the bootstrapping phase. In the EU, multiple overarching funding bodies help you develop your idea like Climate KIC and EIT.
- **Self-funding and credit cards.** Relying on your own funds in the early stage will be essential. It's generally said that a new entrepreneur should have between 6 and 18 months salary in the bank before embarking on their next venture.
- **Crowdfunding.** A whole new access to capital arose with networks like Kickstarter and GoFundMe. Today they've evolved into seed investor marketplaces like CrowdCube which pledges to fund the next generation of businesses.
- **Incubators.** These are undoubtedly one of the most valuable ways to get funding for your startup. If you get accepted into an accelerator or an incubator, you'll not only get funds, but you'll also have access to experienced mentors, potential sources of funding and a supportive community.

The Angel Phase ($100,000 to $1 million)

As your startup begins to grow you need to scale your team and the development of your product to keep the momentum going. If you're beyond your MVP and your business model should be proven, then you might look to angel investors as a way to scale. Angels are exactly what they sound like. Your saviours. They can swoop in and provide your new venture the type of capital that you need to keep going. Angels are accredited high-net-worth individuals who will jump on board your journey for a stake in your business.

Venture Capital ($1 million and above)

Once you've got a proven business model and are looking to scale your venture, venture capital firms are your next likely option for capital. The way that venture capital firms work is they invest in your business and give you access to their network for a percentage of your business. They're investing wealthy individual's money on an institutional basis to give returns back to the individual. They take a gamble on startups in exchange for the possibility of massive rewards (like Facebook's 20X for its original investors), when the startup grows and either their share gets purchased by a later-stage fund or the company goes to an initial public offering. From the stage when a startup gets involved in the process to the point where they exit, there are usually three (but sometimes four) rounds of investment: Series A, Series B and Series C. For those without a long-standing track record in building and selling successful companies, one of the ways to lower access to capital — and Series A funds in particular — is to enrol in an accelerator program.

- **Series A** is usually between $2 million to $20 million and typically, the main investors are venture capital firms. Receiving a Series A round is an important milestone for startup companies as it usually means that they are no longer in the ideation phase, but that they've got something concrete and marketable.

- **Series B** is usually between $20 and $50 million. Series B is all about taking a business to the next level and scaling up. This round has been said to be the most challenging funding round for a business.
- **Series C** can be anywhere from $50 million up to a few hundred million. This round is designed to expand into new markets, increase market share and get businesses ready for a business exit, like an IPO. Beside late-stage venture capital firms, the most common investors of this type of money are private equity firms, hedge funds and banks.

By talking the talk when it comes to investors and venture capital firms and showing that you know your stuff, it will make it much easier for them to trust you with their money. Many entrepreneurs enter into the race to build their business without any thoughts of their exit. This becomes even more apparent if you're an impact entrepreneur — you're building a business to help the world, not looking to sell it to help your own pocket. But if you're looking to raise capital from investors, you have to consider the benefit for them as well as the planet.

The process of applying for funding for your climate tech startup usually comes in five stages. First it's all about measuring your impact — which I'll go into more detail on in the next section — then comes building the perfect pitch deck, identifying a targeted list of prospective investors, outreach to those investors and then negotiation. Each stage comes with their own challenges and can at times require a different form of storytelling.

Raising capital is essential to building your venture and scaling your impact. Whether it's from private impact investors, local or state governments, venture capitalists or multinational enterprises, accessing funding will dramatically shape your path to success. The reason for this is simple. Ideas — no matter how impactful they are — are cheap. The ability to scale them into a business which not only creates meaningful change in the world but also sustains itself, is expensive. Capital is thus, the lifeblood of any startup. But access to it doesn't come cheap either.

Around 60% of an entrepreneur's time is spent on finding capital. That statistic is insane in itself. Think about all time you spend working during your day. Besides sleeping, it would be the next biggest chunk. You wake up, you spend 60% of your day asking people for money. You write a business proposal, give a pitch to an investor and you're nearly ready to go home. Throw on top of another statistic. It usually takes 6 months to raise your first round of investment and you're likely to be continuously raising capital every 12 to 18 months afterwards. Together, these two statistics paint a picture of a lot of an entrepreneur's time being occupied by fundraising, not building a product or service.

However, many of the entrepreneurs I've worked with have been in the dark about this process, inevitably slowing it down. Forgive me if you already know the difference between seed capital and Series A, but you'd be surprised how many impact entrepreneurs don't (another limitation from our days relying on governments and charity for capital to address impact). Lastly, we'll look at the format of a solid pitch deck — a prerequisite for raising capital — and a pre-round communications strategy.

Speed is incredibly important when it comes to raising capital. Because the process takes a lot longer than entrepreneurs usually anticipate, the key to success is preparation. In this chapter I will introduce the different types of capital available, what investors are looking for when they're analysing start-ups, how you can leverage your communications to your advantage in the lead up to a funding round and what are a few red flags which will turn investors off. The purpose of this may seem arbitrary to some, but I have often met impact entrepreneurs with a background in academia, the public sector or non-governmental organizations who don't fully understand the fundraising landscape. This section is dedicated to helping those entrepreneurs navigate the different ways in which you can take your sustainable solution global.

However, keep in mind that the entire premise of this book is to utilise branding and communications to your advantage. A company's worth is much more than its assets, its intellectual property (IP) and its people. A company's worth is based on these things and then multiplied by its potential. Its potential to grow, to create amazing new things. To scale. Think about any of the businesses that we consider unicorns today: Tesla, Airbnb, Uber. When they were just ideas in people's heads, they didn't have much in the way of assets. What they did have however was potential. And how did they express that potential? In their brand's stories, their vision and their brand.

I'm not going to tell you about the importance of a business plan or a strong team. From a branding perspective, I'll assume that you already know that. However I will argue that to attract (the right) investors, branding and strategic communications can help. Many entrepreneurs assume their technology or solution will be enough to win. Some believe their ambition alone can get investors to whip out their chequebooks. And guess what, they fail. As an impact entrepreneur, your social side may open doors but it won't push you over the line. Neither will your solution. It's your obsession with a problem and building a brand around solving it.

Investors want to see their money is safe in your hands. If your startup is built around a technology or innovation and it fails, they will lose their money. However, if you build a strong brand around solving a particular problem and your technology fails, your brand will retain value. The solution you've built is simply proof that you are looking to solve the problem. And a brand can have multiple solutions for the same problem. In this respect, a founder that puts off investing time and energy into branding is a founder that inadvertently shows a disregard for a potential investor's money.

STORYTELLING FOR INVESTMENT

Investors want to be inspired and raising capital is an extensive and elusive process. You have to convince someone sitting on the other side of a desk that you're a worthy choice for their (or their shareholder's) hard-earned cash. That's not an easy job but as we have seen, all humans are hardwired to respond to a great story. It's simple biology. People will forget what you did, but people will never forget how you made them feel. With investors, it's no different. The story that you tell will determine whether or not a meeting goes successfully. But how do you tell a story that gives you a good position within your potential investor's mind? The key is to not only inform them about what your startup is going to do and the solution that you're going to provide but to also involve them in the problem and inspire them. After all, investors are people too.

This shouldn't come as a surprise to you. Throughout this book, time and time again we've discussed the idea of getting away from you and thinking about them. Your target audience. Whilst your goals are obviously different when talking to investors — raising capital rather than selling a service or product — the general principle is the same. You should be doubling down on your niche, finding who you think you need to be talking to based on mutual interests and making your pitch specific to them. A general pitch — just like a general story — won't touch the hearts and minds of anyone.

Many entrepreneurs believe that their product is so good that it will sell itself. Few believe in the need to tailor their pitch to each specific investor. Getting specific and personal with your investors and involving them in your pitch however can create a bond and let them feel like they could be a part of your journey. Make sure you understand their history, their background and their vision for the future. Look for investors who have invested in something similar to your solution before. See how much they gave, try and find a reason why they invested. And before you get in the room, tailor your pitch to their responses.

The most complicated part however is to tell a powerful story, not sell your business idea. Cognitive psychologist Jerome Bruner suggests we are 22x more likely to remember a fact when it's wrapped in a story. Why? Because stories are memorable. I'm sorry about being repetitive, but repitition also helps to drill in a message. Stories help us grab the gist of an idea quickly. They trigger our emotions rather than our rational. To inspire the person sitting on the other side of the desk, you should have at least five stories ready that you can access and use at any time. Each story should correlate to what you want the person in front of you to feel.

- Show that you share their values (based on your research of what they value beyond ROI)
- That you value their opinion (based on a time when you've listened to and taken on advice in the past)
- About why you believe data (and a time when data challenged your own beliefs and values)
- That you understand your strengths and your weaknesses (and can prove it with past examples)
- That you have confidence in your own success (a time when you put everything into something)

Beyond stories, investors are drawn to great startup branding. Entrepreneurs have between 15-20 seconds to capture an investor's attention. Whilst that's almost double compared to a regular audience, it's still not much. Marcin Zaba, Head of Marketing at online investment platform SyndicateRoom says, "Having been involved directly or indirectly in the marketing of nearly 130 successfully funded businesses, I spend a lot of time trying to understand the underpinnings of a successful funding round. There are several factors, but one of the most important is a company's branding and messaging to would-be investors". [1] Zaba has two key tips for entrepreneurs looking to leverage branding if the end goal is investment.

1. **Clarify what you do.** Potential investors need to understand your proposition. Most sustainable start-ups believe they exist on a parallel planet. One where there's no competition and no one is doing anything like they are. Because they're doing good and doing

1 Novanym.

business, they believe that investors will be lining up to talk to them. In a certain way, this is true. But back on this planet, business for good is only good business when it brings in returns. So whilst there's no one else out there with your ideas or exact product, there are thousands out there competing for the dollars that are going to turn it from vision into reality. And today, the competition in the impact ecosystem is getting fiercer. Whilst we've never had so much access to capital, we've never had so many start-ups flooding the market. As a result, having invested in your own personal brand and that of your start-up months before going to the negotiating table is bound to pay off. Why? Because remember, your brand is what people say about you when you leave the room. When you leave the room and investors are discussing whether they want to invest in you or not, what kind of impression do you want to leave behind?

2. **Create an emotional connection.** Just like when you're targeting your niche, targeting the right investors is integral. Most investors will have an agenda that goes beyond making money. For impact investors, it's essential. And it's likely that the impact that they are ambitious to bring about, the world that they want to create, has a backstory. Dig into their history just like they would dig into yours. And make sure you have personal stories ready to tell on a range of topics as well. For instance, when someone asks me "why did you become so interested in sustainability?" I always have the same answer prepared. "During my early 20s, I travelled on and off around Australia, Europe, Asia, Africa and the Americas. Trip after trip, I began to see a pattern. At the intersection of disfranchisement and

social inequality lay a dependence on the earth for survival. And I saw the early signs of a changing planet; rock where there was once snow, bleached coral where there was once reef and sand where there was once trees. It took me a while to put it all together, but once I did, I knew that it would only become worse. That's how I became interested in sustainability." This story doesn't rely on facts and figures, but extends an emotional hand and shows vulnerability. After all, you're preparing to become partners in crime and you'll be responsible for each other's success in the venture. When you find out that you're both on the same page in regards to a certain topic that you care about deeply and can connect about it, it's much easier to enter into a business relationship.

Whilst connecting emotionally and clarifying your proposition can smooth over the story you tell investors, you may still fall short when pitching. All investors need is one reason for them to turn off to your pitch. For example: It doesn't matter how professional your pitch deck looks if you rock up to an interview smelling like you've spent a night in the Red Light District. Similarly, if you have a solid product and business plan, but your pitch is off, you're unlikely to walk away with a check. Attracting investors is all about installing confidence in your company, your ability to lead, your team and your product. So when you give the investor a reason to doubt your pitch, then it's highly likely that you're going to be shown the other side of their office door. Below are few common reasons why things go wrong for founders when raising impact capital.

- Founders don't want to be involved in the soft-side of their business (sales & marketing) so their growth trajectory is dependent on outsiders.

- Founders do not know how to build a network of investors or fail to connect with the right investors. On a basic level, your targets should fund other businesses of your size, stage and business model. On a more fundamental level, they should share the same values as you and have demonstrated behaviour that you feel comfortable aligning yourself with.
- They lack the strategy to close the deal. Many founders believe that they have to go it alone. This mentality can be a red flag for investors and hold them back from investing. Every founder looking to raise capital should have a mentor, help from a professional organization or a network of support. Failing to invest in this crucial form of help can say as much about an entrepreneur's mindset as it will the way they will spend if they do happen to receive investment.
- Founders lack an understanding of the process or the amount of time that successfully raising funds takes. As we've discussed raising capital takes time and energy. The process itself is complicated and requires a lot of thought process, understanding the ins-and-outs of your business and prioritizing fundraising over other core business activities.
- Founders rely on their social and impact ambitions whilst they fail to measure their impact. When you rely on your ambition to create impact over your customer promises and potential payoff for investors and their portfolios, it creates a disconnect between two schools of thought; social and capital. Impact entrepreneurs have to demonstrate their willingness to play by the capitalist rulebook in order to fulfil their promise of impact.

A startup who takes their brand seriously from the beginning can avoid many of these main pitfalls in raising capital. Every successful fundraising campaign has a rock-solid story. A story can open doors and it can generate interest in your startup. And most importantly, when investors like what you're working with — team, technology and vision — a story that investors can relate to and that evokes action can be the difference between a startup being funded or an idea being wasted.

PITCH DECK

A pitch deck is a short PowerPoint presentation or PDF, which summarizes your startup. The purpose of a pitch deck is to communicate to investors or VC firms that they should consider investing in you and your startup. Or at least that they should be open to the possibility of doing so. They're basically a teaser document that should get the investors excited to hear more about your startup. A good deck should communicate what you do, how your startup fits into the firm's investment portfolio, underscore a particular problem and sell your team and solution as a possible remedy for the problem. In most cases, you'll be required to send investors a pitch deck before they agree to meet you. A good pitch deck will help you open doors but with only 15 or so slides to explain your problem, your concept and your solution, you don't have much space to make an impression. Be sure to let your strategic narrative shine through here. So what should you include?

1. **Introduction.** Company Logo & What round of funding you're pitching for.

2. **Purpose.** A condensed yet powerful one-sentence pitch about your startup's mission. Follow Simon Sinek's Golden Circle principle here and lead with why. Remember, your company is the protagonist in this story, so try to visually and metaphorically keep it in the center.
3. **Problem Statement.** A concise articulation of both your customer's problem and the global problem that you are going to solve. Get as specific as possible with your target audience and try and set the scene for the rest of the story.
4. **The Opportunity.** Here you should identify your target market and the opportunity that awaits you if you decide to embark on this journey together. Try to address the investors in terms that they understand like total addressable market (TAM) or credible adjacencies, nascent market potential and frequency of use.
5. **Your Solution.** The unveiling of your product or service. It may be tempting to move this slide further up into your deck, but like we've discussed, the problem and opportunity are more important than the solution. For storytelling purposes, keep the focus on the problem whilst you show your potential investors what your company does.
6. **Why Now?** Because timing is one of the major reasons for startup failure, you should show that a) you've digested this concept and b) why "now" is the best time for your startup to succeed. You can include your impact measurement forecast or metrics on this slide.
7. **Competition.** Competition always exists. I know that I've said it again and again in this book, but sometimes it still doesn't sink

in. Just because you think you're all alone out there in a parallel universe, you'll always be competing against someone else. Showing that you understand the landscape on which you want to make a mark and what makes you stand out can help the investor see that you're serious.

8. **Business Model.** Once you've identified the how, what and why of your business, it's time to talk money. Get specific about how you are going to get your target audience to part with their money. One reason why it's nice to show your competition before your revenue/ business model is that you can identify their own model as a basis.
9. **Marketing & Sales.** The slide you've been dreading. The investor sitting on the other side of the table wants to know what your go-to-market strategy is going to be. How are you going to turn this idea into something that generates sales? Getting to know the metrics of similar business models in terms of cost per customer acquisition (CAC) and demonstrate that you are focused not only on building a product, but building a brand.
10. **Traction & Validation Roadmap.** This slide should ideally show where you are as a company. It should answer the following questions: Have you already received funding? If so, from who and how much? What's your growth trajectory? Do you already have people using your product or service? How are you going to validate the theories behind your solution? How much do you need to raise? And what are you going to do with the money? Answering these questions ahead of time saves the investor having to ask them.
11. **Team.** Your team is one of the biggest assets that you have and investors know it. The reason that they're going to give you a check

with five or more zeros on the end of it is because they believe in your team's ability to execute the story you've told. So why is your team the best fit for this startup idea? On this slide, introduce your team and demonstrate why you have the relevant experience and skills for this business. Show the projects you've worked together on and be open about holes that you need to fill in your management team. It's better than them assuming that you haven't thought about it.

12. **Vision.** Assume that you get your investment, what's the long term goal? "In 10 years, we will be the leading X in our market with Y customers and Z impact."

If you create this deck with your startup, it will surely open some doors for you. Keep in mind that this deck should include the information on the slide that you want the investor to see (as you're not going to be there to present to them). It's OK for it to be a bit heavy on the text, but remember that if you get a meeting then you should adapt the deck to be more slimline: The slides should support your story, not tell it!

PRE-ROUND COMMUNICATION STRATEGY

Ok, so imagine you're an investor and you receive a pitch deck that interests you in an email. What are you going to do now? Sit there and twiddle your thumbs? Obviously not. They'll Google your name, your company's name and they'll look into your history. What they find is up to you. You can influence everything from the press that writes about you, the subjects you're an expert on and the position you hold in your network. In essence, through personal branding, startup branding and public relations, you can assert yourself as a thought leader. In the next half of this book, I'm going to give you all the strategies that you can use to make this happen. Because half the reputation of a company lies on the shoulders of its leader or founder, by simultaneously focusing on your personal brand as well as that of your startup, you'll give your startup the best shot at success possible.

If you're stressing out already at the thought of having to have the right strategy, I'll try to put your mind at ease. Below are a set of tools or tactics that you can use to build your brand. Besides having the foundations (and the story) in place, whether you choose a guest blogging, social media, digital outbound marketing or inbound demand generation strategy, they're all friendly places to start communicating from. And branding is a long haul project, so it's not going to happen overnight. But low-and-behold, if you stick with it, you'll be able to influence the investor's hand in the scenario above and give yourself the best possible shot at success when it comes to getting funding.

In the 6-12 months before you're going to start contacting investors, I would recommend using a few of the following tactics to build a base. This base should focus on learning how storytelling can be both a part of your funding strategy and wider communication's goals, how you can leverage the status quo in your industry to position yourself and build your tribe of innovators and early adopters, how you can build a network of interested reporters and how you can position yourself to your network as a leader in your field. The timing that I'd recommend goes something like this:

- **12 Months Out.** Write your manifesto, your purpose, mission and vision as well as your customer promise.
- **10 Months Out.** Get all of your brand assets in check. Make sure you have your identity consistent across all of your communications channels
- **8 Months Out.** Start rehearsing your brand's story. You need to know it off by heart. Attend as many events as you can and lead with your elevator pitch. If there's one thing that you want this person to remember about your startup, what is it?
- **7 Months Out.** Start pitching out your thought leadership articles to industry specific publications and try to create some contacts within the press which you can leverage when it comes time to announce your funding round.
- **6 Months Out.** Start building your authority on social media by posting on LinkedIn and writing articles about the problem that your startup is solving. My rule of thumb is to write at least one article per month and have at least 6 published on LinkedIn under your own name with 6 being pitched to other industry-specific blogs.
- **5 Months Out.** Google your own name and see what you find. Are there any unfinished blogs out there? What about an old MySpace page or pictures of you drinking beer out of a shoe? By doing a digital cleanup, you can make sure you remove those hiccups ahead of time.
- **4 Months Out.** Measure your impact. Your potential impact should be visible on your pitch deck as well as on your website. Make sure

you present it in a way that a potential investor can understand and digest. Don't confuse them with something that belongs in a business plan from the 1990s.

- **3 Months Out.** Make sure your website displays everything you want it to. Go through it with a fine-tooth-comb for spelling mistakes or outdated information. The last thing you want to show a potential investor is that you're not taking yourself seriously.
- **2 Months Out.** Plan a newsworthy event, invite press and write a press release. By designing a stunt or event which will wow journalists and capture the attention of the press, you can get your startup featured in the press. This shows investors that you're willing to play the game.
- **1 Month Out.** Reach out to other entrepreneurs who've successfully raised a similar amount of capital and ask them to look over your pitch deck and hear your pitch. Never try to go it alone and always remember that whilst you may be building a company, you're also securing our collective future. People will want to help with that.

REFERENCES

Achor, S., Reece, A., Rosen Kellerman, G., and Robichaux, A., 2018, '9 Out of 10 People Are Willing to Earn Less Money to Do More-Meaningful Work' Harvard Business Review, [available online at] https://hbr.org/2018/11/9-out-of-10-people-are-willing-to-earn-less-money-to-do-more-meaningful-work

Akande, Adeoluwa, Cabral, Pedro, Gomes, Paulo, & Casteleyn, Sven, 2019, 'The Lisbon ranking for smart sustainable cities in Europe', Sustainable Cities and Society, 44, 475-487, [available online at] https://www.sciencedirect.com/science/article/pii/S2210670718308138

Alessi, L., Battiston, S., Melo, A. and Roncoroni, A., 2019, 'The EU Sustainability Taxonomy: a Financial Impact Assessment', EU Science Hub, European Commission, [available online at] https://ec.europa.eu/jrc/en/publication/eu-sustainability-taxonomy-financial-impact-assessment

Arguedas Ortiz, Diego, 2018, 'One simple reason we aren't acting faster on climate change?' BBC, [available online at] https://www.bbc.com/future/article/20181115-why-climate-change-photography-needs-a-new-look

Aulet, Bill, 2007, 'Disciplined Entrepreneurship: 24 Steps to a Successful Startup', Wiley.

Aulet, Bill, 2013, 'How to Do Market Segmentation', Youtube, [available online at] https://www.youtube.com/watch?v=ZeIUMuD3QGk

Beal, George M., Everett M. Rogers and Joe M. Bohlen, 1957, 'Validity of the concept of stages in the adoption process.' Rural Sociology, 22(2).

Burk, Kelly, 2020, 'Red Cross under fire for withholding two thirds of bushfire donations' 7 News, [available online at] https://7news.com.au/news/bushfires/red-cross-under-fire-for-withholding-two-thirds-of-bushfire-donations-c-660715

Cade, Adam, Bowden, Rob, 2011, 'YouthXchange guidebook series: Climate change and lifestyles' UNESCO, [available online at] https://unesdoc.unesco.org/ark:/48223/pf0000212876

Chuang, Alex, 2017, 'The Quick and Dirty Guide to Building Your Startup Brand', Medium, [available online at] https://medium.com/startup-grind/the-quick-and-dirty-guide-to-building-your-startup-brand-21834f46740b

Clayton, Susan and Manning, Christie, 2018 , 'Psychology and Climate Change: Human Perceptions, Impacts and Responses', Academic Press

Connick, Wendy, 2020, ' What Is Qualifying a Lead? Definition & Examples of Qualifying a Lead', The Balance Careers, [available online at] https://www.thebalancecareers.com/what-is-qualifying-2917378

Corner, A., Webster, R. & Teriete, C., 2015, 'Climate Visuals: Seven principles for visual climate change communication (based on international social research)'. Oxford: Climate Outreach, [available online at] https://climatevisuals.org/sites/default/files/2018-03/Climate-Visuals-Report-Seven-principles-for-visual-climate-change-communication.pdf

Corporate Finance Institute, 'Beachhead Strategy: The practice of focusing resources on a small market area to turn it into a stronghold in the future', [available online at] https://corporatefinanceinstitute.

com/resources/knowledge/strategy/beachhead-strategy/#:~:text=A%20 beachhead%20market%20can%20be,product%2C%20and%20the%20 market%20itself.

Dallmann, JP, 2018, 'Impact Investing, Just A Trend Or The Best Strategy To Help Save Our World', Forbes, [available online at] https://www.forbes.com/sites/jpdallmann/2018/12/31/impact-investing-just-a-trend-or-the-best-strategy-to-help-save-our-world/#6f3ccd0675d1

Davis, Andrew, 2018, 'At one point, Amazon lost more than 90% of its value. But long-term investors still got rich.'. CNBC, 18 December [available online at] https://www.cnbc.com/2018/12/18/dotcom-bubble-amazon-stock-lost-more-than-90percent-long-term-investors-still-got-rich.html

Davis-Peccoud, J., van den Branden, J., Brahm, C., Mattios, G., and de Montgolfier, J., 2020, 'Sustainability Is the Next Digital', Bain & Company [available online at] https://www.bain.com/insights/sustainability-is-the-next-digital/

DeBord, Matthew, 2019, 'Tesla is revamping its relationship with owners of the original Roadster. Here's a closer look at Tesla's first car.' Business Insider, [available online at] https://www.businessinsider.com/tesla-first-car-roadster-history-revamping-owner-relationships-2019-12?international=true&r=US&IR=T

Edelman, 2019, '2020 B2B Thought Leadership Impact Study', [available online at] https://www.edelman.com/research/2020-b2b-thought-leadership-impact-study

Executive Summary, Edelman Trust Barometer, 2018, 'Annual Global Survey 2018', [available online at] https://www.edelman.com/sites/g/files/aatuss191/files/2018-10/2018_Edelman_TrustBarometer_Executive_Summary_Jan.pdf

Fine, David, Hickson, Hugo, Pandit, Vivek, & Tuinenburg, Philip, 2018, 'Catalyzing the growth of the impact economy' McKinsey & Company [available online at] https://www.mckinsey.com/industries/private-equity-and-principal-investors/our-insights/catalyzing-the-growth-of-the-impact-economy#

Fink, Larry, 2019, 'A Fundamental Reshaping of Finance'. BlackRock [available online at] https://www.blackrock.com/uk/individual/larry-fink-ceo-letter

Funnell, Antony, 2020, 'Insuring your home may get harder and more expensive as climate change increases risks'. ABC News Australia, [available online at] 'https://www.abc.net.au/news/2020-05-14/home-insurance-as-climate-change-and-disasters-affect-industry/12227466

Gilbert, Daniel, 2006, 'If only gay sex caused global warming'. Los Angeles Times, [available online at] https://www.latimes.com/archives/la-xpm-2006-jul-02-op-gilbert2-story.html

Global Impact Investing Network, 2020, 'What You Need To Know About Impact Investing'. [available online at] https://thegiin.org/impact-investing/need-to-know/

Godin, Seth, 2002, 'Purple Cow: Transform Your Business by Being Remarkable', Penguin Publishing Group.

Goodson, Scott, 2012, 'Why Brand Building Is Important', [available online at] https://www.forbes.com/sites/marketshare/2012/05/27/why-brand-building-is-important/#1f759d933006

Green Alliance, 2013, 'Cities: the new green entrepreneurs', Inside Track, 32, [available online at] https://www.green-alliance.org.uk/resources/Inside%20Track%2032.pdf

GuruFocus.com, 2020, 'Warren Buffett Explains His Moat Principle', Yahoo Finance [available online at] https://finance.yahoo.com/news/warren-buffett-explains-moat-principle-164442359.html?guccounter=1

Hodges, Jeremy and Pogkas, Demetrios, 2019, 'These Are the Cities Doing the Most to Combat Global Warming', Bloomberg, [available online at] https://www.bloomberg.com/news/articles/2019-05-15/these-are-the-14-cities-doing-the-most-to-combat-global-warming

Harrison, Kate, 2015, 'A Good Presentation Is About Data And Story', Forbes, [available online at] https://www.forbes.com/sites/kateharrison/2015/01/20/a-good-presentation-is-about-data-and-story/#24b547f3450f

Investopedia, 2020, 'Market Segmentation' [available online at] https://www.investopedia.com/terms/m/marketsegmentation.asp

KPMG, 2018, 'NGOs and the challenge of impact investing: creating value and doing good' [available online at] https://assets.kpmg/content/dam/kpmg/xx/pdf/2018/08/ngos-and-challenge-of-impact-investing.pdf

Labrecque, Lauren and Milne, George, 2011, 'Exciting Red and Competent Blue: The importance of color in marketing', Journal of The Academy of Marketing Science.

LinkedIn, 2015, 'LinkedIn Content Marketing Tactical Plan: A daily playbook for successful content marketing on LinkedIn', [available online at] https://business.linkedin.com/content/dam/business/marketing-solutions/global/en_US/campaigns/pdfs/LNK_LMS_TacticalGuidetoLinkedIn_Rev.pdf

Machiavelli, Niccolo, 1532, 'The Prince'.

Manning, Christie, 2009, 'The Psychology of Sustainable Behavior: Tips for empowering people to take environmentally positive action'. Minnesota Pollution Control Agency, [available online at] https://www.pca.state.mn.us/sites/default/files/p-ee1-01.pdf

Market Watch, 2020, 'Renewable Energy Market: Global Industry Analysis, Size, Share, Growth, Trends and Forecast, 2018-2025', [available online at] https://www.marketwatch.com/press-release/renewable-energy-market-global-industry-analysis-size-share-growth-trends-and-forecast-2018-2025-2020-08-28

McGee, Patrick and Campbell, Peter, 2020, 'Tesla overtakes Toyota to become world's most valuable carmaker', [available online at] https://www.ft.com/content/1fd51f91-ff3c-4723-995c-f75f6629c66e

Miller, Jeremy, 2015, '3% Rule: Engage Customers Before They Need Your Services', Sticky Branding, [available online at] https://stickybranding.com/3-rule-engage-customers-before-they-need-your-services/

Moore, Geoffrey, 1991, 'Crossing the Chasm: Marketing and Selling High-Tech Products to Mainstream Customers', Harper Business Essentials.

Morgan Stanley, 2019, 'Sustainable Signals'. Morgan Stanley Institute for Sustainable Investing [available online at] https://www.morganstanley.com/press-releases/morgan-stanley-survey-finds-investor-enthusiasm-for-sustainable-

Mudaliar, Abhilash and Dithrich, Hannah, 2019 'Sizing the Impact Investing Market', Global Impact Investing Network, [available online at] https://thegiin.org/assets/Sizing%20the%20Impact%20Investing%20Market_webfile.pdf

Murthy, Mahesh, 2019, '$10.5 billion in pre-orders with $0 in ad spend. Tesla is disrupting more than the car market - it's disrupting the marketers.',

LinkedIn Article, [available online at] https://www.linkedin.com/pulse/105-billion-pre-orders-0-ad-spend-tesla-disrupting-more-mahesh-murthy/

Novanym, 2020, Why Branding Can Be Make Or Break For Startups And New Businesses', [available online at] https://novanym.com/pages/start-up-branding-guide

Patel, Sujan, 2020, 'The 2020 Guide to Successful Brand Positioning in Your Market' Hubspot, [available online at] https://blog.hubspot.com/sales/brand-positioning-strategy

Peloza, John, White, Katherine, & Shang, Jingzhi, 2013 'Good and Guilt-Free: The Role of Self-Accountability in Influencing Preferences for Products with Ethical Attributes' Journal of Marketing, American Marketing Association, Volume 77 (January 2013), 104-119, [available online at] http://blogs.ubc.ca/katewhite/files/2017/10/Peloza-J.-White-K.-Shang-J.-2013.pdf

Pollota, Dan, 2013, 'The way we think about charity is dead wrong'. Ted, [available online at] https://www.ted.com/talks/dan_pallotta_the_way_we_think_about_charity_is_dead_wrong?language=en

Pono, Myk, 2016, 'Strategic Communication: How to Develop Strategic Messaging and Positioning', The Marketing Playbook, Medium, https://medium.com/the-marketing-playbook/strategic-communication-how-to-develop-strategic-messaging-and-positioning-3cc59689ca28#:~:text=Strategic%20messaging%20is%20a%20value,the%20solution%20to%20a%20problem.

Popovich, Nadja, Schwartz, John and Schlossberg, Tatiana, 2017, 'How Americans Think About Climate Change, in Six Maps', The New York Times. [available online at] https://www.nytimes.com/interactive/2017/03/21/climate/how-americans-think-about-climate-change-in-six-maps.html

Quelch, John & Harding, David, 1996 'Brands Versus Private Labels: Fighting to Win' Harvard Business Review, [available online at] https://hbr.org/1996/01/brands-versus-private-labels-fighting-to-win

Quintos, Karen, 2020, 'Why sustainability isn't just for green companies', World Economic Forum, [available online at] https://www.weforum.org/agenda/2020/01/sustainability-green-companies-business-partnership/

Randolph, Marc, 2019, 'That Will Never Work: The Birth of Netflix and the Amazing Life of an Idea'. Little Brown and Company. https://www.amazon.com/That-Will-Never-Work-Netflix-ebook/dp/B07QLL7N7D

Shields, Fiona, 2019, 'Why we're rethinking the images we use for our climate journalism https://www.theguardian.com/environment/2019/oct/18/guardian-climate-pledge-2019-images-pictures-guidelines

Sinek, Simon, 2009, 'Start With Why: How Great Leaders Inspire Everyone to Take Action', Portfolio.

Sistemiq, 2020, 'The Paris Effect: How the climate agreement is reshaping the global economy' [available online at] https://www.systemiq.earth/wp-content/uploads/2020/12/The-Paris-Effect_SYSTEMIQ_Full-Report_December-2020.pdf

Steindl, C., Jonas, E., Sittenthaler, S., Traut-Mattausch, E., & Greenberg, J. 2015, 'Understanding Psychological Reactance: New Developments and Findings. Zeitschrift fur Psychologie, 223(4), 205–214, [available online at] https://doi.org/10.1027/2151-2604/a000222

Strauss, Karsten, 2019, 'The Most Sustainable Companies In 2019', Forbes, [available online at] https://www.forbes.com/sites/karstenstrauss/2019/01/22/the-most-sustainable-companies-in-2019/#46f7fdc86d7d

Sukhraj, Ramona, 2018, '7 must-have word-of-mouth marketing strategies', [available online at] https://www.impactbnd.com/blog/word-of-mouth-marketing-strategies-infographic

The Cult Branding Company, 2019, 'How to Create Strong Brand Positioning in Your Market', https://cultbranding.com/ceo/create-strong-brand-positioning-strategy/

Tiwari, Jai Deo, 2017, 'Marketing Research on Tesla Inc. - Strategic analysis', Strategic Engineering Management, Coventry University, [available online at] https://www.researchgate.net/publication/327120498_Marketing_Research_on_Tesla_Inc_-_Strategic_analysis

Vaynerchuk, Gary, 2016, 'The Person That Brings The Most Value, Wins', YouTube, [available online at] https://www.youtube.com/watch?v=JGrd5wXD14M

Vaynerchuk, Gary, 2015, 'Five Core Values Of Business From Gary Vee' [available online at] https://www.garyvaynerchuk.com/5-core-values-of-business-from-garyvee/

Veyrassat, Véronique, 2018, 'The SDGs as a reference framework for measuring impact', 360 Impact [available online at] https://360impact.ch/en/sdgs-and-impact/

Weber Shandwick, 2012, 'The Company Behind the Brand: In reputation we trust' [available online at] https://www.webershandwick.com/uploads/news/files/CEO_Spotlight_ExecSummary.pdf

White, Katherine, Hardisty, David, & Habib, Rishad, 2019, 'The Elusive Green Consumer' Harvard Business Review. July–August 2019 Issue [available online at] https://hbr.org/2019/07/the-elusive-green-consumer

White Jr, Lynn, 1967, 'The Historical Roots of Our Ecologic Crisis,' American Association for the Advancement of Science, [available online at]

https://science.sciencemag.org/content/155/3767/1203/tab-article-info

Wilkie, Kelsie, 2020, 'Red Cross director admits that almost $11million from bushfire donations WON'T go to victims and will be used for 'administration costs',' Daily Mail, [available online at] https://www.dailymail.co.uk/news/article-7918621/Red-Cross-director-admits-10MILLION-not-bushfire-victims.html

Withers, Iain, 2020 'World's financial firms risk $1 trillion in losses if slow to act on climate change: report'. Reuters, [available online at] https://www.reuters.com/article/us-finance-industry-climate-change/worlds-financial-firms-risk-1-trillion-in-losses-if-slow-to-act-on-climate-change-report-idUSKBN20F2FH

Woodside, Martin, 2007, 'Thomas A. Edison: The Man who Lit Up the World', Sterling.

REFERENCES

Printed in Great Britain
by Amazon

10983114R00203